T0305099

# SEX, LIES & POLITICS

## Gay Politicians in the Press

To Mum, Dad, Eve and family

# SEX, LIES & POLITICS

## Gay Politicians in the Press

DONNA SMITH

**sussex**
ACADEMIC
PRESS
*Brighton • Portland • Toronto*

Copyright © Donna Smith, 2012.

The right of Donna Smith to be identified as Author of this work has been asserted
in accordance with the Copyright, Designs and Patents Act 1988.

2 4 6 8 10 9 7 5 3 1

*First published 2012 in Great Britain by*
SUSSEX ACADEMIC PRESS
PO Box 139, Eastbourne BN24 9BP

*and in the United States of America by*
SUSSEX ACADEMIC PRESS
920 NE 58th Ave        Suite 300
Portland, Oregon 97213-3786

*and in Canada by*
SUSSEX ACADEMIC PRESS (CANADA)
8000 Bathurst Street, Unit 1, PO Box 30010, Vaughan, Ontario L4J 0C6

All rights reserved. Except for the quotation of short passages for the purposes
of criticism and review, no part of this publication may be reproduced,
stored in a retrieval system,  or transmitted, in any form or by any
means, electronic, mechanical, photocopying, recording or
otherwise, without the prior permission of the publisher.

*British Library Cataloguing in Publication Data*
A CIP catalogue record for this book is available from the British Library.

*Library of Congress Cataloging-in-Publication Data*
Smith, Donna, 1981–
Sex, lies and politics : gay politicians in the press / Donna Smith.
    A study of how gay MPs in the UK are represented in newspapers.
    p.  cm.
Includes bibliographical references and index.
ISBN 978-1-84519-456-7 (h/b : alk. paper)
    1.  Gay legislators—Great Britain—Press coverage.  2.  Gay
politicians—Great Britain—Press coverage.  3.  Press and politics—
Great Britain—History.  4.  Homosexuality—Political aspects—Great
Britain—Press coverage.  I. Title.
PN5124.P6S55  2012
070.4′49320941—dc23
                                                            2011045358

Typeset & designed by Sussex Academic Press, Brighton & Eastbourne.
Printed by TJ International, Padstow, Cornwall.
Printed on acid-free paper.

# Contents

# List of Figures and Tables

**Figures**

**Table**

# Acknowledgements

I would like to thank Professor Mike Saward and Dr Richard Heffernan from The Open University, for their support and advice and the confidence they showed in my writing and research skills, during my original research and also throughout the publication process.

I am of course very thankful for the support of the team at Sussex Academic Press, whose knowledge and experience made the publication process run smoothly.

And last but by no means least, thanks also go to my family, particularly my mum, dad and sister, for their constant support and love over the years.

# Introduction

"The media have power: they determine the fate of politicians and political causes, they influence governments and electorates. They are, therefore, to be numbered with other political institutions – parliaments, executives, administrations and parties." (Street 2001: 231)

## Background

The changing representation of gay politicians in UK newspapers is an important and intriguing area of research and discussion. Street highlights the power of the media and the impact media institutions and sources, including newspapers, have on democracy. The media also have a big impact on individuals, such as gay politicians caught in the eye of a press storm. A focus on the private lives of gay politicians (and, indeed, all politicians) not only has a potential impact on democracy (such as the amount of attention the press pays to more serious issues, such as policy and debate), it can also affect the ability of individual politicians to do their job. Indeed, gay politicians have had to resign from their ministerial positions or even from Parliament when their personal lives have not lived up to the expectations of the media. For gay politicians this may have an extra edge to it; as there are relatively few "out" gay MPs, particularly in decades past, the destruction of one in the press, and its consequences, can be seen as contributing to a democratic deficit for gay men and women, with a resulting poorer parliamentary representation of gay people and issues. Negative press representation of gay politicians may also discourage gay people from trying to become politicians in the first place, from being "out", from talking about "gay issues" or from voting for gay liberality in Parliament (particularly relevant when homosexuality was illegal or considered immoral, but pertinent to today's politicians too).

While there has been academic discussion of various topics related to the press representation of gay politicians, there is scant research on the actual subject itself. *Sex, Lies and Politics: Gay Politicians in the Press* sets out to readdress the imbalance.

## Gay Politicians

Gay politicians have at times been the subject of academic attention. Rayside (1998), focused on the experiences of three gay politicians (from the UK, USA and Canada), their place in the political world and their impact. There have also been numerous (auto)biographies written about gay politicians, one example being Macintyre's (2000) informative study of Peter Mandelson. While these texts touch on press representation, they do not go into any great detail. Storr's (2001) analysis of changing notions of privacy and acceptable/unacceptable behaviour in relation to gay politicians explored the press coverage of gay politicians in 1998 (a time of numerous "outings"), but lacks the element of changing and historical representation.

## Media Representations of Homosexuality

The representation of homosexuality in the media (press and television) has been the subject of more academic interest. Sanderson's (1995) exploration of the treatment of homosexuality in the UK media is a comprehensive study. However, such studies have only touched on gay politicians, rather than examining them in detail, with a greater focus on celebrities and homosexuality generally, highlighting that there is a significant gap in current research, because much of the press attention received by gay politicians over the years has been controversial, negative and ripe for academic exploration.

## Issues of Public and Private and Homosexuality

Study of the press representation of gay politicians leads to discussion of public and private boundaries (what they are, whether they exist, implications, how they are present in the press *etc.*). There has been much written on issues of public and private (both independent of and relating to homosexuality and the press). The chapters to follow discuss the work of Habermas ([1962] 1991), Fraser (1992) and Steinberger (1999) among many others, with their ideas taken forward and applied to gay politicians and their newspaper representation. Such writers help to inform discussion of the representation of gay politicians in the press: why gay politicians are represented in particular ways; what such representation means; how representation changes.

## Focus and Design

*Sex, Lies and Politics: Gay Politicians in the Press* addresses three main issues. First, how gay MPs in the UK are represented in newspapers. Second, how representation has changed. And third, how the first two points can be mapped and understood using an overarching, tripartite, frame made up as follows:

### 1. *The move towards recognition*
According to the premise of "recognition", marginalized groups are entitled to equal rights and respect, rather than a grudging tolerance, alongside recognition of their particularity. Society has moved from intolerance, to tolerance, to partial recognition of homosexuality, something which has been a halting process, although generally a unidirectional one.

### 2. *Acceptability over time (in relation to "heterosexual public space")*
Sexuality and sexual acts can be rated in terms of public acceptability (as in the acceptance of society) and "heterosexual public space". Generally, public homosexuality has become more acceptable over the last fifty years (again, a halting process), although still has some way to go to reach full acceptability.

### 3. *Mediated personas as "constructed reality"*
Gay politicians are represented in the press through the use of binary themes. Using these themes, their personas (gradients of negative and positive) are created by and mediated through newspapers,

These three interconnected frames comprise an overarching frame of representation. They show how a move from intolerance to tolerance to partial recognition of homosexuality (Frame One) has impacted upon the acceptability of homosexuality in "heterosexual public space" (Frame Two) — and vice versa — with these processes then affecting the representation of gay politicians in the press. Mediated personas and binary themes in the press (Frame Three) then shape (the character/particularly of) and mirror (particular moments of) Frames One and Two, highlighting that public and press opinion and change is not simply enforced by outside factors such as the media: instead, the media influences while *being* influenced, as part of a circular process. In relation to Frame Three, what was private has now become public, pointing to the fact that gay politicians, like celebrities, have mediated personas (through which binary themes operate); their private lives, and sexualities, are lived in and presented through the press. It is Frame Three that has helped to maintain negative and stereotypical representations of gay politicians.

The overarching frame derives from in-depth case studies of the press representation of gay politicians and a literature and theoretical review. It is a product of inductive work, with observations becoming theory, wherein through analysis of case studies and explorations of surrounding literature and theory, key issues have been identified (recognition; acceptability and public spaces; binary themes and mediated personas) and brought together to make an interconnected, overarching frame of representation. The frame is presented as both a preview and as the result of research; it is both a way of organizing the press representation of gay politicians and an account of why the representation takes the form it does.

The argument presented does not undertake comparative analysis; the frame of representation applies to the press representation of gay MPs in the UK. The advantage of such an approach is that case studies can be examined in greater detail, with a fixed focus. It also allows for themes identified to be applied more closely and specifically and acknowledges the fact that conceptions of homosexuality and public and private spaces are not necessarily universal (for example, there may be differences between the UK and USA, or between gay politicians and gay celebrities). A qualitative approach to reading newspapers and understanding case studies has been chosen (*i.e.* identifying key themes and words in relation to their context) because reading newspapers quantitatively (*i.e.* analysing how many times particular words are used over time) does not necessarily reveal an increase or decrease in homophobia or use of binary themes, because words used to describe gay people and homosexuality change over time. After all, just because a particular word is no longer used does not mean that tolerance has increased; it may just mean that that word is no longer in fashion.

## Applying the Frame

Even in recent years there have been major stories involving gay politicians and politicians caught up in gay scandals, all of which can be understood in relation to the frame of representation and which are a useful introduction to its themes. Take 2006 as an example: the then Liberal Democrat MP Mark Oaten was reported as having affairs with rent-boys, sourced via the gay dating website Gaydar, while married with a young family; Simon Hughes was "outed" as bisexual while standing for Liberal Democrat party leadership (he had previously denied being gay); and Conservative MP Gregory Barker was alleged to have left his wife for a man.

The cases of Barker and Oaten are good examples of binary themes in action and positive and negative mediated personas, key concepts discussed. Barker was presented as "good" (*i.e.* comfortable with himself, open and relaxed — an easy to categorize and recognize alleged gay man) and "safe" (*i.e.* his sex life was unthreatening and private) and Oaten as "bad" and "dangerous" — binary opposites of each other. The categorization is partly due to the nature of their cases (Oaten's was deemed more "sleazy", to use a term often employed by the press), but also to do with public and private spheres. Oaten's alleged sexual life was at the forefront of his story, whereas Barker's was not. Barker's sexual life was private and Oaten's public (another binary — private/public), thus Barker's mediated persona leant towards the positive, as opposed to Oaten's negative persona. Barker's press coverage was not 100 percent positive (particularly in the right-wing newspaper the *Daily Mail*), but his and Oaten's cases are excellent examples of the ways in which gay politicians and politicians caught up in gay scandals are categorized and the use of binary themes.

Hughes's press coverage is also of interest in the same way. Hughes had previously denied being gay, and as such, when "outed" by the press received negative press coverage in many tabloid newspapers. He was a "bad" gay/bisexual politician because he was not upfront about his sexuality. While Barker was also "outed", he had not previously lied about his sexuality to the press, making his "transgression" less severe. These cases demonstrate that while gay politicians and politicians caught up in a gay scandal have either a negative or positive persona, these categories are graduated. So, Oaten's press coverage was more negative than Hughes's because he met more negative binary themes. Barker's case also suggests the greater acceptability of (alleged) gay politicians in recent years. His more positive press coverage (apart from the exceptions mentioned above) and the fact that in some newspapers his situation did not receive much comment at all, shows that the press representation of gay politicians has improved. Still, the private nature of his sex life, in comparison to Oaten's, once again emphasizes the fact that public expressions of gay sexuality can be frowned upon and recognition has only been reached *partially*; while Barker's suggested homosexuality was accepted (generally) and he was allowed to stay an MP, his particularity — his supposed homosexuality — was only acceptable because certain criteria were met. These themes are explored with case studies demonstrating that the press representation of gay politicians and politicians caught up in a gay scandal can be examined using the overarching frame of representation, with mediated personas and binary themes, acceptability within public space and recognition, key components.

## Format and Structure

The research is split into three main sections. *Part One* explores theory related to the changing representation of gay politicians in the UK press, leading to the introduction of the overarching frame of representation. Chapter 1 shows how the changing representation of gay politicians in UK newspapers is intrinsically linked to the way the press works and how newspapers treat politicians in general. The intense focus on the private lives of politicians did not begin until the 1960s. From then on, politics has become more and more personalized, with scandal a prime focus of press attention; in terms of news values, scandalous (gay and "outed") politicians are front-page news. The press attention paid to the private lives of gay politicians points to the fact that the private morality of politicians — both heterosexual and gay — is now defined as a public act; if a politician's personal life does not meet strict moral criteria, the press may write about it. As an aspect of the personal, the homosexuality of politicians has thus become a "legitimate" area of press focus. Chapter 2 looks at these issues, paying particular attention to the public/private dichotomy and "heterosexual public space". Finally, building on such discussion, Chapter 3 introduces the overarching frame of representation.

*Part Two* surveys the "traditional" representation of gay politicians in the UK press. There are two case study chapters: pre-1980 (Chapter 5) and 1980–90 (Chapter 6). It builds on *Part One*, showing how the frame of representation identified can be applied to and is borne from press coverage. Chapter 5 examines how the representation of gay politicians in the press pre-1980 was predominately negative, with sensational articles dominating press coverage, often as the result of a "scandalous" event or court case. This was true of representation in the 1950s when homosexuality had yet to be decriminalized and public disapproval was high, but of later decades too after homosexuality had been legalized. When written about, gay politicians were thus the subject of discrimination and demonization, with the personal very political.

Chapter 6 explores how as the 1980s approached the press coverage of gay politicians began to slowly improve — in some parts of the press at least — echoing the improved legal status of homosexuality and more relaxed public attitudes, but a dominant heterosexuality still coloured the press coverage of gay politicians. So, while the 1980s saw Chris Smith's "self-outing" in 1984, demonstrating that "openly" gay politicians could now survive politically, it also saw Peter Tatchell's very negative campaigning experience in the 1983 Bermondsey by-election. However, in the mid-1980s there was a regression in public opinion, with people more intolerant of homosexuality than in the early 1980s, linked to the emergence of HIV/AIDS. HIV/AIDS saw the press representation of gay people become less positive and a rise in the use of homosexuality as a political tool in the tabloid — and broadsheet — press, demonstrated by Harvey Proctor's incredibly negative late 1980s press coverage.

*Part Three* investigates the "contemporary" press representation of gay politicians, focusing on the periods of 1990-7 (Chapter 8) and post-1997 (Chapter 9), also linking to and demonstrating the applicability of the frame of representation. Chapter 8 shows that while the language used to describe gay politicians became more moderate towards the mid-1990s, especially in the broadsheet newspapers (echoing — and influencing — public opinion), politicians such as Michael Brown were still being "outed" by tabloid newspapers, with the sensationalist tone and stereotypical language used by many newspapers (particularly the tabloids) still considered unsatisfactory by many gay activists. It is perhaps unsurprising that Smith remained the only "self-outed" gay MP at this time, with the "outing" of numerous "sleazy" and "untrustworthy" Conservative MPs contributing towards a fevered atmosphere surrounding the personal lives of politicians.

Chapter 9 discusses the positive reaction of the press to the election of openly gay politicians in 1997, which suggested that gay politicians would no longer have to hide their sexuality in order to get ahead in politics (in fact, it could be a plus point), something emphasized by the promotion of gay men and woman to ministerial posts. However, soon after various gay politicians were "outed" by tabloid newspapers, with stereotypes and discriminatory language utilized, and the public interest criteria of the Press Complaints Commission (which regulates the UK press via self-regulation) disregarded. While many political commentators felt that tabloid newspapers such as *The Sun* went too far in their press coverage, other tabloid newspapers, and broadsheet newspapers too, covered the "outings". While on the surface the press representation of gay MPs has improved, and in the 2000s the repre-

sentation of "scandalous" gay politicians increasingly echoes the representation of heterosexual politicians caught up in a scandal (with
non-scandalous gay MPs not receiving much attention at all), the
portrayal of gay MPs and homosexuality as a whole can still have murky
undertones.

*Part Two* and *Three* each begin with a contextualization: an exploration of relevant social, political and legal issues, alongside an
assessment of how newspapers have portrayed homosexuality generally. For homosexuality has an intricate, multi-layered history, with the
concept of "homosexuality" in itself particular to a moment in time,
with the law, medical developments, political and public opinion and
concepts of morality having an impact on each other and the definition
and perception of homosexuality. And, of course, these issues also have
an impact on the representation of homosexuality in the press (and vice
versa), hence the importance of the contextualization. Chapter 4 of
*Part Two* and Chapter 7 of *Part Three* examine the historical status
of homosexuality relevant to their respective eras, from the mid-twentieth century to the present — with attention also paid to the late
nineteenth century when homosexuality first became an "identity".
They look at the ways in which legal developments (for example, the
criminalization of and then the later legalization of homosexuality),
social issues and public and political opinions have had an effect on the
media landscape regarding homosexuality.

It is appropriate to note that there is of course a certain irony in
writing a book which explores the negative consequences of the press
discussion of the sexuality and private lives of politicians and then
writing about their private lives in some detail, but that cannot be
avoided. To prevent unnecessary intrusion, though, only politicians
who are either openly gay (or in some cases bisexual), or who have
received press coverage focusing on their sexuality and/or been caught
up in a publicly reported "gay scandal", are discussed (as such, the
press coverage of some heterosexual politicians is explored because
their sexuality has been discussed and speculated on in the press). As
a result, politicians rumoured to be gay, but without publicly available
confirmation or press supposition (based on, for example, a court case,
exposé or published speculation), are not discussed. Neither is the
press representation of every known gay politician examined. Apart
from the need to focus on politicians whose sexuality has been publicly
commented on, some politicians — particularly in recent years — have
not received much press coverage about their sexuality (which in itself
says something about contemporary representation). The text concentrates on MPs only, not members of the House of Lords, members of

the European Parliament or local politicians, in order to have a defined area of discussion and comparison.

In summary, *Sex, Lies and Politics: Gay Politicians in the Press* provides a much-needed analysis of the changing representation of gay politicians in UK newspapers. Focusing on the 1950s onwards, it uses theory, case studies and socio-political analysis to develop and discuss a frame of representation which can be used to understand and map the press coverage of gay politicians. It reveals insights about representation and the construction of identity through its focus on sexuality, politicians and the media, with the changing line between the private and public an essential concept. Sensationalism and scandal are key issues, with the press coverage of politicians caught up in gay scandals, as well as gay politicians, explored. It is sincerely hoped that the work contributes to political, media and social history.

# PART ONE

# Building a Frame of Representation

# 1

# The Press, the Personal and News Values

"In the immediate postwar period the British people knew little; political leaders were looked up to as moral leaders, and the public and the press did not pry into their private affairs . . . [it was not until] the scandal-ridden 1960s and 1970s, deference collapsed and the veil of secrecy which protected the privacy of the political class was torn." (Baston 2000: 8–9)

## From Deference to Exposure

It would be mistaken to believe that the private lives of politicians, of any sexuality, have always been subject to press exposure. Up until the 1960s the press did not typically focus on the private lives of politicians. After then, and scandals such as the Profumo affair in 1963, deference ended and the private lives of politicians became fair game to press exposure.[1] Baston (2000: 9) uses the phrase "veil of secrecy" to describe a time of deference, when those in power were looked up to by the people they were supposed to serve and when their private affairs were hidden from the public. It is not the case that political misdemeanours were never published in the "age of deference", or that if they were exposed, the politicians concerned were not punished. John Belcher (Labour MP for Sowerby 1945–9), for example, a minister in the 1940s Labour Government, was forced to resign as a minister and MP for accepting gifts from a corrupt businessman. But, overall, the "veil of secrecy" remained firmly in place. The task ahead is to explore the shift from the "age of deference" to the personalization of politics and politicians and — linked — notions of scandal and news values and the idea of mediated personas, giving background to the overarching frame of representation through which the press coverage of gay politicians can be mapped.

## A New "Publicness"

Changes to the communication process were at the heart of the move from deference to exposure. Thompson (2000: 34) describes how developments in the "cultural sphere" — from the development of the printing press in the early fifteenth century to newspapers and then electronic communication — changed the way society communicated. These changes led to a growth in what he calls "mediated forms of communication" and, in turn, changes to the way in which people interacted with each other and their elected representatives. Information could be transmitted to those who were not witnessing it immediately (face-to-face at a public meeting, for example) and could therefore become "open-ended". Such open-endedness is even more relevant in the twenty-first century, the age of the Internet, a communication tool which has led to an even greater rise in mediated communication, with information stored and dispersed for (potentially or theoretically) the whole world, or large portions of it, to access.

Of course, developments in the "cultural sphere" do not in themselves account for the rise in coverage of the personal lives of politicians. According to Thompson (2000: 36), a new "publicness" occurred, wherein politicians could be viewed by the public via the media. "Open-ended" forms of media and communication meant that politicians could become detached from immediacy and extend their reach; the new form of "publicness" changed the ways in which the media and the public viewed politicians. It was possible for political leaders to reveal aspects of their character and inner lives to the wider public as they were no longer constrained by the limitations of one-to-one contact, meaning, in turn, that politicians could become more personal and present themselves as ordinary people in touch with their public, rather than be seen as remote and inaccessible figures. Mediated personas could come into play.

The idea of politicians presenting or "spinning" their public personas is not a new one. Goffman ([1959] 1990: 203) used the phrase "impression management" to describe the process of controlling and influencing the impressions that people have about a person as part of social interaction. Impression management is related to social settings: people may present different aspects of themselves in different situations (so a politician can present him or herself as tough and hard-talking while debating in the House of Commons, and friendly and approachable while visiting school children). Virtual public spaces such as newspapers, through which politicians can stage their public selves, have been important public arenas for politicians since the rise of "publicness". Through newspapers (and other forms of media), politicians can promote themselves to various audiences in ways both beneficial to the audience and to themselves. The process of impression management is not necessarily a cynical exercise, something suggested by Goffman's rather cold terminology; while politicians (and people in general) may try to deliberately mislead their audience, they may also genuinely believe in their performance.

## Mediated Scandal

By revealing aspects of their character (whether authentic or not), politicians operating within the new field of "publicness" could be judged in ways they were not previously: how "human" they appeared; how well they were perceived to empathize with the problems of "ordinary" people; and their personal behaviour, character and appearance. As Thompson recognizes, this led to further problems for a political class used to distance between itself and the public: political character could be negatively as well as positively judged. Consequently, a new visibility and "publicness" created an environment in which scandal — "mediated" scandal — was much more likely, implying, in turn, that scandals do not exist in isolation; instead, they are fed and created by the media. Thompson suggests that there are three types of political scandal — all of which can be created and enhanced by the media: sexual-political scandals; financial-political scandals; and power scandals. The concern here is the first category of scandal (although scandals can cross categories and become, for example, sexual-financial scandals), but what is significant is that all these "types" of scandal involve the transgression of "norms" and values, even though scandals in themselves can be very diverse. Owing to the new "publicness", activities which the "veil of secrecy" would have hidden from the public (activities which may have conflicted with a public political image) could now be categorized as a ("type" of) scandal and exposed, leading to published conflicts of interest, public scandal and political disgrace. Obviously, such a move does not mean that there were more political scandals than in the past, but that they were now much more likely to be revealed to the public.

Within "mediated scandals" there are "mediated personas", sometimes working to the benefit of politicians, sometimes against. Corner (2000) argues that there are three different spheres of action related to mediated personas: first, the sphere of political institutions and processes; second, the sphere of public and popular; and third, the private sphere. He states it is in the sphere of public and popular that politicians develop reputations and are judged. That sphere then relates to the private sphere because the latter sphere is "used as a resource in the manufacture of political identity and in its repair following misadventure" (Corner 2000: 394). Therefore, the private sphere connects to the public spheres, mediated personas can be projected within the private sphere and, importantly, the private sphere can also be engaged with in terms of "risk", such as repairing a negative mediated persona following a so-called sexual scandal. Interestingly, Corner (2000: 404) goes on to say that personalization via mediated personas is not necessarily a negative thing because political personas are a source of "democratic engagement". So, while a focus on the personal can have negative consequences for politicians, it can also have positive ones for both them and their audience.

Corner's idea of spheres of action connects with Habermas's ([1962] 1991) notion of the public sphere. However, distinctions between private and public can be debated. Fraser (1992) problematizes Habermas's definitions, noting that there are no naturally given boundaries between what we think of as public and what we think of as private (she discusses domestic abuse and states that this once private issue has now become an issue of public concern). Fraser (1992: 122) also says that Habermas's idea of the public sphere is not an inclusive one; marginalized groups form their own public spheres (counterpublics), which can be seen as a positive thing: "In stratified societies, arrangements that accommodate contestation among a plurality of competing publics better promote the ideal of participatory parity than does a single, comprehensive, overarching public." As discussed in Chapter 2, while boundaries of public and private can be contested, the concept is a useful one here because the press itself engages with such a distinction. That said, ideas such as Fraser's are interesting because they suggest that the "move to the personal" — which itself connotes that there are private issues and public ones and what we define as such, and what we regard as "scandalous", has changed over the years — involves notions of public and private which are contestable as well as the idea that there is more than one public. The idea of multiple publics certainly ties in with the notion of emerging gay and lesbian spheres, explored in Chapter 2.

## A "Lighter" Style of Journalism

The "move to the personal" points to the fact that there also had to be a willingness on the part of the press to write about the private lives of politicians. Thompson makes the point (in relation to sexual scandal) that the newly emerging focus on the private lives of politicians could be helpful to newspapers; such reporting made easy headlines, grabbed the reader's attention, and most importantly, was considered a good story. The development has a historical basis, one that is broader than the press simply responding to politics and politicians. In the mid-1800s journalism can be thought of as entering a new phase. As Williams (1998: 50) explores, instead of a focus on serious news, "new journalism" focused on "entertainment and amusement instead of instruction." What is considered a "good" story — one thought to appeal to readers — is not historically static. It responds to the socio-political factors of the time, public tastes and industry developments (such as industrial change and press ownership).

Williams discusses how the rise of the "popular" press and "lighter" stories from the mid-1800s onwards (itself a result of factors such as higher levels of literacy, new technology like the telegraph, the abolition of press taxation and the industrialization of the press) saw stories focus on scandal, romance, crime and sport, instead of independent political commentary. So, while the rise of campaigning journalism in the 1880s, characterized by W. T. Stead's work on child prostitution, saw more socially responsible topics discussed in the press, these stories were still written in a "popular" fashion, utilizing interviews, personal testimony and lurid headlines, demonstrating that a "lighter" style was becoming the norm, even if the subject matter itself was serious. Williams points out that changes in the economics and content of newspapers were accompanied by changes in layout, style and typography. Some newspapers resisted the changes more than others, leading to differentiation within the media market.

## Tabloidization

Humanization extended to political coverage as well, what could be thought of as an emerging "tabloidization", an idea Franklin (1997) engages with, albeit in reference to the 1980s and 1990s. Franklin notes that contemporary newspapers, echoing the earlier period, are now much more likely to adopt a tabloid agenda, with emphasis on the sensationalist and the scandalous. Indeed, Franklin's writings about "lighter" contemporary journalism could just as easily be related to the nineteenth century. So, the "serious" reporting of politics has been replaced by a focus on the "less serious" side of politics: personality, private behaviour and character, rather than parliamentary debate, political analysis and comment. As the term "tabloidization" suggests, the change has in fact moved on to broadsheet newspapers as well, a form of media Franklin refers to as "broadloids" (1997: 7–10). Franklin argues that parliamentary journalism (journalism focusing on reports and debates from the Houses of Parliament) has declined and been replaced by humorous and less serious sketches by politicians turned journalists. Consequently, when Parliament is reported upon, it is often trivialized. As Thompson (2000: 238–9) writes, the result has been "a 'tabloidization' of the media and a 'privatization' of the public sphere."

## Media Economics

So far a link has been shown between a changing media and communication process, a new "publicness", a decrease in serious political coverage and a greater focus on the personal lives of individual politicians, raising the issue of *why* there has been a change of focus. One commonly held belief is that "dumbing down" is exactly what the readers of newspapers want. As Franklin (1997: 4) supposes, "Journalists are more concerned to report stories which interest the public than stories which are in the public interest." They are also more likely to write stories that interest themselves. So, a move from the serious reporting of politics and parliamentary debates to a focus on sex, scandal and personality can be observed. Essentially, the customer drives the market. Street (2001) writes how politics is often framed as soap opera in newspapers and discusses how the boundary between news and entertainment has become blurred, which in turn strongly emphasizes the idea of the news media as "infotainment". Entertainment is deemed to be of more interest to the public and more likely to sell newspapers (or gain viewers). Certainly, Franklin claims that the vast majority of journalists he spoke to believed that the decline in reports from the House of Commons and Lords was demand led. He goes on to note that news is delivered in snippets which do not demand too much of the audience. The aforementioned argument is emphasized by Street, who not only notes the increased demand for space in newspapers (between political and sports coverage, for example), but also challenges by other forms of media and the resulting competition for readers.

Media economics is an important factor in the increased focus on the personal lives of politicians in UK newspapers. It should not be forgotten that newspapers are a commercial enterprise, and owners of newspapers want their products to sell. As such, focusing on the personal is another commercial decision which may reap benefits. At the very least, it differentiates publications within the media market. Thus, some publications (such as the *News of the World*, before it ceased publication in 2011) focus their content on "lighter" stories (Thompson 2000). Newspapers (and different media formats as a whole) have different agendas, such as political (supporting one party above another), moral (presenting a particular way of life as correct) and intellectual (presenting as "highbrow"). Therefore, a broadsheet newspaper such as the *Guardian* is not just concerned with pleasing its readership when deciding to have a greater focus on "serious" issues than "light" ones: it is trying to present an image of gravitas and social conscience to the market as a whole.

Thompson (2000: 78) states that there are four reasons why the press may focus on mediated (political) scandals (scandal being a way in which the personal lives of politicians may be presented): "(1) financial gain, (2) political objectives, (3) professional self-conceptions, and (4) competitive rivalries." The first and fourth points are of most importance when discussing the relationship between media economics and the rise of the focus on the personal. Thompson suggests in relation to financial gain that scandals equal sales. Political scandal stories thus make financial sense. Of course, it may not be the case that journalists are necessarily thinking about financial gain when they focus on scandal and aspects of the personal. It may be more the structure of the media which has ensured that these kinds of stories are written about, rather than individual personnel (Thompson 2000).[2] Competition (point four) is the key issue. As Thompson (2000: 83) writes, "Media organizations do not exist in isolation: they stand in complex relations — often competitive in character — to other media organizations . . . [This has] a bearing on the production of mediated scandal." In audience terms, it therefore makes sense for a newspaper to expose, for example, the sexual proclivities of a politician: such articles will probably be more interesting and gratifying to read for many readers than the details of a complicated political issue. "Structure" (competition, economics and technology) and "agency" or "agents" (consumers, reporters *etc.*), are key components in the production of news and mediated scandals. Outside organizations also play a role (perhaps the police) (Thompson 2000), as do the subjects of the news — those whose "scandalous" activities are being written about. And, it should not be forgotten that news takes place within a socio-political context.

## Reader Demand and Expectation

Interestingly, Street (2001: 45) writes in relation to the reporting of the personal lives of politicians, "Readers are there to be amused rather than informed; they are expected to laugh and mock." This is a claim about how readers are treated, rather than how they actually are, suggesting that readers may not necessarily want "infotainment", but are fed a diet of it by sections of the press anyway. Research has suggested that journalists think that "infotainment" is what readers want. Franklin (1997: 246), for example, states that the journalists he wrote to described readers as "bored" and "uninterested". However, newspapers may not actually need to focus on "lighter" (political) stories in order to sustain their readerships. To echo Thompson, they have become a routinized feature of newspapers, rather than an audience-required one.

Even if readers do want to be entertained by the articles they read and are interested in the personal aspects of politics, it can be contended that it is certainly not the case that "the trivial has triumphed over the weighty" (Franklin 1997: 4) in a *complete* sense. Just because an article is phrased and presented "lightly", it does not mean that it cannot expose, for example, political wrongdoing: while the presentation may be entertaining, the message may be very serious (as suggested in relation to W.T. Stead).[3] Plus, personal issues can be serious ones. A story about a "personal" matter (the lifestyle of a politician for example) could actually end up raising serious issues. Alternatively, a story which is about a "serious" matter (say, the economy) could become a personal one by focusing on an individual at the centre of the story.

It could be claimed that the idea of personal issues as serious issues is the essence of politics. As Downs (1957) famously argued, politicians want power first and foremost. The personal, as something which can increase the chance of success, is therefore an extremely serious issue: think 1994 and Tony Blair's (Prime Minister 1997–2007 and Labour MP for Sedgefield 1983–2007) promotion as a family man, over the then unmarried and childless Gordon Brown (Prime Minister 2007–10 and MP for Dunfermline East 1983–2005 and Kirkcaldy and

THE PRESS, THE PERSONAL AND NEWS VALUES

Cowdenbeath 2005– ). While it can be debated how much the topic mattered to the actual public (and the politicians), it was something discussed in the press, even if it was on an oblique level. Certainly, the idea that personalization takes away from politics is not necessarily the case. Van Zoonen (2005: 146) suggests that personalization is a way in which people can engage with politics: through "political personas" (a combination of a politician's personality and the responsibilities that are projected onto them), similar to mediated personas, political selves are revealed and perceived by other people, with personalization perhaps offering a way into politics for people otherwise disengaged (of course, it should be recognized that there is a vast difference between personalization and invading privacy).

It may also be the case that modern readers do not actively choose their newspaper (McQuail 2005). People may read newspapers chosen by other people in their household or circle. As a consequence, the readership numbers of a "light" newspaper such as *The Sun* may be as much to do with its easy availability and commonplaceness rather than people actively choosing it — and its content and message — over another newspaper. The way the modern media works is certainly a key factor in the "move to the personal". After all, we now live in a twenty-four hour media age, meaning that news is available more quickly and there is a greater demand on the journalist by the industry and on the product by those who buy it. Street remarks that the media focuses on the personal because of the organization and structure of the media, limited space for stories and tight deadlines. Therefore, it is much easier to report on a political sex scandal, with column inches taken up by sensationalist paparazzi photographs and lurid quotes, than to report on a complicated international development debate in the House of Commons. A circular process perhaps: the more the public knows, the more its appetite needs to be fed.

There are also social and cultural factors to consider. The distance between politicians and the public has narrowed. Although many politicians today have had a good education and benefit from the opportunities that follow, and it is the case that they often come from similar, advantaged backgrounds (Moran 2005), it is certainly no longer the case that politicians are automatically of a different class or upbringing. Theoretically, anyone can become a politician today, meaning that many voters will be able to see themselves represented in the person they have elected (even if the parallel relates to some, rather than all, politicians). As Ridley (1995: 72) neatly comments, "If John Major [whose father worked in the circus] can become Prime Minister then Jack will be inclined to say he is as good as his master — and entitled to criticize the behaviour of those who rule him."

The "move to the personal" and the collapse of deference required means that the public have different expectations and demands of politicians. The public as a whole will no longer allow misdemeanours to be swept under the carpet and expects politicians to remain sleaze free. As suggested in relation to Goffman, politicians themselves have played a big role. For example, many politicians and political parties have portrayed themselves as family orientated in order to gain favourable media coverage and more public support. It is legitimate to argue that by portraying themselves in such a manner (*i.e.* by consciously utilizing "impression management") politicians are actively encouraging the media's focus on their private lives. Many people have argued that politicians do not have the right to complain if their personal lives become the focus of the media's attention because they have often played such an active role in the process.

## News Values

Having explored the move to the personalization of politics and politicians in the press, it is necessary to look at news values. By doing so, the reasons why the press focuses on the personal is further contextualized, and it also starts to become clear why gay people and politicians in particular are represented in certain ways. Contemporary articles on gay people are more positive than at any other time: the press (both tabloid and broadsheet) often publishes articles focusing on gay public figures and members of the public, which either positively highlight homosexuality or ignore it altogether (for homosexuality is now so "normal" there is no need to draw attention to it). However, as *Part Three* illustrates, even in the twenty-first century gay people have still been depicted in the (often tabloid) press in a derogatory manner. Homosexuality has certainly always had great news value.

As far back as 1889 and the Cleveland Street scandal, when the Earl of Euston and Lord Arthur Somerset were accused of visiting a male brothel, "scandalous" tales of homosexuality have always caught the attention of the press and the public.[4] As homosexuality was illegal in the late 1800s the news value of the scandal was immense. The story began in late 1889, when the *North London Press* (a radical paper which focused on the underprivileged) printed an article headed "'OUR OLD NOBILITY': CHARGES OF INFAMOUS CONDUCT AGAINST PEERS" (28 September 1889), which mused on "a scandal of so horrible and repulsive a character that it would be better unmentioned if it were not necessary to expose the shameless audacity with which officials have contrived to shield the principal criminals." The names of Euston and Somerset were not mentioned in the article, just the line "amongst them [those who escaped prosecution] were the heir of a duke, the younger brother or another duke, and an officer". However, Euston then engaged a libel trial against the editor of the *North London Press*, which then reported on the court case under the headline "THE WEST END SCANDALS" (30 November 1889). In the article Euston and Somerset's names were mentioned in connection with the "indescribably loathsome scandal in Cleveland-Street." The article reported on the notion that Euston and Somerset had escaped prosecution because it would have disclosed "the fact that a few more distinguished and more highly placed personages than themselves were inculpated in the disgusting crime".

As these short extracts show, while condemning the crimes the newspaper promotes their "shocking" and "scandalous" nature: the articles' news values are based around the fact that homosexuality was illegal at the time. Thompson explains that the Cleveland Street scandal was one of many scandals presented in the late nineteenth century English press which involved sexuality (heterosexual and homosexual) shaped by the morals and laws of late Victorian England. The legal status of homosexuality has always been a major factor in the press treatment of homosexuality. Due to the fact that it was once illegal and the age of consent for gay men has changed over the years (and until recently has always been higher than the age of heterosexual consent), the press has had plenty of opportunity to write about public figures caught in "compromising" situations. In fact, the Cleveland Street scandal, along with Oscar Wilde's trial for gross indecency in the 1880s, is representative of a time in which sex and sexual scandals became more relevant subjects for the press. As Chapter 4 explores, these events occurred at a time when the private was regulated against (in the form of the 1885 Criminal Law Amendment Act), the public became involved in private sexuality and homosexuality itself became a criminally punishable, public identity.

## Selection

Although homosexuality has strong news value, particular stories and issues are the subject of press attention: stories are selected, part of a "gatekeeping" process, wherein the media selects the information to be presented to the public, for reasons such as available time and space, moral and political agendas and the process and structure of news. Critcher *et al.* (1997) explain that the media chooses news rather than simply reports events as they happen. As such, events are sorted and selected according to socially created categories. While news values may be unconscious in actual editorial practice (Fowler 1991), news is still an active process. As Philo (1983: 135) writes: "News is not 'found' or even 'gathered' so much as made. It is a creation of a journalistic process, an artefact, a commodity even."

So, a married politician reported in a newspaper as having a private affair with another man *becomes* a news story, even a "scandal"; the situation does not naturally and automatically present itself as a smoothly packaged news item. Their mediated persona would almost certainly be *presented* as a negative one, utilizing negative binary themes. Stories can be categorized as being reported (*i.e.* a newspaper reports "outside" events as they happen, for example, reports on a court case involving a politician) or manufactured (*i.e.* a newspaper manipulates events in order to produce a story), a division which echoes the difference between reporting on the sexuality of a gay politician and actually "outing" them. Although there can be some crossover between manufacturing and reporting, it is useful to think in terms of such a division because it helps to understand the motivations of the press, as well as the impact of press representation. The case studies in *Part Two* and *Part Three* demonstrate the reporting/manufacturing difference.

In relation to the idea of categorization, Fowler (1991: 17) writes that newspapers make reference to "frames", "paradigms", "stereotypes", "schemata" and "general propositions". He believes that newspapers are preoccupied with categorizing people and putting discriminatory frames on them. So, a married but secretly gay politician has news value as a stereotype; he may be presented as a scandalous, amoral and "bad" gay man. Galtung and Ruge (1973) identify twelve 12 actual news values. The more a story meets, the greater news value it may have:

1 Frequency (the time span of an event — how quickly meaning can be arrived at)
2 Threshold (the magnitude of an event)
3 Unambiguity (the clarity and simplicity of an event)
4 Meaningfulness (cultural immediacy and relevance)
5 Consonance (the predictability of/desire for an event)
6 Unexpectedness (the unpredictability/rarity of an event)

7  Continuity (the running time of an event)
8  Composition (the mixture of different sorts of event)
9  Reference to elite nations (linked/well-known nations are likely to be reported)
10  Reference to elite persons (it is assumed their activities are more relevant)
11  Personalization (events are linked to particular people)
12  Negativity (bad news equals good, interesting news).

News values ten (reference to elite persons), eleven (personalization) and twelve (negativity) are particularly applicable to the representation of gay politicians in the press. Certainly, in relation to "reference to elite persons", it is assumed by the press that the activities of gay politicians and other public figures are more important than the activities of "ordinary" individuals (one of the reasons why the press often references the "public needs to know" argument in relation to the publication of articles on homosexual political scandal). And, as Hartley (1995) explores, the actions of famous, "elite" people such as gay politicians can serve as representative actions: the reader can see their own lives within the press through these people. With "personalization", Hartley (1995: 78) suggests "events are seen as the actions of people as individuals." Further, as individuals are easier to identify with than institutions, institutions are often personalized. Therefore, individual people can be presented as representative of institutions. So, a gay politician caught up in a sex scandal and described by the press as "sleazy" and lacking in morals, can be used to symbolize a "sleazy", morally bankrupt government. "Back to basics" in the early 1990s is a good example, when the individual peccadilloes of Conservative MPs (some gay, some heterosexual) came to be seen as representative of a failing, morally unsure government. In relation to "negativity" most sexual scandal stories (particularly pre-2000) involving gay politicians are presented in a negative light — for the individual concerned, their families if married and their political party (but not for the newspaper concerned, for whom the story is positive). It does not seem to occur to the press (particularly the tabloids) that stories concerned with homosexuality may turn out to be extremely positive for the person concerned. For example, a politician may have finally become comfortable with his or her homosexuality after years of struggle and embarked upon a loving, happy relationship with someone of the same sex.

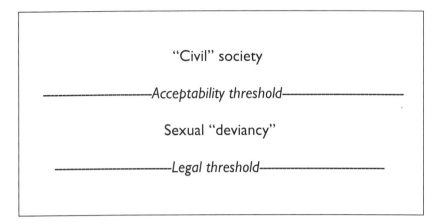

**Figure 1.1** Mapping consensus and dissent.*
*Influenced by Hall *et al.* (1978).

## Homosexual "Deviancy"

Within Galtung and Ruge's structure, Hartley (1995: 81–2) states there are maps which assume society to be: "fragmented" into spheres; "composed of individual persons who are in control of their destiny" (actions are the result of personal choices); "hierarchical" (some people/spheres are more important that others); and "consensual". While the categorization of people in such a way does not necessarily reflect the personal views of journalists (news is often an impersonal process), groups outside consensus are often portrayed by the media as dissenters or deviants. The media's treatment of homosexuality fits in well with Hartley's notion of consensus and deviancy.

Homosexuality can be mapped using the ideas contained in figure 1.1. It can be seen (or has been seen) as a threat to what Hall *et al.* (1978: 226) call "civilized society" — or at least deviant when compared to it — and "permissiveness" (termed "civil society" and "acceptability" in figure 1.1). "Civilized society" can be thought of as heterosexual society and public space. At times homosexuality has of course fully breached the legality threshold (*i.e.* pre-1967 when homosexuality was completely illegal). The further away from "civilized society" homosexuality has existed, the more newsworthy homosexuality has been. Hartley notes that moral disapproval (which is beyond "civilized society" but within law) can be applied to non-family sexuality. As suggested by "moral", other factors besides its legal status have placed homosexuality outside of "civilized society". HIV/AIDS, for example, caused gay people (men in particular) to be seen as a threatening, immoral presence.

As figure 1.1 intimates, politicians caught up in gay sexual scandals and/or "outed" as gay have been presented as sexual deviants outside the realm of "civilized society" and acceptability. The legal status of homosexuality contributed to the process pre-1967, with various aspects of moral disapproval (alongside legal issues) the main driving force post-1967. According to Thompson, sexual political scandals normally transgress moral codes, but this is not necessarily the case, because the media can exploit sexual activities. Thus, the media impacts upon Hall's ideas and can make issues such as homosexuality and sexual "scandals" appear to be further away from "civilized society" than they may initially appear.

Linked to the notion of "civilized society", the issue of who dominates the press (particularly in the past) is significant, which has largely been white, middle class, heterosexual males, something that has undoubtedly had an impact on what is presented as "normal" and what is seen as "unusual" and thus newsworthy. As Gillespie and Toynbee (2006) recognize, dominant social groups have power over others which is in turn reflected through the media. Homosexuality (whether in the form of an "outed" gay politician or an age of consent debate) is thus a newsworthy topic: it is or was outside of the day-to-day experiences of many of the people who produce newspapers, and for those that read them (although this has changed over the years and may continue to change). Such an idea leads to the notion of "us" and "them" (or what could be termed the "other") — consensus — being represented in newspapers, something touched on by Fowler (1991: 53) amongst many others, who states that people who practise behaviours outside of the consensus are considered "deviants".

While things have undoubtedly improved since Fowler made this assessment, gay people (men in particular), as an "outside" group, may still be presented in opposition to "mainstream" heterosexual society. Their news value is high, particularly if linked to a sexual scandal. However, in recent years many gay politicians or politicians involved in a gay "scandal" have received the same kind of press coverage that politicians caught up in heterosexual sexual scandals have received. As *Part Three* will illustrate, while particular stereotypes and themes are often still utilized in the 2000s, explicit homophobia (*e.g.* use of particular words) is far less common; it is often the "kiss and tell" aspect of a gay sexual scandal story which is utilized, rather than its homosexuality. So, there is almost sexual scandal "equality." "Almost" because gay sexual scandal stories are inherently more "scandalous" than heterosexual sexual scandal stories, for the simple fact that homosexuality is often portrayed by the (tabloid) press and thought of by some of the public as "other". Therefore, gay political scandals are not only newsworthy because of the suggestion of political scandal, they are newsworthy because the scandal involves homosexuality.

## Conclusion

Changes and issues in the way the press works are central topics in the representation of gay politicians in the UK press. The focus on the personal present in today's newspapers would not have taken place without developments in the communication process, a move to mediated forms of communication and a new "publicness" which changed how politicians could interact with and present themselves to the public. It is no surprise that homosexuality, as an aspect of the personal, has been seen as particularly newsworthy, from the 1800s to the present day. Its "news value", as different to the supposed "norm", is still present in the press today. Chapter 1 has given background to Frames Two and Three of the overarching frame of representation described in the *Introduction*: the notion of homosexuality being rated in terms of acceptability and "heterosexual public space" and the idea of (gay) politicians having mediated personas. These issues will be explored in more detail in Chapter 2, alongside Frame One — recognition — leading to the introduction in Chapter 3 of an overarching frame of representation through which the changing representation of gay politicians in the UK press can be mapped. Throughout this process the notion of public and private bubbles away: the idea that there are different "spheres" of action; the idea that some things are deemed private and others public; the idea that divisions can change and have changed over the years. The following chapter explores these issues in more detail.

### Notes

1. John Profumo (Conservative MP for Kettering 1940–5 and Stratford-on-Avon 1950–63), Minister for War, was forced to resign from Parliament after it was revealed he had lied about an affair with a young woman who was also having an affair with a Soviet military official.
2. The market concept in itself can also be problematic: it treats audiences as consumers rather than a public. As McQuail (2005: 399–400) writes: "It links sender and receiver in a 'calculative' rather than normative or social

relationship . . . People in audiences do not normally have any awareness
of themselves as belonging to markets, and the market discourse in relation to the audience is implicitly manipulative."

3.  In fact, Cole (1997: abstract) suggests that "while there has been changes
    in news reporting it is not strictly one way and down; indeed, there is some
    evidence to indicate an upmarketing amongst the tabloid press and televi-
    sion." In this article material is presented from *The Sun, Daily Telegraph,
    The Times* and a number of television channels for comparison.

4.  In the late 1800s a house on Cleveland Street in London was run as a male
    brothel. The brothel came to police notice when a fifteen-year-old boy
    called Charles Swinscow was accused of having an unusual amount of
    money on his person (money had been stolen from the Central Telegraph
    Office where he worked as a telegraph messenger). When questioned, the
    boy admitted that he had earned the money by "going to bed with
    gentlemen" in the house on Cleveland Street.

# 2

# Issues of Public and Private

"Since . . . the arrival of the 'mediated society' in all its forms, sexualities have become more and more entrenched within media forms. People increasingly have come to live their sexualities through, and with the aid of, television, press, film, and more recently, cyberspace." (Plummer 2003a: 275)

## Private Acts made Public

Plummer illustrates that the press is now a public space in which sexualities are discussed, defined and even disputed — a place in which private morality is defined as a public act. Although the research presented here upholds the notion of the private/public binary (at least in relation to the idea that society generally has about "appropriate" behaviour in private and public), in many ways the division is an artificial one. As Plummer (2003b) also writes, the personal and the public cannot be spilt up so easily; in fact, they actually shape each other. However, UK governments have attempted to regulate homosexuality in terms of the private and public. In 1967 when homosexuality was partially decriminalized, the notion of privately acceptable but publicly unacceptable homosexuality came to the forefront. Weeks (2000) notes that the role of the law was to enshrine and maintain proper standards of order and decency *in public*. While the private and public domains were legislated against in this strict way in the mid-twentieth century, the public has encroached on the private (and vice versa). As Weeks explains, while sexuality is a private and personal activity, it is a very public one as well; while we may be embarrassed to discuss it, at the same time it is sensationalized and publicized in the media. This chapter explores private and public spaces and definitions in order to flesh out some of the issues present in the changing representation of gay politicians in the UK press. It gives background to the overarching frame of representation to be defined in Chapter 3, which will then be applied to the case studies of *Part Two* and *Three*.

## Definitions and Boundaries

Although the parameters of the private/public binary (in relation to sexuality and in general) can be debated, Habermas's ([1962] 1991: 1) definition of the public, although contested, is a helpful one to engage with: "We call events and occasions 'public' when they are open to all, in contrast to closed or exclusive affairs." An individual's homosexuality, although something which can be discussed and viewed by and in the public, can therefore be considered a private matter in that it is not something that the public ordinarily has any part in.[1] As such, a useful definition of the private realm comes from Inness (1992: 140): "privacy is the state of possessing control over a realm of intimate decisions." One can also think in terms of private and public morality. Public morality refers to ethical standards within a society (which may become laws and regulation). Private morality refers to the idea that individuals can decide for themselves what is moral (linking back to Inness's idea of "intimate decisions"), although decisions may be influenced by the ideas of, and understood by, others. The difference between public and private morality does not necessarily relate to different values, but how they are applied in different situations. What is defined as acceptable public behaviour, and moral private behaviour, can obviously differ from person to person, but there is a general shared definition of, or consensus about, what is "right" or "wrong" in society (something which changes over time). Of course, laws may not always reflect the general consensus (they may be more or less liberal than people would like), and the consensus may be strong or weak.

It is not just the notion of the private/public binary which is disputed: the notion of "spheres", "spaces" or "realms" has also been contested. Steinberger (1999: 294) believes that the private/public binary needs to be considered in relation to "acts" performed: "[it is better] to think of public and private as denoting not primarily — perhaps not at all — separate realms of endeavour but different ways of being in the world, what I shall call different 'manners of acting'." This is not to say that he believes the distinction between the private and public should be abandoned altogether; he goes on to state that the difference is a very important one and our job is to work out how the distinction between private and public can be maintained, while acknowledging that for many people such a rigid separation is unsustainable. For Steinberger it is the act performed rather than the space in which it is performed that is important. As he explains, there are no spaces that are specifically public or private, but there are manners of acting that are distinctly public or private. Steinberger (1999: 311) takes marriage as an example and notes that it is not an entirely private event between two people or within a family; the "realm of marriage", in common with all realms or spheres, is instead a mixture of private and public manners of acting. Thus, a private marriage has implications of a public nature — laws, political and religious issues *etc.*

He also writes about sexual intimacy and notes that while in many ways sex is a private matter, it can become a public one (for example, the sexual abuse of a minor is a matter for the police). However, Steinberger (1999: 310) states that while society tends to agree that sexual intimacy is a private matter (aside from issues such as sexual abuse or incest), "we are much less inclined to agree about . . . sodomy or sadomasochism." So, some types of sexual intimacy and even sexuality are more public than private to begin with. In fact, he writes that society can turn a private activity into a public one if it decides that interference is needed. The public can therefore override control over our private and intimate decisions. The media play a big role in the process and can decide whether something is a public rather than private matter, according to the socio-political factors of the time.

## "Heterosexual Public Space" and Acceptability

Homosexual sexual intimacy has definitely been dragged into the public realm over the last hundred or so years, much more so than heterosexual sexual intimacy. As Steinberger suggests when he mentions sodomy, society has regarded, and perhaps still regards to an extent, homosexuality as an issue of "public concern" (hence the reams of political and press discussion about issues such as the age of consent). In fact, it could be said that homosexuality equals public sexuality and — linked — the public is a "heterosexual space"; but it is not to say that heterosexuality is not discussed in public. What is of importance is that homosexuality has had its very acceptability debated and judged in public, in a way in which heterosexuality has not, because heterosexual sex is "natural" and the "norm" to many people.

It could be argued that it is not being gay in itself that is or has been problematic for gay people (gay men in particular, as lesbianism has

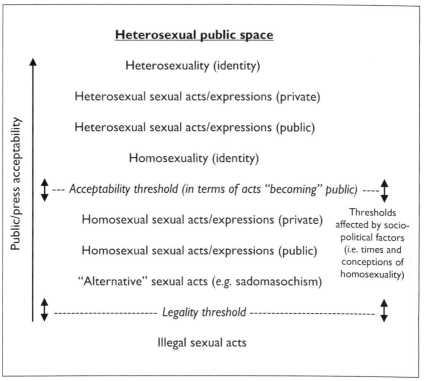

**Figure 2.1** The relationship between sexuality, sexual acts and public space (c.2000s).

never been directly legislated against), particularly in recent years. More accurately, it is the actual act of sodomy. So, homosexual penetration can be categorized as not only a breach of "normal" sexuality, and in the past law, but as a breach of the "proper" way of acting in "heterosexual society"; even though homosexual sexual acts may be carried out in private, they become public acts, something to be judged by "heterosexual society" in "heterosexual public space". As much then as it is not a homosexual identity in itself which is problematic (at least in recent times), private and public spaces or manners of acting may be a secondary issue: it may be the homosexual sexual act which is of concern in the first instance, whether that takes place privately or publicly, if those terms are used.[2] Of course, homosexual sexual intimacy which takes place in the privacy of, for example, a home, is generally less problematic (at least in relation to the visibility of homosexuality) than public homosexual sexual intimacy, showing that the private/public binary is still important, as explored in figure 2.1, which has been influenced by Steinberger's ideas as well as figure 1.1: sexuality/sexual acts can be rated in terms of public acceptability and "heterosexual public space".

What is acceptable has changed over the years, hence the dating of figure 2.1. In the 1950s, for example, all homosexual acts would be below the legality threshold. Concepts of the private and public and acceptability may also be different for the press and for individuals (whether public figures or not). It must also be taken into account that heterosexual opinions of acceptability are not one and the same; while some heterosexual people are fully accepting of homosexuality, others are not. There are also "cohorts" of homophobia, with factors such as religion and culture having an impact on the views of particular "groups". Plus, there may be differences between different *types* of public space: rural versus urban spaces, local versus national newspapers or tabloid versus broadsheet newspapers. Thus "heterosexual public space" as a concept, can be debated, analysed and contextualized. As figure 2.1 suggests, legality and acceptability may not tie in with one another; something may be legal but considered unacceptable by the press, or illegal but considered acceptable. Generally, in the contemporary UK, legality and acceptability have moved in one direction, towards liberality, although in the 1980s the appearance of HIV/AIDS affected public opinion negatively; British Social Attitudes data suggests that public attitudes towards homosexuality became less liberal in the 1980s — post HIV/AIDS — before becoming more positive as the 1980s ended.[3]

While it could be argued that private homosexual sexual acts should be categorized as being above the acceptability threshold in figure 2.1, and they have without doubt moved in such a direction over the last ten years, it may be that they are not quite there yet in terms of full acceptability, something suggested by the amount of press attention given to issues such as the age of gay consent in recent years and public opinion data: the issue has been regarded as still being of public concern. British Social Attitudes data reveals that in 2010 36% of people thought that sexual relations between two consenting adults of the same sex were "always" or "mostly wrong", down from 62% in 1983 (Natcen 2010).[4] While a big increase in liberality, the statistic suggests that full acceptability still has some way to go (only 39% said it was "not wrong at all" — other categories included "rarely wrong" or "sometimes wrong"). Generational change is important when it comes to changing public attitudes, with younger people often more open-minded. It therefore follows that as time progresses, attitudes towards issues such as homosexuality are likely to become even more liberal. In relation to how public opinion changes, McQuail (2005: 501) suggests the media acts as a "channel and facilitator" thus reflecting society and providing the means for debate and change: it mirrors and shapes boundaries, to use an important term from the frame of representation. If newspapers are led by their readers, mirroring and shaping, rather than directly setting public opinion (although it may sometimes occur), the move towards acceptability has been driven by the public. There are other social factors involved in mirroring and shaping (such as families, culture *etc.*). Indeed, the idea of the media as a "gatekeeper" suggests there is one "gate", whereas there are actually multiple "gates". So, the move towards liberality is influenced by multiple factors, the press being one.

While the heterosexuality of public space(s) can be debated and should be contextualized, it is a concept well discussed in academia (see Binnie 1997; Duncan 1996; Johnston 1997; Myslik 1996; Namaste 1996; Valentine 1993; and Valentine 1996, amongst many others). Brickell (2000) suggests that public space is heterosexual in two ways:

- Heterosexuality is regarded as unproblematic in public spaces, unlike homosexuality which is policed
- Heterosexuality is not marked in public in the same way as homo-sexuality.

The idea of a dominant "heterosexual public space" can be read in relation to the feminist notion of the feminine private sphere/masculine public sphere dynamic. Feminist writers have suggested that this is what the feminist struggle is all about. Pateman (1988) suggests that through a sexual contract men control women; through marriage and sex, patriarchy is upheld. The public sphere can be interpreted as a patriarchal space through which women are dominated, therefore rele-gating them to the private or domestic sphere. Heterosexuality and homosexuality can be understood in a similar way: through the domi-nation of public space, homosexuality is pushed into the private sphere, so the public sphere is a dominant, heterosexual space. Accordingly, it is not surprising that gay women were excluded from many of the early laws relating to homosexuality. Not only is public space predominately heterosexual, it is (or was particularly so in the past) a male space, thus contributing to the "invisibility" of gay women in society.

Even though the private lives of gay politicians have become more public over the last fifty years, and the dominance of heterosexuality in the public sphere is being challenged, gay politicians and gay people more generally may still be expected to limit public "displays" of their sexuality (including campaigning about gay rights); this is echoed in figure 2.1, with the mention of "expressions" in relation to public/private homosexuality, as well as "sexual acts". The notion of "expressing" or "displaying" sexuality does not usually apply to heterosexual people, unless their actions are considered inappropriate. Brickell (2000: 166) explains, "The boundaries of permissibility are set in different places for homosexuality". As he goes on to recognize, same-sex expressions of affection, unlike heterosexual ones, are not common to the front pages of newspapers (or at least, in the UK in the 2000s, not *as* common). Heterosexuality is "unmarked" within society (Brickell 2000; Young 1990); it is not noticed, even though it is ever present.

The notion of "heterosexual public space" can be related to newspapers. As something written for and mediated by the mostly heterosexual public (if one understands sexuality in terms of homo/heterosexual identities, something which can be disputed, but with which the press engages), newspapers can be seen as a heterosexual space, contributing to the publicness of heterosexual sexual intimacy and relegation of homosexual sexual intimacy. As the *Gay News* (THE EXPERIMENT THAT SUCCEEDED, 24 June 1982) noted in an editorial in the early 1980s: "A free press, they say, is the great defence against tyranny. There is no free press in this country for homosexuals. Apply a simple test: who can you think of who writes for the quality or popular press, whenever it would be relevant, as an out gay? If people cannot be open about their homosexual viewpoint to the same degree that heterosexual writers are about their viewpoint, then a significant section of opinion finds no expression in Britain's 'free press' and that press is not free."

Of course, there are many more openly gay journalists now than in the 1980s, and positive articles by and about gay people do now appear in the press (although negative articles about gay people increased post-1982 as a result of the appearance of HIV/AIDS). A gay "public sphere" (one overlapping with/existing alongside the "heterosexual public sphere") has begun to emerge, something Clarke (2000) discusses in relation to America. While heterosexuality dominates the press, "alternative" voices are coming through, challenging the dominance of heterosexuality. Plummer (2003b) recognizes that the gay and lesbian movement is developing its own culture while making inroads in public culture more generally, therefore bringing gay public spheres into the "mainstream" public. Yet, while the representation of gay politicians and gay people as a whole has improved as gay voices and

---

"Acceptable" gay politicians  = "Out" gay politicians
= Private acts/spaces

"Unacceptable" gay politicians  = "Closeted" gay politicians
= Public acts/spaces

---

**Figure 2.2**  The private/public frame.

experiences have penetrated the heterosexual media, to a certain extent the private/public dichotomy of 1967 still exists. As explored in *Part Two* and *Three*, while the press (particularly the tabloid press) likes gay people to be "upfront" about their homosexuality, private "acts" or "displays" of homosexuality are more acceptable than public ones. Further, certain "types" of gay people and behaviour are more acceptable than others: "safe" sexual behaviour is acceptable, "dangerous" sexual behaviour (which does not fit a sexual "norm") is not (again, particularly in the tabloid press). As such, definitions of private and public spaces or acts can be used to frame the changing representation of gay politicians in the (mainly tabloid) press (see figure 2.2).

Out/in and private/public are key binary themes, identified in Frame Three of the overarching frame of representation. A third category exists: "acceptable" can also equal gay politicians who are known or believed to be gay, but who do not publicize their sexuality, *i.e.* they believe their sexuality to be a private matter. Such a category is also representative of the old Conservative Party mantra of keeping homosexuality private. There have always been gay politicians in the Conservative Party, an unproblematic fact (privately, the Party was always very tolerant). Problems only arose when the sexuality of gay Tory politicians became publicly known/exposed (the private/public "boundary" — if that term is used — was transgressed). Indeed, if one thinks of Oscar Wilde's arrest and trial, he was punished not just because he was partaking in illegal sexual acts, but because his behaviour transgressed boundaries, or to use Steinberger's terminology, because his manner of acting (in relation to his homosexual sexual behaviour) was inappropriate.

It should be recognized here that the legitimacy of a binary or dichotomous approach has been challenged. Prokhovnik (1999) suggests that dichotomy can entrench division, and Grosz (1994: 3) states that such an approach "hierarchises and ranks the two polarised terms" so that one is deemed negative. As an alternative to binaries, a "relational" theory and practice has been proposed. A relational approach eschews twofold difference and instead allows for other possibilities. However, people often *do* see the world through binaries or by using binary reasoning, with one binary ranked higher than its opposite: a gay politician is good *or* bad, safe *or* dangerous for example, with the latter binaries deemed negative. In the same way, the press defines sexuality as heterosexual *or* homosexual: there is rarely an engagement with a relational idea of sexuality. The press certainly uses binary reasoning, as demonstrated in *Part Two* and *Three*. By doing so, they simplify matters and can "sell" their argument more easily.

While gay people and politicians have become more visible over time in what could be called the dominant, "heterosexual public sphere", certain norms of behaviour are still expected of them. It is still the case that the (tabloid) press and perhaps society as whole defines the private sexual acts of gay people in terms of the heterosexual public. Following on from Padgug (1992) and Richardson (1996), Brickell suggests that if gay people try and inhabit public spheres, an insupportable breach occurs. It is no surprise that some gay men and women may prefer to "exist within" the gay public sphere (*i.e.* the gay media, gay leisure spaces *etc.*). That said, Brickell maybe goes too far in his statement; in some public spaces displays of same-sex affection are not (as) marked (the central London location of Soho perhaps, or a liberal broadsheet such as the *Guardian*). Perhaps it is the case that some gay people do not always want to be fully integrated. After all, in order that the gay community and gay public spaces are strongly defined, there has to be some appreciation of difference within and in relation to heterosexuality. And, as much as an appreciation of difference does not necessarily equal homophobia on the part of heterosexual people, an acknowledgement of difference does not necessarily mean that gay people want to withdraw from "mainstream" society.

## Recognition and Norms of Behaviour

The norms of behaviour which gay men and women are supposed to uphold in relation to "heterosexual public space" can be related to "recognition", as can the idea of acknowledging difference. According to "the politics of recognition" (C. Taylor 1992), marginalized groups are entitled to equal rights and respect rather than a grudging or reluctant tolerance, alongside recognition of their own particularity. Certainly, acceptance suggests that full approval has not been given because if it has, there is nothing to accept. The politics of recognition is an extension of the politics of equal dignity (Abbey 1999; C. Taylor 1992) or identity politics, the belief that people are entitled to equal rights and respect. Identity politics calls for marginalized groups, identified by shared characteristics, to gain equality, or at least advance towards it, via political action. There is tension between the politics of recognition and identity politics. The politics of recognition calls for distinct identities rather than equality (although people should be treated equally in common practice). One could call it normalizing (identity politics) versus difference (recognition). Taylor (1992: 38) writes: "With the politics of equal dignity, what is established is meant to be universally the same, an identical basket of rights and immunities; with the politics of difference, what we are asked to recognize is the unique identity of this individual or group, their distinctness from everyone else."

A good example of the dichotomy is UK civil partnerships. Some gay activists believe that the legislation introduced in 2005 did not go far enough; while it gave the same legal rights to gay couples as marriage gives to heterosexual couples, it is not marriage. It did not give absolute equality in relation to its name or religious context. Gay rights campaigner Peter Tatchell, for example, called it a "watered down version of marriage" (*Daily Post*, GAY MARRIAGE PLANS DON'T GO FAR ENOUGH, 30 June 2003). On the other hand, some gay activists do not want "gay marriage" legalized; they are satisfied with civil partnerships in name and as a legal device because they do not want to be the same as heterosexuals. As gay men and women they want a distinct identity, to celebrate their difference at the same time as gaining *legal* equality. The singer and activist Elton John, for example, stated in relation to debates surrounding gay marriage in the USA, "I don't want to be married. I'm very happy with a civil partnership . . . You get the same equal rights that we do when we have a civil partnership. Heterosexual people get married. We can have civil partnerships" (*USA Today*, ELTON JOHN: WHERE PROP 8 WENT WRONG, 13 November 2008).[5] Of course, it could be said that what is important is equality of *opportunity*. So, gay men and women should have the opportunity to get married or to reject marriage, civil or religious, in the same way as heterosexual couples.

While public opinion polls suggest that homosexuality has become increasingly tolerated as time has gone on (allowing for setbacks such as public and press opinion towards HIV/AIDS), *full* recognition has not yet been reached. In the case of gay politicians, they are generally accepted but not yet recognized as whole individuals, particularly in relation to public spaces. For example, gay politicians are accepted by the press if they are asexual, private individuals: their sexuality must not be overt, and they must definitely not "flaunt" it in public. If they do, they lose their acceptance. Therefore, they are not recognized as "whole" or "full" sexual individuals, as explored in the case studies of *Part Two* and *Three*.

Taylor's concept of recognition is not unproblematic in itself or when applied to gay people and politicians. In his work Taylor suggests that for minority groups/sub-cultures (such as the Québécois) there is "one" recognition. However, this suggests that all the members of the group share the same characteristics at an individual level and have the same goals and opinions *etc.*, but it may not necessarily be the case, leading on to the question: who decides what those characteristics should be? It is doubtless the case that some people will disagree with the characteristics identified, leading to a two-tier system of identification, with minorities within a so-called homogeneous group. In relation to homosexuality, it has to be asked whether group recognition works for gay people. The press presents gay people as having different characteristics and lifestyles, but gay men and women may also not see themselves as a homogeneous group. As a result, expecting recognition from others can be difficult if the members of the group concerned are not settled on what it means to be a member of the group. That said, Taylor's concept of recognition can still be applied to the press representation of gay politicians. The argument presented here discusses recognition of *particularity*; gay politicians do not necessarily have to share all of the same characteristics as part of the process (although the presence of negative binary themes affects the likelihood of recognition). So, recognition of particularity equals recognition of the fact that someone is a *gay individual*.

## Intimate Citizenship

In many ways, the private sphere as a whole has shrunken (or, to use Steinberger's terminology, what were private acts are now public ones): private lives are now defined in and judged by the public. As Plummer (2003b: 68) writes in relation to "intimate citizenship": "In the late modern world, the personal invades the public and the public invades the personal." Is this problematic? What effect does a shrunken private sphere, to use that term, have on the way society works? It could be argued that the erosion of the private sphere impacts upon the freedom that people have to live their lives the way they want to, free from public interference (assuming that their actions are legal). Consequently, privacy is actually undermined unless there is a strict boundary between the private and public, something articulated by Arendt (1958). Equally, it could be maintained that people should be allowed privacy in their lives; just because something is private or not discussed in public (for example, a gay politician's sexuality), it does not mean that the public will necessarily suffer.

It can be argued that by denying the existence of a wholly private realm, privacy is "always enjoyed only at the sufferance of public authority" (Steinberger 1999: 312). Steinberger disagrees, noting that privacy, as a fundamental aspect of life, can be defended against public life, an analysis that is rather optimistic, given the difficultly of defending privacy in the face of the move to the personal and mediated society. Steinberger is correct though to note that the distinction between the public and private is a fluid one today, although one could maintain it is (or should be) more robust than he presumes. While private acts often become public ones if they require public judgement and accountability, Steinberger (1999: 310) comments that "No such [private] realm exists." However, the opposite could be stated: the private realm does exist, and only in extreme cases should it be violated. For, how do we assess when public judgement and accountability are needed? Also, it must be acknowledged that society acts as if there are strict boundaries, something supported and influenced by time-specific moral codes and laws focusing on what is and is not appropriate (public) behaviour. It is all well and good to say that these strict boundaries do not exist, but in practice many believe that they should. Another interesting point of Steinberger's work is his comment that "any act is presumed to be private unless shown otherwise" (1999: 312). Conversely, it could be argued that the press as an institution believes that any (sexual) act is a *public* one unless shown otherwise; the press can easily argue — and has done on numerous occasions — that a politician's homosexuality is a public matter because the public has the right to know about the private lives of politicians. Indeed, it is often claimed that the public interest overrides any right a politician has to a (relatively) private life. The politician concerned, however, is likely to disagree.

## Conclusion

The idea of the erosion of the private sphere goes hand in hand with the notion of a mediated society; people's private lives, including those of gay politicians, are lived in and presented through the media. In fact, people in the public eye, including gay politicians, now have "mediated personas", discussed by Evans (2005) in relation to celebrity and Corner (2000) in relation to politicians. The notion of private lives being lived through the media — what could be termed a (re)presentation of reality — is not a new one. Baudrillard ([1981] 1995), for example, judged that reality and meaning within society had been replaced by symbols and signs, and what society thinks is real is just a simulation of the real — the "hyperreal". The media can be seen as a space in which the hyperreal — or artifice — is presented.[6] In Baudrillard's world, communication becomes a means to an end, something which impacts upon the public and private and sexuality. Wulf (2005) suggests that the private and public spheres are disappearing under one dimension of information, making sexuality too visual. As such, the homosexuality of politicians, as an aspect of the personal — and something which can be mediated — becomes an area of press focus. In particular, if a politician's personal life does not meet particular (moral) criteria, the press may comment on it, with homosexuality an issue of "public concern". The changing representation of gay politicians in the UK press is therefore not only linked to how the press works and how newspapers discusses politicians and homosexuality generally, it also relates to the shrinking of the private sphere, notions of acceptability and "heterosexual public space" and recognition. In Chapter 3, these issues come together to form an overarching frame of representation through which the press representation of gay politicians can be mapped.

### Notes

1. Although people sometimes make highly ("political") celebrations of their sexuality with the aim of making it a public issue.
2. It is important to note that the sexual act does not necessarily equal sexuality; a man may have sex with another man, but it does not mean that either of them identify as gay or bisexual.
3. When asked about sexual relations between two people of the same sex, the following percentage of people answered that they were "always" or "mostly wrong" in relation to the following years: 1983 — 62%; 1985 — 69%; 1987 — 74%; 1989 — 68% (Britsocat 2011; Brook *et al.* 1992 cited Rayside 1998: 40). Other options included "sometimes wrong", "rarely wrong" and "not wrong at all". Percentages rounded to whole numbers.

4. Percentages rounded to whole numbers.
5. Although he was later reported as condemning America's ban on gay marriage (*Guardian*, ELTON JOHN ATTACKS BAN ON GAY MARRIAGE, 24 January 2011).
6. Baudrillard's musings on scandal are actually another interesting way of examining political scandals; scandals are simulations of scandal, engineered to strengthen morality.

# 3

# Unifying Key Themes

"Frames are principles of selection, emphasis and presentation composed of little tacit theories about what exists, what happens, and what matters." (Gitlin 1980: 6)

## Introducing the Frame

Chapter 1 and 2 have suggested that the press focus on and representation of homosexuality has a historical and theoretical basis which creates conditions of possibility for the ways in which gay politicians are written about. In particular, three key themes have been explored so far:

- Recognition
- Acceptability and public spaces
- Binary themes and mediated personas.

These themes can be brought together to make an overarching frame of representation, demonstrating why the representation of gay politicians in the UK press takes the form it does, how it has changed and key issues in press coverage. After a brief overview of the overall concept of frames and framing, the chapter explores the overarching frame of representation in more detail. It is presented as both a preview and result of research, building on the preceding historical and theoretical discussion, before the case studies to be presented in *Part Two* and *Three* show how the frame was induced and how it can be applied.

## Frame Analysis

Frames can be understood as a social scientific method of understanding the world around us, a concept attributed to Goffman (1974).

Konig (2007), for example, notes that frames are "cognitive structures which guide the perception and representation of reality." Frame analysis as a concept is not unified; there are different approaches within the qualitative and quantitative fields. A qualitative approach is taken here, identifying themes and the use of key words, categories and concepts (a quantitative approach might count the use of particular key words).

Entman (1993: 52) notes that framing is taking aspects of a "perceived reality" and making them more prominent in a text, thus promoting a point of view. While Goffman did not believe that frames were consciously manufactured — he felt they were unconsciously adopted — Entman and other theorists such as D'Angelo (2002) and Tankard (2001) and Reese (2001), suggest that frames are *selected*. A midway point between these two opposing standpoints seems appropriate in relation to the ideas proposed here. So, while journalists may not actively frame their work, through their training and immersion in their own newspaper's moral and political environment, the frame is present: journalists see gay politicians in a particular way.

The overarching frame of representation discussed here can be understood in relation to frame analysis. As such, the binary themes identified in press coverage can be thought of as metanarratives or "master frames" (McAdam 1994: 41–3). These metanarratives/master frames do not exist in isolation: they draw on codes already present in society. Therefore the press draws on public opinion, law, medicine *etc.* when employing these themes.

The ultimate aim of the press is frame alignment (Snow *et al.* 1986). When the frames employed do not align, or perhaps resonate with the reader, their incongruity is apparent. For example, *The Sun*'s coverage of Peter Mandelson and Nick Brown's "outings" in 1998 was deemed by some broadsheet newspapers, commentators and members of the public to be a step too far (something later admitted by the then editor, as discussed in Chapter 9), suggesting that there are perhaps limits to the overarching frame of representation: the binary themes/metanarratives employed were inappropriate. As Cappella and Jamieson (1997) recognize, journalists and the audience may frame news differently, suggesting that while newspapers aim to reinforce public opinion and align their frames with the public, they may be unsuccessful. If a newspaper crosses the line, as *The Sun* apparently did in 1998, they have to step back within an appropriate frame pretty quickly in order that their press coverage resonates with their readership.

## The Frame of Representation

The representation of gay politicians in UK newspapers can be understood in relation to frames and framing. In particular, three interconnected frames, making up an overarching frame of representation, are present in press coverage:

### 1. The move towards recognition

The move towards recognition suggests that gay politicians have become increasingly tolerated as time has gone on — although it has been a halting process, quicker at some times than others, with some backward steps. Full recognition is a status which has not yet been reached by gay politicians; they are generally accepted (bar "bad" acts), but not yet recognized as whole individuals. While there may not be "one" recognition for gay people — because what it means to be gay may be different for individuals — wholeness has the potential to be achieved; recognition of particularity (*i.e.* a gay politician's homosexuality) can be an acknowledgment of the fact that someone is a *gay individual*, meaning that gay politicians can have different characteristics within recognition.

### 2. Acceptability over time (in relation to "heterosexual public space")

Sexuality and sexual acts can be understood in relation to the acceptance of society and "heterosexual public space". Public homosexuality has become more acceptable over the last fifty years, although has not reached full acceptability. Although homosexuality has grown in acceptance (legally and socially), the "heterosexual public space" part of the frame is very important: there is an acceptability threshold in terms of acts becoming public. Indeed, homosexuality is marked in society because public space as a whole is heterosexual. Therefore, gay politicians are expected to act a certain way in public and not cross the acceptability threshold.

### 3. Mediated personas as "constructed reality"

The binary themes present in the press representation of gay politicians suggest that there are two main types of persona for gay politicians as presented by the press: negative and positive. Although they are stronger at certain times than others (for example, negative themes, while still utilized, were stronger in the 1980s when HIV/AIDS was classified as a gay disease), these personas are still in play. It is, however, important to note that there are gradients within the mediated personas

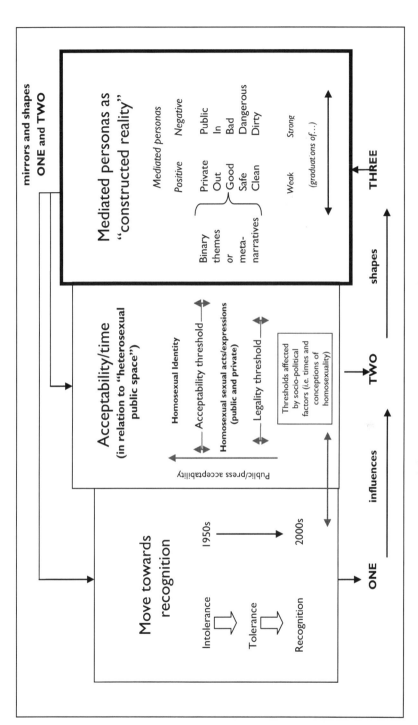

**Figure 3.1** The changing representation of gay politicians in the UK press: a frame of representation.

and binary themes. As such, some politicians have a stronger or weaker negative or positive mediated persona than others, or may meet a particular binary theme more conclusively. Tabloid and broadsheet differences apply here; tabloid newspapers are more likely to write about the personal lives of gay politicians and cover sexual "scandals" and are therefore more likely to portray gay politicians using negative themes and personas.

The interconnected frames create conditions of possibility for press representation and are present throughout recent history. So, while the representation of gay politicians in the 2000s is less discriminatory than the early 1990s or earlier, the frames are still in place. While aspects of the three frames have been addressed in literature, the ways in which the frames are linked within an overarching frame, and the application of them to the press representation of gay politicians, is new.

Figure 3.1 conceptualizes the overarching frame of representation. It shows that Frame One influences Frame Two (with Frame Two also influencing Frame One), which shapes Frame Three: the move from intolerance to tolerance to partial recognition impacts upon the acceptability of homosexuality in "heterosexual public space" (and vice versa), with these processes then affecting the representation of gay politicians in the press. Frame One, recognition, is about public and press attitudes and Frame Two, acceptability, about behaviour. Frame Three then shapes and mirrors Frames One and Two, showing that the media influences and is also influenced. Indeed, while the research here concentrates on the influence of the press, there are other social factors which are part of the process too. The (predominantly) unidirectional trajectory of Frames One and Two (in that there is generally a move towards liberality) is supplemented by Frame Three, which has the most impact on a day-to-day basis: readers can see the binary themes and mediated personas when reading their newspapers. Frame Three is "constant" in that the binary themes and mediated personas are always present. However the strength of the themes and personas change over time, and thus link back to Frames One and Two.

The interconnected frames used to illustrate the changing representation of gay politicians in the UK press show that newspaper coverage is a representation of reality: gay politicians are *filtered through* press representation. Herewith is the key framework used to discuss the changing representation of gay politicians in the UK press. Through piece by piece theory construction, the overarching frame is built up over the course of the book. While Frames One and Two provide context and background to the press representation of gay politicians, Frame Three reveals *how* gay politicians are represented. As such, *Part*

*Two* and *Three* use binary themes and mediated personas as an explanatory tool.

## Conclusion

Chapter 3, and *Part One* overall, has provided theoretical background to the ways in which gay politicians are represented in the UK press. Through its discussion and definition of an overarching frame of representation through which the press representation of gay politicians (as well as politicians caught up in a gay "scandal") can be mapped, this chapter has set the scene for the case studies of *Part Two* and *Three*. In the case study chapters, elements of the overarching frame will be emphasized, discussed and debated in relation to relevant newspaper articles. In particular, Frame Three, mediated personas as "constructed reality", will be focused on, because it is the most visible and "real" frame; as demonstrated by the case studies of Mark Oaten, Simon Hughes and Gregory Barker explored in the *Introduction*, when someone picks up a newspaper and reads an article about a gay politician or a politician caught up in a gay scandal, the binary themes are present, whether explicitly or implicitly. Through such a focus it will become clear how gay MPs are represented in the press, how that representation has changed over time and how it can be mapped using an overarching frame of representation.

# PART TWO

# Exploring "Traditional" Representation

# 4

# Histories of Homosexuality: Definition and Discrimination

"The recent history of homosexuality could best be interpreted as a complex process of definition and self-definition. On the one hand we could trace the social, cultural and political forces that shaped the creation of homosexuality as a minority, and generally socially execrated, experience: religion, the law, state activities, family ideologies, class consolidation, popular prejudice, the institutions of medicine, psychiatry and even sexology. On the other hand there were forces of resistance: individual struggles, subcultural developments, nascent organizations for homosexual rights." (Weeks 2000: 7)

## Understanding Sexual History

Sexuality is not timeless. In fact, homosexuality has a complex, multi-layered history. As recognized by Weeks (2000: 1), sexual history is *made*: "Who makes sexual history? . . . It was taken for granted that the truths of sex were timeless. Attitudes, legal forms, religious injunctions, moral codes, literary expressions, subcultural patterns might change, but the substratum of erotic energy and gendered (as it was not then called) relationships remained locked into biological necessity, beyond the realms of history of social science . . . Today that has all changed." So, not only is "homosexuality" — as a sexuality or perhaps, more accurately, as a concept — particular to a moment in time, legal and medical developments, political and public attitudes and moral ideas also affect each other and the definition and perception of homosexuality. These issues also have an impact on the representation of homosexuality in the press, with the press having an impact in return ("mirroring and shaping", to use a phrase from the overarching frame of representation).

From the mid-twentieth century onwards, UK law has moved in the direction of greater homosexual equality and tolerance. The process has been slow and difficult: while sexual acts between men were partially decriminalized in 1967 (after the 1885 criminalization of homosexual sexual activity), politicians and campaigners continue to fight for further equality. Jeffery-Poulter (1991) notes that up until the early 1980s public opinion towards homosexuality gradually became more liberal echoing advancements in legal rights. However, the 1980s were in many ways a difficult time for gay rights; the AIDS crisis of the early 1980s saw public opinion towards homosexuality become less liberal, and although the legal status of homosexuality became more regularized over the decade, the introduction of Clause 28 (also known as Section 28) in the late 1980s was seen by the gay community as a direct attack on homosexuality by the Conservative Government (although it was perhaps more of a reaction against the *assertion* of gay rights, not necessarily gay rights and people themselves). This chapter surveys these tumultuous changes, investigating the ways in which legal developments, social issues and public and political attitudes affected the media landscape and status of homosexuality, contextualizing the press representation of gay politicians. It is spilt into two sections: pre-1980 and 1980–90. As well as echoing the structure of the case study chapters, Chapter 5 and 6, the division is representative of the UK's socio-political climate. In relation to the overarching frame of representation, the chapter shows a process of intolerance to partial tolerance: recognition (Frame One) was not achieved. Homosexuality, as an identity, became more acceptable as the 1990s approached (Frame Two), but there were still issues of private and public, with public homosexuality problematic, and negative binary themes (Frame Three) prevalent.

## Homosexuality Pre-1980: Criminalization and Legalization

### The 1885 Criminal Law Amendment Act

The Criminal Law Amendment Act of 1885 brought forth new restrictions on homosexual activity: for the first time all forms of sexual activity between men were criminalized. Before then, only sodomy was an actual criminal offence, with the 1861 Offences Against the People Act seeing sentences of ten years to life (replacing the death penalty) introduced for buggery. The 1885 Act did not originally refer to homosexuality at all, and was instead concerned with protecting women through the suppression of brothels, but the clause introduced by Henry Labouchere (Hansard 1885) stated that: "Any male person who, in public or private, commits or is a party to the commission of, or procures or attempts to procure the commission by any male person of any act of gross indecency with another male person, shall be guilty of a misdemeanour". Homosexuality therefore became a criminal, punishable, public identity, and the need for gay men to hide their sexuality became more vital. Weeks (1981a) states that before the 1885 legislation it was sexual *acts* that were the subject of hostile laws, rather than a particular "type" of person; in direct contrast, "homosexuality" was a legal, psychological and medical category, something which could be the subject of speculation but also a new self-articulation. The French philosopher Hocquenghem (1978) wrote that there is a difference between "desire" and the psychological category of homosexuality, but here we see the labelling of desire in legal and medical terms.

## A Homosexual Identity

Homosexuality became unmentionable apart from when it was being condemned (or "speculated" against) which, ironically, became more and more prevalent due to lurid press coverage of court cases. Foucault ([1976] 1998: 36) argues that a "discursive explosion", of which the 1885 Act can be considered part, attempted to banish from society forms of sexuality "not amenable to the strict economy of reproduction". Through the "discursive explosion" laws against so-called perversions increased, sexual difference became linked to mental illness and a norm of sexuality developed. He describes how figures, such as those who were attracted to the same sex, were made to confess what they suddenly "were". The "homosexual" was thus named and became a sexual identity. Foucault ([1976] 1998: 43) believes that the process occurred when sodomy was no longer a forbidden act practised by its subject, but had actually become part of someone's person, and dates it to 1870 when Westphal wrote an article on "contrary sexual sensations". In fact, the word "homosexuality" was not invented until 1869 and did not become commonly used in England until the 1880s and 1890s (Weeks 1981b). Like Foucault, Weeks (1981b: 93) argues that sexuality is organized through "definition and regulation", rather than repression, through the construction of sexual categories such as the homosexual. So, sexuality is constructed and "of its time".

Weeks explores Foucault's theories and writes that the history of sexuality discussed by Foucault is actually a history of discourses about sexuality. Further, Weeks (1981b: 100) claims that "this ever expanding discursive explosion is part of a complex growth of control over individuals, partly through the apparatus of sexuality." So, if one accepts Foucault's analysis about control and power and the construction of sexuality arising from that, then homosexuality was identified in order to protect a natural, productive heterosexual identity. Moreover, power tries to make the process appear natural. However, as Foucault identifies, what is sexually natural differs according to the period being referred to. Medicine — which can be seen as a form of control — played a big part in the categorization of "the homosexual". Certainly, the emergence of homosexuality as a concept tied in with the development of new medical terms used to describe people interested in those of the same sex (Weeks 1981a). It is important to recognize that Foucault's arguments are not universally accepted. Sinfield (1994), for example, believes that the change identified by Foucault, while correct, is a gradual one, with medical and legal discourses of less importance than stated by the author. Sinfield notes that the sexual oppression of working-class women by middle-class men was the main focus of legislation in the period concerned, and the penalization of homosexual men occurred opportunistically within the pattern; the Labouchere amendment was tacked on to the original Criminal Law Amendment Act, rather than focusing entirely, and originally, on homosexuality.

## 1885 Political Opinion

Weeks (1981a: 103) highlights that the 1885 Act was not universally popular at a political level (at least in relation to its form, rather than the general ethos), stating that there was opposition to the Labouchere Amendment at a government level because it applied to private behaviour, as well as public: "The Director of Public Prosecutions noted in 1889 'the expediency of not giving unnecessary publicity' to cases of gross indecency; and at the same time he felt that much could be said for allowing 'private persons — being fully grown men — to indulge in their unnatural tastes in private'." Note the distinction between public (unacceptable) and private (tolerable) behaviour, the same kind of attitude expressed by some politicians and newspapers as late as the late twentieth and even twenty-first centuries, and a binary recognized in the overarching frame of representation (Frame Three).

That distinction aside, in the late nineteenth century politicians of all political colours appeared disgusted (publicly and politically at least) with homosexuals and homosexuality as a whole. Sanderson (1995: 4) argues that the Government echoed the desire of the press to "look away". As he notes, soon after Oscar Wilde's 1895 trial there were calls for the public mention of homosexuality to be forbidden; in 1896 Lord Halsbury introduced the Publication of Indecent Evidence Bill into Parliament with the specific aim of suppressing newspaper articles which focused on prosecutions brought under the Labouchere Amendment. The Prime Minister, Lord Salisbury, backed the Bill (Hansard 1896): "The reason why the publication of that class of cases is so much to be deprecated is not merely because it offends our taste, and makes the reading of the newspapers disgusting, but because it is a well-ascertained fact that the publication of details in cases of that kind has a horrible, though undoubtedly direct, action in producing an imitation of the crime by other people." Sanderson believes the Bill was not passed in Parliament due to pressure exerted by newspaper editors and publishers (demonstrating that even in the nineteenth century, the press was keen to assert the importance of press freedom), but homosexuality continued to be thought of as an unfit topic for discussion: there was a "philosophy of silence" (Sanderson 1995: 5). This certainly applied to the general public as well at the time although, as with issues of a sexual nature today, people revelled in their intimate details. The Wilde trial of 1895, for example, saw newspapers double their circulations by reporting on every minutiae of the case (Sanderson 1995).

## The Impact of the 1885 Act

One of the results of the 1885 Criminal Law Amendment Act was ever-increasing (negative) coverage of homosexuality. In fact, through sensational reporting of court cases, many people were actually made aware of something that previously they did not even know existed or cared to think about, something Labouchere obviously did not intend (Sanderson 1995). One of the first cases to be subject to garish press coverage was Wilde's court case in 1895. The *News of the World* wrote on 26 May 1895 under the headline "THE WILDE CASE", "Oscar Wilde . . . has been convicted of the foulest crime that man can commit — a crime so foul that to call the criminal a beast is to insult the animal." The use of the words "foulest", "beast" and "animal" in the article is remarkable. While warned of the terrible crime of homosexuality, the reader is encouraged to read on through use of these salacious words: in Wilde's case, sex certainly did sell.

Sanderson (1995: 4) notes that the *London Evening Standard* wrote after the Wilde Case: "England has tolerated the man Wilde and others of his kind too long. Before he broke the law of the country and outraged human decency he was a social pest, a centre of intellectual corruption. He was one of the high priests of a school which attacks all the wholesome, manly, simple ideals of English life . . . We venture to hope that the conviction of Wilde for these abominable vices, which were the natural outcome of his diseased intellectual condition, will be a salutary warning to unhealthy boys who posed as sharers of his culture." The way in which the *Standard* article links Wilde's sexual practices to his intellect is revealing because, as stated by Foucault, the sexual act had become intrinsic to the person as a whole. Paradoxically, this was something taken up by those who fitted the new "category" of the homosexual; while the Wilde trial can be thought of as a "labelling process" which drew a line between acceptable and unacceptable behaviour, it also gave gay people a self-consciousness and confidence to acknowledge their difference (Weeks 1981a: 103). At the time there was therefore an emergence of a "whole" homosexual identity. As Foucault ([1976] 1998: 101) writes: "homosexuality began to speak on its own behalf, to demand that its legitimacy or 'naturality' be acknowledged, often in the same vocabulary, using the same categories by which it was radically disqualified."

Homosexuality in the late nineteenth century was irrevocably linked to class identity. Weeks (1981a: 113) discusses how in the period there was a belief that working class people were indifferent to homosexuality because they were "closer to nature", with a much more defined sense of homosexual identity amongst the middle and upper classes and more possibility of homosexual encounters through money and the mobility that it brought. Crossing the class divide through sexual encounters was common (Wilde being the most famous example). As Weeks explores, there was a belief that sex across classes was reconciling. The public attitude of much of the "ruling" class towards homosexuality was in fact rather ironic, for it was that class of men that was key in articulating the homosexual voice (through literature, drama and the early homosexual reform movement) at the end of the nineteenth century.

## Post-1885 Politics

Following the 1885 Act, the law against homosexuality was further strengthened. The 1898 Vagrancy Act tightened up laws in relation to importuning for "immoral purposes" — in reality, the law was applied against homosexual men exclusively (Weeks 1981a). Through the subsequent Criminal Law Amendment Act of 1912, the offence was set at six months imprisonment, with flogging applicable for a second offence, on summary jurisdiction. Sexual acts between women were not covered by the 1885 Act at all, and later attempts to legislate against lesbians failed to get through Parliament. It was thought that laws against lesbians would actually do more harm than good (Weeks 1981a). When in 1921 such legislation was attempted, Lord Desart (Director of Public Prosecutions when Wilde was charged) exclaimed (Hansard 1921): "You are going to tell the whole world that there is such an offence, to bring it to the notice of women who have never heard of it, never thought of it, never dreamt of it. I think that is a very great mischief." So once again, lesbian women remained invisible.

While no other legislation against homosexuality appeared in the first half of the twentieth century, sex and sexuality were topics at the forefront of discussion. The "theorisation of sex" (Weeks 1981a: 141) in the 1920s achieved respectability as a result of the work of Havelock Ellis and Sigmund Freud, with Ellis suggesting that "normal" behaviour was "no more than what societies defined as the norm" (Weeks 1981a: 144). A major concern of the 1940s and 1950s was the decline of moral standards, homosexual behaviour being a key worry. As such, the police stepped up prosecutions of homosexual behaviour as a result of public and official anxiety, which was in itself related to the post-war stress on monogamous heterosexual relationships and family life, seen as a stark contrast to so-called homosexual "deviancy" (Weeks 1981a).

## The 1967 Sexual Offences Act

The Criminal Law Amendment Act remained in place until 1967, when the Sexual Offences Act decriminalized private sexual activity between consenting men over the age of 21. The Sexual Offences Act was preceded by the Wolfenden Committee, set up in 1954 to look into the law surrounding homosexuality and prostitution (the two issues still being linked, as in 1885), a response to the moral concerns of the 1940s and 1950s but, paradoxically, as suggested by Weeks (1981a), serving as a blueprint for the permissive movement of the 1960s and the need to effectively regulate "deviancy". From the 1885 Act onwards, homosexual prosecutions were common (as were newspaper stories about the resulting court cases, especially in the 1940s and 1950s). Indeed, the number of recorded offences of indecency between two men reached their highest levels ever in the mid-1950s: 2,034 in 1954 and 2,322 in 1955 (Jeffery-Poulter 1991). While taking part in gay sexual activity was an offence, declaring oneself gay was not, highlighting that it was the *act* of homosexual penetration that was deemed most offensive.

The Wolfenden Committee reported in 1957 after 62 meetings at which evidence was gathered from over 200 organizations and individuals. The Committee's report — officially known as *The Report of the Committee on Homosexual Offences and Prostitution*, but more commonly known as the Wolfenden Report — stated (Wolfenden 1957: 43) that "We do not think that it is proper for the law to concern itself with what a man does in private unless it can be shown to be contrary to the public good that the law ought to intervene in its function as guardian of that public good." As the extract suggests, the report was revolutionary in that it debunked so many common ideas about homosexuality. The report found that: homosexuality does not menace the health of society; homosexuality (*i.e.* a homosexual husband) was no more damaging to the family than, for example, adultery (so, if a husband had a heterosexual affair); and, men attracted to other adult men and men attracted to young boys tended to be mutually exclusive categories. The report concluded that all forms of homosexual behaviour between adult men in private should be decriminalized. Crucially, adult did not equal 16, the age of heterosexual consent. Instead, the Wolfenden Report (1957: 51) decided that 21 was the appropriate age for men to have homosexual sex as this was the age that "a man is deemed to be capable of entering into legal contracts".

## 1960s Political and Public Opinion

During the gap between the Wolfenden Report and the implementation of the 1967 Sexual Offences Act, the law surrounding homosexuality was discussed in great detail in the House of Commons. In 1960 a motion asking the Government to take early action to implement the Report's recommendations was defeated by 213 votes to 99.[1] In 1962 a Bill to implement some of the recommendations was talked out in the Commons.[2] And in 1965 a Labour member's attempt to introduce the Sexual Offences Bill in the Commons under the Ten Minute Rule was defeated by 178 votes to 159.[3] Although the Bill was reintroduced in the Commons in 1965, and passed its first and second reading, Parliament's dissolution for a general election meant that the Bill lapsed (Jeffery-Poulter 1991). While the Common's attitude was, as a whole, disappointing, the Sexual Offences Bill was introduced in the House of Lords in 1965 and was passed by the Lords up to its third reading. The Bill was reintroduced in 1966 in the Commons and Lords, and was eventually passed and then given Royal Assent in 1967. Post-1967 campaigns for gay law reform continued (including the struggle to extend the Sexual Offences Act to Northern Ireland and Scotland), but it was a slow process.

Many politicians were not in favour of decriminalizing sexual activity between men in the 1950s and 1960s and did not hesitate to say so in the Commons and Lords. As highlighted by Jeffery-Poulter, when in 1965 a Labour Member attempted to introduce the Sexual Offences Act in the Commons under the Ten Minute Rule, a Conservative backbencher (Hansard 1965) declared "do we wish to encourage sodomy? It is as simple as that . . . This is an age of lawlessness, violence and crime. What we need is sterner discipline, and not more licence." Opposition to gay law reform was not limited to Conservative politicians. While the Bill was supported by the Labour Government of the time, many Labour politicians (mostly traditional, trade union supporting figures) opposed it. The politicians' disapproval not only reflected contemporary moral beliefs, but also perhaps the heterosexual "boys club" atmosphere of the Palace of Westminster and a pronounced private/public divide. Certainly, many heterosexual politicians tolerated homosexuality and gay politicians privately (for example, Tom Driberg, Labour MP for Maldon 1942–55, whose sexuality was an open secret) but "visible" homosexuality — whether practised or discussed — was most certainly not tolerated.

Even supporters of a change in the law were careful to assert that their backing did not mean that Parliament wished to encourage homosexual activity. As Lord Arran (Hansard 1966a), a Liberal peer and champion of the Bill said, "No single Lord or noble Lady has ever said that homosexuality is a right or good thing. It has been universally condemned from start to finish, and by every single member of this House." It is made clear that homosexuality, while permitted in private, had to be banished from the public. Another key supporter of reform, Leo Abse (Labour MP for Pontypool 1958–83 and Torfaen 1983–7), also tempered his support saying (Hansard 1966b), "The paramount reason for the introduction of this Bill is that it may at last move from our community away from being riveted to the question of punishment of homosexuals which has hitherto prompted us to avoid the real challenge of preventing little boys from growing up to be adult homosexuals." Abse later said that the approach he took was necessary in order to get measures of reform through a male-dominated, heterosexist Commons (*Observer*, COMING OUT IN THE DARK AGES, 24 June 2007).

Public attitudes towards homosexuality gradually improved up to and after the 1967 Sexual Offences Act, although class boundaries have to be considered; from the 1960s onwards better-educated middle class people became more liberal towards homosexuality and gender issues, but the change did not reach the lower middle classes, who retained their traditional views (Rayside 1998). So, growing toleration of homosexuality did not necessarily cut across class boundaries, emphasizing the need for two thresholds — acceptability and legality — in Frame Two of the overarching frame of representation.

While the legal changes of the 1960s were obviously regarded by campaigners as positive, they were actually modest. Homosexuality was not fully legalized and there was, as Weeks (2000: 147) writes, "no attempt to create new rights, or . . . to assert the values of different sexual lifestyles." The Wolfenden Report instead vocalized the belief that the law could better protect public decency if it ceased to be concerned with private morality (Weeks 1981a), once more emphasizing a sharp distinction between the private and public, and the furtherance of the idea that public homosexuality was especially problematic and something which needed to be controlled. Of course, for many people (whether politicians, religious leaders or members of the public) the 1967 Act, even with its limitations, was certainly not a cause for celebration; instead, it represented the abandonment of moral standards to be replaced by moral relativism (Weeks 2000).

The permissiveness of the 1960s became for many a symbol of everything that was wrong with society. Perhaps linked, further attempts in the 1970s to improve gay rights were not successful. In 1977 a Bill to reduce the age of gay consent to 18 was defeated in the Lords by 146 votes to 25[4] and in the same year the "Save Ulster from Sodomy" campaign was launched by the Democratic Unionist Party (DUP) in Northern Ireland (homosexuality was still illegal in Northern Ireland). And, in 1972, the Law Lords found a magazine guilty of "conspiracy to corrupt public morals" for publishing gay contact adverts. Paradoxically, though, in the 1960s and 1970s homosexuality became more "visible" (in the arts for example) and by the 1970s a public gay liberation movement was in full flow. In 1970 the first gay demonstration took place in London, in the same year the London Gay Liberation Front (GLF) was founded, the first UK Pride Carnival took place in London in 1971 and in 1976 the Lesbian and Gay Christian Movement (later known as Lesbian and Gay Christians) was founded. Ironically, while the 1967 Sexual Offences Act condemned public "displays" of homosexuality, gay men and women were becoming more and more vocal and political (something which in itself may not have been possible without the 1967 Act).

## Press Opinion Post-1967

Sanderson argues that at the time of the 1967 Act newspapers had generally supported reform (the *Daily Express* being the exception), recognizing the cruelty of the law and the unfairness of destroying men for no good reason. As the *Daily Telegraph* (12 February 1967) wrote: "It will end a law that is equally disreputable for being largely unenforceable and often cruel where enforced; it will shift a great fear from many people, no more sinful than most of their neighbours; it will cut the blackmailer's income; not least it will end a controversy that has become unseemly and disproportionate, and rob homosexuality of the false glamour which always attaches to persecuted minorities." While the majority of newspapers were (guardedly) positive about the Act, it did not cause them to change their general attitude towards homosexuality; newspapers still disliked homosexuality as a general rule and continued to refer to it using moralistic terms (Sanderson 1995).

As the 1980s approached press coverage of homosexuality slowly began to improve, but heterosexuality still coloured gay representation. Sanderson (1995: 2) writes: "Gay events and opinions were certainly being covered in the papers but they were overwhelmingly filtered through straight journalists. We were written about rather than being allowed to speak for ourselves." Gay men and women began to demand representation on their own terms. By the 1960s a few magazines contained contact adverts for gay men, in 1972 the UK's first gay newspaper was founded (the *Gay News*) and by the 1970s *Spartacus*, the first magazine to cater openly for gay men, was available in over 200 gay venues in the UK. *Spartacus* was written by and for gay men; it featured stories, news and articles and made unapologetic reference to gay sex (Jeffery-Poulter 1991). The gay press was part of an emerging gay "public sphere". The "mainstream" press and its negative language were finally being challenged; the invisible were loudly demanding visibility and would no longer accept the way that the national press represented them. Here was a huge step in gay representation. While the gay public sphere is still surrounded by hostility, gay public spaces are now part of public life (Plummer 2001).

## Homosexuality 1980–1990: The Thatcher Years

### Clause 28 and the Thatcher Government

Soon after coming to power in 1979 the Conservative Party, led by Margaret Thatcher (Prime Minister 1979–90 and MP for Finchley 1959–92), made it very clear that furthering gay rights was not part of its agenda. Even though Thatcher, like many Conservatives, was said to be privately tolerant of homosexuals (one of her Parliamentary Private Secretaries was thought to be gay), it became clear very quickly that her Government's priorities lay elsewhere. Indeed, in March 1980 a Labour amendment to the Housing Bill, which would have given gay couples security of tenure in their council accommodation, was defeated.[5] The new Environment Secretary described the amendment as "quite unacceptable . . . it is not part of the philosophy of this Bill to take the lead on an issue of social policy" (Jeffery-Poulter 1991: 139). The statement was negated, however, with the introduction of Clause 28 in 1987.

Clause 28 — an amendment to the Local Government Bill of the same year, and a response to left-wing (relatively) pro-gay Labour councils and their assertion of gay rights (Sanderson 1995) — became one of the most controversial pieces of legislation affecting gay men and woman to ever be passed in the House of Commons. The amendment stated that a local authority should not promote homosexuality or publish material with the aim of doing so, or promote the teaching of homosexuality as an acceptable family relationship via such material. Clause 28 did not have an easy journey in the Commons. A bill attempting to prevent local authorities promoting homosexuality was first introduced and passed in the House of Lords in 1986.[6] The Bill was then introduced into the House of Commons in 1987, but as the Chamber was not quorate the debate was suspended.[7] Later that year the amendment was introduced in the Committee Stage of the Local Government Bill and was accepted without a vote as Clause 28 of the Bill. The Clause was debated and voted on over the next year and became known as Section 28 of the Local Government Act, coming into force on 24 May 1988.

Clause 28 was deemed by many gay men and women as a direct assault on their community and as characterizing homosexuality as less than normal, something which innocent children needed to be protected from, and as Sanderson (1995: 66) writes "an unprecedented politicization of the gay community in Britain." The politicization can be seen as a backlash to the permissive movement of the 1960s and 1970s and the liberalism of many individuals and groups in the 1980s which were seen as undermining the hegemony of family life (Weeks 2000). In fact, Clause 28 can be interpreted as defining homosexuality as "other" and as putting gay men and women "in their place". It helped to restrict homosexuality to its 1967 interpretation with anything beyond that a threat to family (Weeks 2000).

## 1980s Legislation

Clause 28 was not the only legal failure of the 1980s for the gay community and campaigners. The 1983 Sex Equality Bill (introduced by a Labour MP) sought to, amongst other things, outlaw discrimination in employment on the grounds of homosexuality. The Conservative Government did not support it and it was defeated by 198 votes to 118.[8] The failure was symptomatic of the Government's desire to "rein in" homosexuality or perhaps to not allow it free rein. There is a distinction between the two: rolling back gay rights or stopping the advancement of gay rights. As with left-wing councils and the notion they were attempting to promote homosexuality, the Government appeared to be more concerned with halting advancement than actually taking away rights (although it does not take away from the belief many have that legislation such as Clause 28 was a serious infringement of gay rights).

While Clause 28 and subsequent legal failures were disappointing for gay men and women, the 1980s did see some legal gains regarding gay rights. Despite the many difficulties and painful experiences endured by gay people in the decade, there were some significant legal steps forward, accompanied by the increasing visibility of gay people and causes, as well as political figures, in the media (Weeks 2000). It is perhaps the case that the advancements which were made happened at a slower pace and in an often-hostile environment. It is certainly the case that the Government did not enthusiastically push for the gains that were made. For example, the Sexual Offences Act was extended to Scotland in 1980 (as an amendment the Criminal Justice [Scotland] Bill, introduced by a Labour MP, with a free vote allowed by the Government) and Northern Ireland in 1982 (as an Order in Council introduced and therefore supported by the Government) after years of legal confusion. While the Government's position was officially one of neutrality when Scotland was being debated, the Secretary of State for Scotland tried very hard to indicate that the neutrality of the Government actually equated to disapproval of the proposal (Jeffery-Poulter 1991). In addition, the case for extending the Act to Northern

Ireland was bolstered by a ruling in the European Commission of Human Rights that the Government's position was illegal, meaning that the Government had no choice but to act.

## 1980s Political and Public Opinion

The Conservative Government of the 1980s did not operate in a vacuum. It was able to push forward legislation like Clause 28 because the public mood towards homosexuality had also become more negative, something the Labour Party was also sensitive to. Labour tried to distance itself from gay issues in the 1980s for fear of being characterized as "extreme". As Rayside explains, while more supportive of gay rights than much of the Conservative Party, the Labour Party was still heavily influenced by its working class membership. Towards the end of the 1980s Labour did become more assertive in its support of gay rights (then Labour leader Neil Kinnock [Labour MP for Bedwelty 1970–83 and Islwyn 1983–95 and Labour leader 1983–92] spoke against Clause 28, after initial front-bench floundering), reflecting the growing number of pro-gay Labour politicians. However, as Rayside (1998: 32) goes on to discuss, fears of electorate opinion meant that the pronouncements of party leaders, through the late 1980s to the next decade, continued to be cautious, with Labour leaders more comfortable with "tolerantly liberal views" on these matters than "fully inclusive views". The Liberals (becoming the Liberal Democrats in 1988) were the most publicly pro-gay rights major political party in the 1980s. But, while from the early 1960s to late 1980s the Liberals had the most progressive official record, the support for gay rights policies was stronger *outside* the Commons than in (Rayside 1998). The Liberals no more opposed Clause 28 when it was first being discussed than the Labour Party (although both parties became very publicly opposed as time went on).

Politicians were not alone in finding homosexuality a difficult issue to deal with in the 1980s; as discussed in Chapter 2, public attitudes towards homosexuality worsened (Britsocat 2011; Rayside 1998), emphasizing that the move towards recognition (Frame One), while generally unidirectional, is a halting process, with occasional backwards steps. As with Clause 28, this can be interpreted as a backlash to the permissiveness of the previous decades and, in particular, the emergence of HIV/AIDS in the early 1980s. HIV/AIDS was at first predominately thought of as a gay illness. Content analysis of the media has found that this was a very strong theme and, further, media messages about how easily the disease was transmitted were inconsistent. As Lilie *et al.* (1993: 126) write, "early media accounts of AIDS (during most of 1982) emphasized its association with a life-style outside of the morally acceptable cultural mainstream, so the question of contagion was given less play." HIV/AIDS therefore fed the anti-gay moralistic fever of the 1980s, indirectly fuelling policy such as Clause 28.

The Conservative Government's response was relatively slow. Weeks (2000) believes that the association between HIV/AIDS and homosexuality coloured the Government's reaction. It could certainly be described as confused and even purposely ignorant (although one has to allow for the fact that the medical profession's initial reaction towards HIV/AIDS was also relatively uncertain). As Jeffery-Poulter writes, HIV/AIDS challenged the very core of Thatcherism: conservative individualism versus state interference in the way people live their lives, a free market economy and a commitment to reduce state spending versus public money spent on an issue linked with a minority group. He goes on to suggest that the Thatcher Government was content to ignore the many warnings about the dangers of the spread of HIV/AIDS because it was seen as a gay issue, and by refusing to be properly involved in the initial debate about HIV/AIDS (which was raging in the media at the time), when it finally *did* get involved the Government could claim that it was reacting to public pressure and opinion.

## Press Representation and HIV/AIDS

While both politicians and the medical profession genuinely felt that HIV/AIDS was a gay crisis in the early 1980s (it was first officially labelled "Gay Related Immune Deficiency" or GRID), the press reacted very negatively, very quickly. The emergence of HIV/AIDS can be seen as the opportunity some sections of the press were waiting for, as it provided a "genuine" excuse for homophobia. Sanderson (1995: 206) argues that the press created "categories of blame": "the innocent (haemophiliacs, children, those who had caught the virus through blood transfusions) and the guilty (homosexuals, drug abusers, prostitutes)." Gay men were presented by the press as selfish and a dangerous presence in society, and their suffering was deemed just punishment for their "unnatural" behaviour. While tabloid newspapers were at the forefront of the homophobia, typically using stronger and more colloquial language, broadsheet newspapers did not hesitate to play to basic fears. *The Times* (LIFE-BLOOD, OR DEATH, 21 November 1984), for example, wrote in an editorial: "The infection's origins and means of propagation excites repugnance, moral and phys-ical, at promiscuous male homosexuality. Conduct, which tolerable in private circumstances, has, with the advent of 'gay liberation,' become advertised, even glorified as acceptable public conduct, even a proud badge for public men to wear." While the newspaper goes on to note that "Many members of the public are tempted to see in AIDS some sort of retribution for a questionable style of life but AIDS of course is a danger not only to the promiscuous nor only to homosexuals.", there is still the notion in the article that the heterosexual public needs to be protected from gay men, emphasized by the article's suggestion that gay men should not be allowed to donate blood anymore. The broad-sheet's notion of (relatively) acceptable private behaviour and unacceptable public behaviour is rather ironic considering the fact that much of press was happy to publicly highlight and condemn the private sexual behaviour of gay men at the time. Indeed, Rayside (1998: 36) remarks that the tabloid newspapers "were feeding off sensationalist probes into private lives, just as their predecessors had".

The approach of the tabloid newspapers to HIV/AIDS was some-what hysterical. *The Sun* (THE SUN SAYS: PLAGUE IN OUR MIDST, 12 December 1986), the worst culprit, wrote in an editorial response to a speech made by James Anderton, Chief Constable of Greater Manchester: "Three cheers for James Anderton . . . For the first time a major public figure says what the ordinary person is thinking about AIDS. He accuses homosexuals of spreading the deadly virus through their obnoxious sexual practices . . . Their defiling of the act of love is not only unnatural. In today's AIDS-hit world it is LETHAL. Predictably, the gays are quick to deliver Mr Anderton a limp-wristed slap. They brand him an uncaring, Bible-thumping bigot. *The Sun* hopes Mr Anderton will treat these perverts with the contempt they deserve. What Britain needs is more men like James Anderton — and fewer gay terrorists holding the decent members of society to ransom." Here there is a clear division between what can be thought of as "clean" heterosexuals and "dirty" homosexuals. In effect, through use of the word "terrorist", homosexuals are explicitly presented as a dangerous threat to "decent" heterosexuals. Even the left-leaning *Daily Mirror* (GUARDING AGAINST GAY PROPAGANDA, 22 June 1986) allowed a columnist to write in response to a *Church Times* advert for Church of England primary school teachers which stated that applica-tions were welcome regardless of sexual orientation, "This presumably means that Ealing Borough Council does not mind if paedophiles and pederasts teach their infants . . . Just as pederasts flit from boy to boy, so do homosexuals flit from one to another. Their promiscuity, together with their fondness for anal intercourse, is responsible for their terrible vulnerability to aids. Any encouragement of homosexual behaviour is likely to encourage the spread of AIDS." The mediated personas of gay people were thus very negative, with strong use of binary themes (Frame Three).

Obviously, it should be recognized that many journalists, both tabloid and broadsheet, chose not to echo the above bigotry. It is also important to understand that while HIV/AIDS had an enormously negative impact on the gay community (and gay men in particular, with whom the disease was most associated), the debates surrounding HIV/AIDS did have one positive effect. As Weeks (2000) argues, the gay community enhanced its voice greatly, with gay men and women achieving a new openness and presence in the "mainstream" public sphere. So, an illness that was presented by the press as a gay "plague" actually increased the visibility of gay men and woman (and even, eventually, humanized them), with gay men and women taking part in political debate and represented in the political field as never before (Rayside 1998).

## Conclusion

In order to fully understand the changing representation of gay politicians in the UK press, examination of applicable social, political and legal issues, as well as an assessment of how newspapers have depicted homosexuality over the decades, needs to take place. This chapter has revealed that homosexuality is "of the moment"; what is meant by the term "homosexuality" or the category of the "homosexual" has changed over time, from the late 1800s when homosexuality became a "whole" identity (rather than an act), through to the 1980s, when homosexuality was seen as a dangerous and threatening opponent of heterosexuality. The socio-political status of homosexuality has therefore changed over the decades; law, political and public attitudes, medical matters, political parties and the gay community itself, have all impacted upon one another and changed the status of homosexuality and gay men and women in society.

Having surveyed the socio-political status of homosexuality pre-1990, it is clear that there was a halting process of intolerance to tolerance (Frame One), with a backward step in the 1980s: at first homosexuality was not tolerated (with transgressions of "boundaries" completely unacceptable), then over the years it became more acceptable in private (taking into account socio-political factors), before

HIV/AIDS impacted negatively, publicly and privately. "Toleration" and "acceptance" suggest that homosexuality was still regarded as somewhat problematic even towards the approach of the 1990s and, as such, "recognition" was not reached. Chapter 5 and 6 will show how the changing representation of gay politicians and politicians caught up in a gay "scandal" in the UK press, from the mid-twentieth century to the late 1980s, can be understood in relation to the (halting) progression of tolerance. For example, while in the 1950s suspected homosexual politicians (and homosexuality as a whole) were not (publicly) tolerated (something reflected in newspaper coverage), in the 1980s it was possible to be an "out" gay politician. However, full recognition (Frame One) was not possible, and gay politicians were often depicted in the press in a derogatory manner, with their sexuality a negative defining feature rather than positive one, with negative binary themes and personas the norm (Frame Three). In terms of acceptability and public spaces (Frame Two), public expressions of homosexuality were deemed negative, even if all they involved was the support of gay rights; while it was possible to be "out", gay politicians who campaigned and spoke out for gay rights were quickly labelled as obsessed and militant.

## Notes

1. Hansard House of Commons Debates (vol. 625) 29 June 1960 (Wolfenden Report: Part Two).
2. Hansard House of Commons Debates (vol. 655) 9 March 1962 (Sexual Offences Bill).
3. Hansard House of Commons Debates (vol. 713) 26 May 1965 (Homosexual Reform).
4. Hansard House of Lords Debates (vol. 384) 14 June 1977 (Sexual Offences [Amendment] Bill).
5. Standing Committee F Official Report, Session 1979–80. Vol. IX, Cols 967–8.
6. Hansard House of Lords Debates (Vol. 483) 18 December 1986 (Local Government Act 1986 [Amendment] Bill).
7. Hansard House of Commons Debates (Vol. 115) 8 May 1987 (Amendment of Local Government Act 1986).
8. Hansard House of Commons Debates (vol. 50) 9 December 1983 (Sex Equality Bill).

# 5

## Private Lives, Public Consequences: Representation Pre-1980

"In some ways being a self-confessed lesbian has ruined my political career." Maureen Colquhoun, Labour MP for Northampton North 1974–9 (The Knitting Circle 2001)

### Outing the "Other": Early Innuendo and Sexual Scandal

Pre-1980, "mainstream" press coverage of (alleged) gay politicians was limited to "outings" and "scandals", all ending unhappily (politically at least) for the politicians concerned. Gay men and women did not have much of a voice in the "mainstream" media, and when they were written about — by heterosexual journalists — the language used was overwhelmingly negative, with dominant heterosexuality colouring representation and therefore the press coverage of gay or "outed" politicians. At the time it was very difficult for gay politicians, or politicians caught up in a gay "scandal", to separate the personal from the political. Indeed, all of the "outed" politicians in the period were either forced to resign or had their careers irreparably damaged by their experiences and press coverage, ranging from politicians in the 1950s brought to court for sexual misdemeanours, to politicians in office when homosexuality was legal. Binary themes were present in the press, contributing to negative mediated personas (Frame Three of the overarching frame of representation). The notion of private versus public was strong, with public homosexuality frowned upon (even when homosexuality was legal). However, private lives were still deemed public property, with every detail of personal lives covered in the press once a politician was "outed". So, while recognition (Frame One) and public acceptability (Frame Two) were still a long way off, the news value of homosexuality pre-1980 is very clear. It is now time to explore these issues in more detail.

## William Field and Ian Harvey

In the mid-twentieth century there was no such thing as good publicity when it came to non-heterosexual political scandal. In 1953 William Field (Labour MP for Paddington North 1946–53) appeared in court charged with importuning men for an immoral purpose after being arrested in a public toilet in Piccadilly tube station, and in 1958 Ian Harvey (Conservative MP for Harrow East 1950–8) was fined for indecency with a Coldstream Guard. Both paid with their careers for their misdemeanours: Field was forced to resign a few days after his appeal against his conviction failed (he pleaded guilty when originally arrested) and Harvey chose to resign despite Prime Minister Macmillan (Prime Minister 1957–63 and Conservative MP for Stockton-on-Tees 1924–9 and 1931–45 and Bromley 1945–64), who wanted to avoid a by-election, asking him to think about it over the weekend (Parris 1995).

The press reported the results of their misdemeanours, "outing" them by default, with their negative press coverage contributing to their exclusion from political society. Field's case was reported in a straightforward manner, but in detail, with every twist and turn of his court case covered. *The Times*'s headlines, for example, include "BIOCHEMIST AGAIN IN COURT (17 January 1953), "MP FINED" (26 January 1953) and "APPEAL LOST BY MP" (21 February 1953). Journalists placed Harvey's case on their front-pages, but lost interest in his case once he resigned his seat (Jeffery-Poulter 1991). *The Times* (11 December 1958) reported Harvey's case with the headline "£5 FINE ON IAN HARVEY. 'HE WILL PAY TO THE END OF LIFE'" noting that he "bitterly regretted the shame and disgrace he had brought on himself and his family" and that "For him it must be the end of his hopes, at any rate in the sphere of public life, and nothing remained for him when the case was over but the obscurity of private life which he had already sought to withdraw." In one headline and a few short sentences the paper's condemnation of Harvey's actions is very clear: he is classed as a criminal (as he was at the time), a man who will not be forgiven. In relation to Frame One of the overarching frame of representation, they were not tolerated at all; in the 1950s homosexuality, whether actual or admitted or not, was not something which the political and media establishments — and public — accepted, particularly sexual behaviour in public (Frame Two).

## Tom Driberg

Tom Driberg's (Labour MP for Maldon 1942–55) relationship with the press was an unusual one, in that while ostentatiously gay, he was never actually "outed", and although he went to court on a charge relating to homosexuality before he became an MP, he escaped police prosecution while an elected figure even though he was well known for soliciting gay sex in public places. His case is still of interest though, precisely *because* his sexuality was not discussed in the press. As to why, Baston (2000) writes that Driberg was proud of his life and felt no shame, unlike Field and Harvey. So, when questioned, he would react pro-actively, threatening the police with a legal battle, meaning his fame protected him. Driberg's high-placed friends (many of whom were journalists, as was Driberg before he became an MP) also protected him from adverse press coverage, as did his openness; because he was so open about his sexuality, seemingly not caring what people thought about his life, the importance of "outing" him was negated. Driberg's case serves to remind that the press did not expose all (alleged) gay politicians at the time; to be "outed" in the 1950s politicians had to be accused of some kind of contemporaneous sexual misdemeanour which resulted in an arrest and court case, *à la* Field and Harvey. However, the lack of scandalous press coverage of Driberg's personal life is of note because, without a doubt, Driberg's activities, as discussed by Driberg (1977) himself in his unfinished autobiography and by Wheen (2001) his biographer, were far more colourful and news-worthy than anything known about Field and Harvey.

The press can be seen as classing Driberg as a "good" homosexual and Field and Harvey as "bad" (a binary theme of Frame Three), although it should be noted that Field denied the charges made against him and never admitted to being gay (Harvey later became honorary president of the Conservative Group for Homosexual Equality). As such, Driberg was completely open and relaxed about his sexuality (but not "out", an important definition: a gay politician can be "in" but "good") and was therefore not a threat to the "norm", unlike Field and Harvey who had not defined themselves as gay (at the time of initial press coverage in Harvey's case) and did not appear relaxed and open. Their lack of openness (whether expressed privately or publicly) meant that the press could not pigeonhole them into a neat, safe category. By reporting the cases of Field and Harvey, thus suggesting their homosexuality, the heterosexuality — and "nor-mality" — of the press and public could be reaffirmed. Driburg was also helped by the fact he married in 1951, something his political and journalistic contemporaries reacted to with wry amusement (Parris 1995). But, gaining a wife undoubtedly contributed to the protection of his public image (the reason why many gay public figures choose to marry). Marriages of convenience can be very beneficial for gay politicians because if a husband or wife happily poses with a sus-pected — or even "outed" gay politician — then heterosexuality can be asserted more successfully. It did not work for Harvey though, who had married with an eye to aiding his political ambitions (Parris 1995), suggesting such a strategy only succeeds up to a point.

## Jeremy Thorpe

Moving on to the 1970s, one politician who was not classed as "good" by the majority of the press was Jeremy Thorpe (Liberal MP for North Devon 1959–79 and leader of the Liberal Party from 1967–76). Thorpe was first alleged to have had an affair with a young man called Norman Scott in 1976 and then, in a bizarre twist of events, was accused of incite-ment and conspiracy to murder Scott in 1979. Thorpe, having lost his seat, was acquitted after a sensational trial in 1979, and to this day, denies that he and Scott were anything other than good friends (Parris 1995). Even by the late 1970s rumours of homosexuality could finish a political career. As Parris (1995: 192) explains with reference to Thorpe, "The ink had dried on the 1967 Sexual Offences Act, but twelve years on homosexuality was barely tolerated, and this respected politician's choice of partner made it worse: there was public and press revulsion against the young man one judge called a 'spineless neurotic character'."

Scott's original claim that he and Thorpe were lovers irrevocably damaged Thorpe's career, with Thorpe forced out as leader as a result. The tabloid press reaction towards the alleged affair was gleeful in its sensationalism (although the press could claim to be reacting to outside events, reporting rather than manufacturing his press coverage). *The Sun*, unsurprisingly, told Thorpe he should stand down. The front-page of the *London Evening News* (29 January, 1976) stated "THORPE DENIES SEX AFFAIR ALLEGATION". Through the use of the words, "sex" and "affair", the alleged relationship is reduced to its most basic form with no mention of possible affection or love; the headline suggests that the relationship, if true, consisted simply of sex and nothing else. Broadsheets were not necessarily better, with even a liberal broadsheet such as the *Observer* (30 January 1976) shouting "SEX WITH MAN: CLAIM DENIED", highlighting the importance of attention-grabbing headlines.

*The Times* used a softer tone when Thorpe actually resigned in 1976, stating "MR THORPE RESIGNS OVER 'PLOTS AND INTRIGUE'" (11 May 1976), highlighting Thorpe's denials and the future of his Party, rather than explicit details of the charges against him. Some broadsheets therefore appeared somewhat sympathetic towards Thorpe. *The Sunday Times* (THE MURKY ROAD TO DAVID STEELE, 11 July 1976), for example, in a comment piece, stated "Yet it is by no means clear that public opinion at large can any longer be said to consider good personal morals and sexual relations between men to be incompatible. It is not even clear that the question commands much public interest." The *Observer* (16 May 1976) was also understanding, stating in an editorial headed "OUR INTOL-ERANT SOCIETY", "The law has legalised some homosexual relationships, but continuing public prejudice against homosexuals makes it probable that any politician against whom such an allegation is made will deny it and attempt to hush it up . . . to find whipping boys may satisfy many people's feelings, but it solves nothing." Even the traditionally right-wing *Daily Telegraph* was relatively supportive, with the paper (LIBERAL MISFORTUNES, 11 May 1976) regretting in an editorial that Thorpe had become a "sacrifice to the well-established convention in British politics — the convention that a public man must be free from all publicly sustainable suspicion about his personal morals. This is a harsh doctrine, one which exposes politicians to the constant danger of insidious attack and imposes on their colleagues the duty constantly to give them the benefit of doubt. It is arguable that the doctrine should be abandoned, though the evil consequences of doing that are not to be underrated either." However, the *Daily Telegraph*'s support seems to be based on the fact that Thorpe was only *suspected* of homosexual behaviour. An actual admission of homosexuality may have resulted in a more dismissive tenor.

Thorpe's trial in 1979 brought more attention on his alleged homo-sexual affair with Scott. The *Observer* (THE HAUNTING OF JEREMY THORPE, 24 June 1979) commented "In an ideal world, Jeremy Thorpe's sexual preferences should not have been of the slightest interest to anyone but his sexual partners. But we do not live in an ideal world. Even today, twelve years after the passing of the Sexual Offences Act . . . for anyone in public life, let alone a politician, to admit openly that he is a homosexual is to court disaster." The *Observer*, while sympathizing with Thorpe, actually excused the behav-iour of the press through such a statement, therefore contributing to the wide-scale punishment of Thorpe for his supposed homosexuality. The quote from The *Observer* is also a useful demonstration of Frame

Two of the overarching frame of representation, acceptability over time in relation to public space; an admittance of homosexuality in public was seen as crossing the acceptability threshold, even though homosexuality was by then legal.

## Maureen Colquhoun

In the mid-1970s Maureen Colquhoun became the UK's first known lesbian MP, after being forced out of the "closet" by the *Daily Mail*. In 1975 Colquhoun left her husband of 25 years for a woman, Babs Todd. She did not keep a low profile and in 1976 threw a housewarming party for herself and her partner at their new home. The *Daily Mail* diary columnist Nigel Dempster published details of the invitation stating that it featured "Two entwined females, with the names of Maureen and Babs above the forms" (MP MAUREEN QUITS HOME AND MOVES INTO VICAR'S CLOSE, 15 April 1976), leading to widespread press coverage. While the article did not mention explicitly that they were lesbian partners, it did note that "Until recently Babs was living at the elegant Connaught Square, Bayswater, home of broadcaster Jackie Mackenzie . . . coordinating editor of *Sappho*, which describes itself as 'the only lesbian magazine in Europe.' Only last month Babs gave up her job on *Sappho* as one of the regional directors". The implication is clear. Colquhoun did not deny her sexuality and actually took the *Daily Mail* to the Press Council (precursor to the Press Complaints Commission) for invasion of her privacy (her initial press coverage was certainly manufactured, with the *Daily Mail* making the decision to "out" her). Colquhoun lost the case. As Hemmings (1980: 159) writes about the case, "Lesbianism is the news, so if you want to stay out of it give it up or stay invisible." So, here is another example of the acceptability threshold (Frame Two) in relation to public space, wherein crossing the line from private to public was problematic.

Other newspapers were not wholly unsympathetic to Colquhoun's case. *The Times* (PRESS COUNCIL REJECTS WOMAN MP'S PRIVACY COMPLAINT, 8 December 1976), for example, summarized the Press Council's belief that "The methods used to obtain information from her [Colquhoun's partner] were a gross intrusion into privacy, and harassment of a serious kind" and that "the methods employed to obtain information from Mrs Colquhoun's husband constituted harassment of a serious kind" rather than white-washing the coverage. But, as Parris notes, her personal life was relevant as she had been vocal on feminist issues, meaning that her decision to move in with a woman after leaving her husband was of public interest. As the Press Council stated, and *The Times* reported, "Mrs Colquhoun, as an MP, had taken a strong stand on feminist issues" taking the case "just over the border into what is permissible". The private is thus political, a fact strengthened by Colquhoun's feminism. As Seaton (2003: 182) observes, the rise of feminism, and the idea of the private as political, created a "legislatively constructed 'private' life", demanding consistency between private and public lives: hypocrisy was untenable. Colquhoun was classified as a "bad" gay MP (Frame Three) even though she was open and relatively relaxed after her exposure. While it is possible for a gay MP to become "good" if they react the "correct" way to an "outing", the homophobia of the time meant that such a possibility was not available to Colquhoun.

Later tabloid stories about Colquhoun highlighted her homosexuality. In December 1976 Colquhoun was accused of hitting a car-park attendant in an argument about a complimentary parking ticket. Parris (1995: 221) writes that one journalist described her as a "cheery butch battleaxe". The *People* headlined a story with "WOMAN MP SOCKED ME" (5 December 1976), noting that "A woman MP who has struck many a blow for women's lib has been involved in a real punch up with a man." The words "butch" and "battleaxe" are used to make Colquhoun appear more masculine, and the terms "socked", "struck", "blow" and "punch" used to liken her to a boxer. The paper categorizes her in order that the reader can understand who and what she is, tying in with Fowler's (1991) idea that in order to make sense of the world we categorize people. Colquhoun was no longer allowed to be an individual. Instead, she was presented as looking and behaving a certain way to fit a lesbian stereotype.

Colquhoun found that support in the House of Commons came from heterosexual male MPs, rather than female or gay politicians, with support from the left lacking, something she attributed to people being threatened by her later openness (Parris 1995). The fear of being labelled "other" is a common heterosexual reaction to homosexuality (Swim *et al.* 1999), and is perhaps the reason why some MPs did not support Colquhoun. The reaction of the left emphasizes that homophobia was not limited to right-wing politicians. The apparent response of gay politicians towards Colquhoun is very striking. It suggests that gay MPs of her era could not only expect negative and discriminatory press representation, but also political isolation, not just from (some) heterosexual politicians, but also fellow gay politicians. It suggests that recognition (Frame One) was a long way off, not just from heterosexual people, but also in the minds of many gay people. Perhaps outside homophobia impacted on self-image and affirmations of solidarity and confidence.

## Conclusion

Apart from Driberg who managed to avoid press focus on his sexuality, the politicians discussed in the chapter all suffered politically when their (alleged) homosexuality became public knowledge or their sexuality was speculated on: Field and Harvey resigned from Parliament, Colquhoun was deselected by her constituency party (although the deselection was a result of general dissatisfaction with her conduct, Colquhoun's sexuality certainly did not help matters) — a decision eventually overturned by the Labour Party's National Executive — (Parris 1995) and Thorpe, while forced to stand down as Liberal leader because of criminal allegations rather than suggestions of homosexuality as such, had his career and reputation damaged beyond repair by Scott's claims of an affair. The press coverage of Thorpe and Colquhoun was more detailed than the coverage of Field and Harvey, and both MPs became defined by their (alleged) sexuality and, in Thorpe's case, sexual scandal. Partly because the press focused on their sexuality and sex lives for longer (although their careers were irreparably damaged, both carried on as MPs for a few years after their sexuality was first discussed in the press), but also because politics had become more personalized generally and deference towards politicians had collapsed.

Negative mediated personas and binary themes (Frame Three) are clearly in use pre-1980, although binary themes are not as vivid as in later years, perhaps because press coverage in general was not as sensationalist (although it was more so in Thorpe and Colquhoun's time than in Field and Harvey's). Although, generally, broadsheet newspapers did not cover "outings" in a sensationalist manner (as the tabloids did in the case of Thorpe and Colquhoun in particular), utilizing stereotypes and negative language, they did not ignore the stories: they just presented them in a more straightforward and serious manner. In fact, broadsheets often perpetuated the focus on sexuality, while sympathizing, emphasizing that even for the "quality" press (left and right), the trials and tribulations of (allegedly) gay politicians were too interesting a story to ignore, particularly when the details were salacious. That said, the hints of sympathy in Thorpe and Colquhoun's press coverage are clear, suggesting that tolerance (Frame One) was moving closer, if only in some broadsheets, intermittently.

Colquhoun told *Gay News* (BATTLING MAUREEN, 6 October 1977): "I am not 'Britain's Lesbian MP.' I am the working Member of Parliament for Northampton North and I am carrying on with my job. My sexuality is of no more relevance to that work than is the sexuality of heterosexual MPs — something people do not continually question." Unfortunately for Colquhoun, and other gay politicians at the time, dividing private lives from public office was extremely difficult. Certainly, while the Press Council was partially in place to consider public complaints about press behaviour, its ethos was one of protecting press freedom, thus giving more weight to the press than to the subjects of press coverage (PCC 2009). Of course, one can argue that the "right to know" ensures that political morality is upheld and politicians and political institutions are kept in check. Boling (1996), for example, writes that respecting privacy can actually reinforce privilege. Nevertheless, it is difficult to argue that some of the press coverage described here (particularly since decriminalization in 1967) was for any reason other than its newsworthiness and sensationalism (even if the press could fall back on a public interest defence). There was a paradox: public homosexuality was problematic (Frame Two), but gay politicians were defined by their sexuality and were not allowed to "keep it private" even if they wanted to. This is even more apparent in the 1980s, with the onset of HIV/AIDS having a big impact on press coverage. Chapter 6 will explore this decade, a time when homosexuality was used as a political tool, with recognition seemingly further away then ever.

# 6

# Immoral Sexuality, Moralistic Press Coverage: Representation, 1980–1990

"My homosexuality was made into an issue by the tabloids. They repeatedly and gloatingly focused on it." Peter Tatchell, Labour candidate for the 1983 Bermondsey by-election (Tatchell 1983: 62)

## Backlashes and Successes: Battling the Media Storm

The backwards shift in public opinion in the mid-1980s, in which people were less tolerant of homosexuality that in the early 1980s, saw the press representation of gay men and women become more vicious (Jeffery-Poulter 1991; Rayside 1998) and an escalation in the use of homosexuality as a political tool in the press (Sanderson 1995) — both tabloid and broadsheet. As Gronfors and Stalstrom (1987: 53) write: "AIDS drowned the budding optimism. Once again homosexuality and homosexual people were being thought of primarily in negative terms, control policies again dominating the discussion in such volume and ferocity as never before." Against such a background, it is unsurprising that there was only one voluntarily "out" gay MP at this time. While in 1984 Chris Smith (MP for Islington South and Finsbury 1983–2005) "came out", showing that "openly" gay politicians were now able to survive politically (have successful careers, keep the support of their party or, if unelected, run a proficient election campaign), 1983 saw Peter Tatchell's extremely negative campaigning experience in the Bermondsey by-election, wherein stereotypes and discriminatory terms where utilized in order to characterize him negatively and damage him politically. So, even before the worst of the HIV/AIDS media hysteria, gay politicians could have a difficult time.

| Positive | Negative |
|---|---|
| Private (sexual behaviour) | Public (sexual behaviour) |
| Out | In |
| Good | Bad |
| Safe | Dangerous |

**Figure 6.1** The mediated personas of gay politicians or politicians caught up in gay "scandal".

By analyzing the press coverage of gay politicians and politicians caught up in a gay "scandal" in the 1980s, it becomes clear that they were represented in the press through the use of particular binary themes and stereotypes; using these linguistic tools, their mediated personas (gradients of positive or negative) were created by and mediated through newspapers (Frame Three of the overarching frame of representation). These binaries were stronger than in previous decades and, in particular, the above binaries were common (figure 6.1). Analysis shows that public homosexuality continued to be very much frowned upon (Frame Two), with recognition (Frame One), and even tolerance at times, still some way off, even as the 1990s approached. Despite the different "statuses" of gay politicians or politicians caught up in a gay "scandal" at the time (*i.e.* "closeted", "out" and "outed"), they all suffered from discriminatory press coverage and the use of negative binary themes. However, Smith's coverage was much more moderate than Tatchell's; the fact that he was a "good" and "safe" gay MP who voluntarily "came out" to the press undoubtedly contributed, showing binary themes in action. So, gay politicians *were* able to stay in post, but, they had to fulfil strict criteria to do so.

## Allan Roberts and Keith Hampson

The tabloid press's homophobic campaign against Tatchell in the 1983 Bermondsey by-election at first suggests that in the early 1980s it was very difficult for any politician whose sexuality was the focus of press attention to survive politically. However, such a proposition would not only fail to take into account the unique circumstances of Tatchell's experience (the fact he was not an elected politician, his lack of party support and his unpopular political leanings), but also the experiences of other politicians. In fact, along with the "openly" gay Smith, in the early 1980s Allan Roberts (Labour MP for Bootle 1978–90) and Keith Hampson (Conservative MP for Ripon 1974–83 and Leeds North-West 1983–97) both managed to carry on as MPs when their sexuality became the focus of intense press speculation.

In 1981 the *News of the World* (following on from an investigation by *Private Eye* magazine) reported on suggestions that Roberts had visited a gay S&M club in Germany and while there had donned a studded dog collar and been whipped by men in Nazi uniforms. The experience apparently led to him needing emergency hospital treatment, paid for, as Parris (1995) notes, by a Conservative MP (emphasizing once more that while publicly hostile as a party, many Conservative MPs were privately very liberal). The front-page article (15 February 1981) stated "GAY ROW MP IS BACK AT WORK", and went on to say: "The MP at the centre of what he calls a homo-sexual 'smear campaign' yesterday resumed his political work for the Labour Party. Bachelor Allan Roberts . . . refused to talk about his visit to a homosexual nightclub in West Berlin . . . The nightclub Mr Roberts visited is the Buddy Club, one of West Berlin's most famous haunts for homosexuals. Bare-armed, muscular men stand around surveying the more submissive clientele, who perch on bar stools sipping frothy German beer. On one wall, video cassettes show well-built men in naked homosexual romps." The *News of the World*'s sensationalist splash did not move Roberts. He refused to "come out" to the press and was quoted in the article as saying "suggestions that I was dressed in a dog collar and was whipped are utter rubbish", noting that while he visited the club he only needed medical treatment because he was involved in an accident there. In fact, the *News of the World* and *Private Eye* magazine (which originally published details about Roberts's supposed antics in Germany) were forced to pay libel damages to Roberts over later allegations that the police were investigating him over sexual offences (Parris 1995). The luridness of Roberts's expo-sure demonstrates that his press coverage was not just about sexuality; it was also about the (tabloid) press's love of scandal (whether hetero-sexual or gay), a focus made possible by the increasing "visibility" of politicians (Thompson 2000). Indeed, Roberts's personal life was discussed (with his press coverage manufactured) because it was a good story, rather than in relation to any public interest issue or in response to outside events such as a court case.

Although Roberts never admitted being gay, he was still a staunch defender of gay rights; he voted to extend the Sexual Offences Act to

Scotland in 1980[1] and Northern Ireland in 1982,[2] and to neuter the effect of Clause 28 in 1987[3] and 1988[4] (the latter two votes were unsuccessful). Why then did he survive his adverse tabloid press coverage, eventually becoming a member of Labour's frontbench environment team, when other parliamentarians whose sexuality was speculated on in the press met disastrous fates? Undoubtedly, Roberts was very popular with his constituency party (as Parris writes, they gave him a unanimous vote of confidence after his travails), but so were other less fortunate "outed" MPs. Perhaps the answer lies with the fact that Roberts, like Driberg before him, appeared to be comfortable with his alleged sexuality and did not let the press intimidate him. It did not matter what the press threw at him — and it cannot get much more politically embarrassing than being accused of being beaten by men in Nazi uniforms — Roberts refused to be cowed by the press and continued to speak on gay rights in the Commons.[5] Charges of hypocrisy could not be levelled at Roberts; he had never been married and so could not be accused of misleading his constituents (unlike Colquhoun, however unfairly) and did not make anti-gay remarks or vote against gay rights. Like Driberg, Roberts was "good" in terms of his relaxedness, even if he was "dangerous" sexually (binary themes of Frame Three).

In 1984 Hampson was accused of indecently assaulting an undercover police officer in a gay club in Soho. He was brought to trial and a verdict of not guilty was recorded after the jury had failed to reach a verdict. The Attorney General announced that there could not be a re-trial due to the widespread publicity of the case (highlighting the fact that his case was reported because of outside events). There is no suggestion that Hampson is gay. As Parris (1995: 247) writes, the judge in the case said "to suggest Hampson was a homosexual was 'absurd and unthinkable'." However, the circumstances of the case (for example, allegations of public sexual behaviour, a binary of Frame Three) still lend him a negative mediated persona. He survived the bad publicity and remained an MP until the 1997 Labour landslide, refusing to go quietly, something which undoubtedly benefited him (Parris 1995). Like Roberts, Hampson refused to buckle under his press coverage and survived his ordeal, although he did have to resign as a Parliamentary Private Secretary. He was undoubtedly lucky: he had a wife to underline his heterosexuality and had no skeletons in his closet. Hampson was also fortunate that the press (tabloid and broadsheet) was unimpressed with his apparent entrapment, perhaps making his negative mediated persona a bit weaker. As *Gay Times* (MEDIA-WATCH, July 1984) noted, commentators were "unanimously favourable in their support for an end to entrapment". *The Times* (HOMOSEXUALS AND THE POLICE, 16 May 1984) wrote "It is increasingly true that the way the police treat sexual and racial minorities affects the trust in which they are held by the wider public. And so it should." Even *The Sun* (1984 cited Jeffery-Poulter 1991: 172) stated that "the real crime that worries the public is out on the streets. For most people safety on public transport and in their homes comes before private morals". While *The Sun*'s stance is admirable, the newspaper is somewhat hypocritical; *The Sun* has "outed" and focused on the sexuality of numerous politicians and public figures, suggesting that "private morals" are of interest to the newspaper, if not the public.

Roberts and Hampson were both fortunate in that unlike Colquhoun, both received the support of their local parties, perhaps reflecting growing public tolerance (Frame One) of (suggestions of) homosexuality (before much of the moral and media panic relating to HIV/AIDS). Of course, their constituency parties may have supported them because they denied being gay (or, in Roberts's case, stayed silent on the issue), in contrast to Colquhoun. However, while Roberts and Hampson survived politically, staying on as MPs for many years after their negative press coverage, their cases should not be taken as a signal that gay politicians or those who were "outed" suddenly had it easy. While politicians (gay or not) no longer necessarily lost the support of their parties and their seats when their sexuality was the focus of press attention, their private lives were often still ruthlessly exploited. Tatchell's press coverage is a prime example of such exploitation.

## Peter Tatchell

### The Tabloid Approach

The Bermondsey by-election (the official campaign — January to February 1983 — but also the pre-campaign as well) is infamous for the slurs, discrimination and outright homophobia faced by Tatchell. The source of much of the homophobia were tabloid newspapers such as the *News of the World* and *The Sun*, whose journalists took it upon themselves to damn Tatchell not just as a left-wing politician, but also as a "suspected" gay man. In fact, Tatchell's pro-gay stance was used to signal that he was part of the so-called "dangerous" and pro-gay (and therefore anti-family) "loony left" and consequently an unsuitable candidate for the people of Bermondsey to vote for. The Liberals (who eventually won the seat) also courted anti-gay feeling during the campaign (Rayside 1998), indicating that a good historical record on gay rights counts for nothing during a fiercely fought campaign. However, the impact of the press representation of Tatchell's (then unconfirmed, but suspected) homosexuality must not be underrepresented; it was used as a way of discrediting him as a politician in an election described by *Gay News* as "THE MOST HOMOPHOBIC BY-ELECTION OF OUR TIMES" (3 March 1983).

The lengths the tabloids would go to get proof of Tatchell's homosexuality were amazing. The *Daily Mail* and *Sun* newspapers camped outside Tatchell's house and sorted through his rubbish to try and find "incriminating" evidence, with the *Daily Mail* apparently compiling a list of 20 supposed ex-lovers from whom they hoped to extract a scandalous sexual story (Tatchell 1983). The articles which *were* published were over-the-top and frequently untrue. *The Sun* (25 September 1982) decided to construct the story that Tatchell had deserted his constituents to attend the Gay Olympics — something emphatically denied by Tatchell — and printed it under the headline "RED PETE 'WENT TO GAY OLYMPICS'". The story characterized Tatchell as a militant gay man more interested in gay issues than "ordinary" members of the public, stating: "Left-wing Labour candidate Peter Tatchell has upset his tough dockland supporters, who say he has been to the gay Olympics. They claim the 36 year old bachelor spent two weeks in the company of homosexuals at the bizarre sports event in San Francisco." Public homosexuality (Frame Two of the overarching frame of representation) was thus unacceptable in relation to active *campaigning*, as well as expressions of sexuality or identity. *The Sun* (5 December 1981) headlined another story "MY FIGHT FOR THE GAYS — BY RED PETE", claiming that "Left-wing parliamentary candidate Peter Tatchell — disowned by Labour leader Michael Foot — talked yesterday about his controversial links with the gay rights movement." The paper damned Tatchell on two fronts: first, he was identified with gay issues, and second, he was portrayed as left-wing. The article goes on to describe a trip Tatchell made to the World Youth Festival ten years earlier: "In 1973 Mr Tatchell was involved in a violent scuffle in East Berlin when he raised a banner calling for solidarity with East German gays. Fellow members of his student delegation at a world youth rally ripped down the banner and attacked him, reducing him to tears." As Tatchell (1983: 62) states, the article was a "crude propagandist" effort at promoting the stereotype that all gay men are "simpering queens".

Further ammunition came from the *News of the World*, which Tatchell (1983) claims doctored a photo to make it look as if he was wearing make-up, thus further equating his homosexuality with effeminacy. As McIntosh (1996) notes, heterosexual people often assume that gay men will be effeminate. Tatchell certainly does not make that correlation himself and was angry that the newspaper pushed the stereotype to its readers. Tatchell (1993) described further negative press coverage in his submission to the National Heritage Committee on the Press: "There was the constant abusive, sneering and ridiculing tone of the tabloids . . . 'Red Pete', 'immigrant upstart', 'gay rights extremist', 'a rather exotic Australian canary' . . . Objectivity was largely abandoned. News became fused with hostile and denigratory comment. Editorial opinion replaced factual reporting." The words "exotic" (often used when describing gay men, as demonstrated in relation to the press coverage of Peter Mandelson in Chapter 9) and "canary" characterize Tatchell as atypical and preening, and the word "extremist" as out of touch with "real" issues. Tatchell is justified in claiming that opinion replaced facts; after the election *The Sun* (26 February 1983) ran a full-page editorial headed "THE TRUTH HURTS — LIES, SMEARS AND PETER TATCHELL", blaming Tatchell for his defeat, rather than the truthful journalists employed by *The Sun*, declaring that "At Bermondsey they had an attractive and energetic candidate in Simon Hughes. But above all they benefited from the revulsion of the electors at a farcical campaign and a travesty of a candidate."

## The Broadsheet Approach

Most of the broadsheet newspapers did not target Tatchell for his homosexuality and instead focused on the politics of his candidacy, such as his political beliefs, the hostility of the Labour leadership and the ways in which tabloid newspapers portrayed him. Indeed, the more liberal *Guardian* newspaper noted that Tatchell's beliefs were "less exotic" then his opponents alleged (THE WORDS AT THE BACK OF THE BOOK, 15 January 1983). The *Guardian* (WHY I'LL NOT BE STANDING IN BERMONDSEY, 18 April 1983) also gave Tatchell a platform post-election, to explain why he would not stand again. He wrote: "What Fleet Street really objected to was my radical socialism rather than my homosexuality. It merely played on my gayness to discredit my politics." *The Times* also gave space to two opinion pieces defending Tatchell during the campaign, "HOUNDS OFF PETER TATCHELL" (20 October 1982) and "STOP BEING BEASTLY TO TATCHELL" (19 February 1983). Both articles note the personalization of the campaign against Tatchell, politically and in the press, with the October piece stating: "most popular papers have sought to discredit him by whipping up atavistic prejudices against him as a deviant . . . he has been projected in a succession of reports as a simpering, neurotic stereotype of a 'gay rights supporter'. He wears "a symphony in brown', chortles the *Daily Mail*. 'His pouting lower lip hardens if anyone dares to argue with him', warns the *Sunday Mirror*".

There were a few exceptions to the broadsheets' political, rather than personal, focus. The right-wing *Daily Telegraph* (DISOWNED TATCHELL SAYS HE BACKS FOOT AS LEADER, 5 December 1981) emphasized that Tatchell was a "draft-dodger and a supporter of homosexuals" and "Mr Tatchell, a bachelor, has been a consistent supporter of the gay rights movement. In 1973 he attended the World Youth Festival in the Soviet-controlled East Berlin, and carried a banner calling for solidarity with East German homosexuals." Echoing the approach of tabloid newspapers, the *Sunday Telegraph* (THE KNOCK-OUT BATTLERS OF BERMONDSEY: THE CANDIDATE, 6 December 1981) also personalized Tatchell's press coverage, noting that he was "a willowy, curly-haired and softly spoken 29-year-old bachelor". Tatchell describes similar articles as examples of "trivialisation, ridicule and personalisation" and also claims that reporters were obsessed with his clothes and appearance (Tatchell 1983: 61). While the appearances of many politicians and public figures — heterosexual and gay — are scrutinized, the use of the words "willowy" and "softly" in the above article is of significance; Tatchell is almost sexualized, with an implicit correlation between homosexuality and overt sexuality. In fact, he is feminized by the focus on his appearance. As Tatchell himself (1983) recognizes, it is much more common for the appearances of *female* MPs to be commented on than males.

## The Personal as Political

The focus on Tatchell's appearance was not just about sexuality; it was also about his left-wing views. Tatchell (1983: 61) summarizes that the press focused on the personal in order to undermine the political: "We could reasonably ask why the . . . papers were giving up so much space to such trivia . . . [well] ridiculing my apparel was just an additional weapon in their armoury to assassinate the character of a Left-wing Labour candidate." He believes that the press attempted to portray gay rights as a personal crusade even though he was only supporting national Party policy. Indeed, the *News of the World* (UPROAR AS LABOUR IS HIT BY GAY ROW, 26 September 1982) named

Tatchell as a key figure in the fight for gay rights policy within the Labour Party: "The Labour Party was plagued with fresh turmoil yesterday in a row over demands for freedom for homosexuals. The far Left accused Party leader Michael Foot of butchering a plan to sweep away restrictions on the activities of 'gays.' The row erupted as Left-wing candidate Peter Tatchell was attacked by members of his Bermondsey party over allegations he went to a bizarre gay Olympics sports meeting in the U.S. Mr Tatchell — who denied the claim — is a key figure in a massive campaign to make homosexual rights a domi-nant issue at this week's Labour Party Conference in Blackpool."

Rayside (1998) writes that a link with gay issues and rights was disadvantageous for any political party in the 1980s. As such, Tatchell's local party advised him to keep quiet about his sexuality in order to avoid negative press coverage (Tatchell 1983), demonstrating that while the already elected (and, if he was gay, technically still "closeted") Roberts received the support of his local party, standing as an "openly" gay candidate was still unthinkable. Although Tatchell's left-wing views were the biggest concern of the Labour Party (Tatchell 1983), it is not unreasonable to suppose that the assumed tabloid reaction to his homo-sexuality contributed to the lack of support he received from Labour headquarters. Certainly, while Labour was committed to protecting gay people from unfair discrimination, it had backed away from a commitment to equal rights (Jeffery-Poulter 1991). The Labour Party sensed the damage a strong link to gay rights could have, hence the distancing of Tatchell, and was also aware of the more "traditional" opinions of working class members (Rayside 1998). Recognition (Frame One) was obviously a long way off, with tolerance of homo-sexuality not exhibited by all.

## In versus Out: Binary Themes

While it is unfair for Tatchell to be criticized for not openly declaring his sexuality — aside from the advice of the Labour Party, the threats made to Tatchell about his sexuality left him fearing for his safety (Tatchell 1983) — his decision had an unfortunate side effect. As with Harvey and Field decades earlier, his lack of "openness" meant that the press was unable to define "what" he was, leading to innuendo and suggestion — maybe more than if he had just followed his heart and "come out" as gay in the first place — meaning that he was a "bad" gay man. Tatchell's press coverage demonstrates the good/bad, private/public and out/in binary themes of Frame Three. As a "bad", "closeted" gay man — who nevertheless supported gay rights —

Tatchell was a threat to "normality", leading to his hounding. Paradoxically, while public "displays" of homosexuality (for example, expressing solidarity with other gay people and causes, something Tatchell was accused of even though he was not "out") was frowned upon by the tabloid press (in terms of Frame Two, it was below the acceptability threshold), "private" homosexuality (homosexuality unconfirmed in public) was also deemed suspicious. By characterizing Tatchell as effeminate and therefore gay, the press could right the ostensible wrong.

## Defeat

Tatchell's case exemplifies the inherent difficulty of being a gay politician in the 1980s. Although homosexuality had a more tolerant legal status, many parts of the press still portrayed it as shameful and somehow indecent. The press's obsession with damning Tatchell contributed to the scale of his defeat (Labour's vote fell from 63.6% in 1979 to 26.1%). In an ironic twist, the candidate who won the election was Simon Hughes, "outed" many years later. Tatchell (1983) has stated that the tabloid press actually compromised democracy in the by-election. He feels the press abused its power and manipulated the news for political reasons, leading to readers being given a biased view of what he stood for. Even the Labour supporting *Sunday Mirror* (27 February 1983) condemned Tatchell after his defeat, stating "WHAT A FREAK" alongside his picture and the point that "Mr Tatchell's crusade for gay rights and the suggestion that he is himself a homosexual (as are several MPs) did not help him. It is the kind of cause that goes down better in the middle-class world of Mr Tatchell's own background. He would have been the wrong candidate even if he had not written that article in a Marxist sheet." The broadsheet newspapers played a much straighter bat, although hostile newspapers such as the *Daily Telegraph* were certainly not averse to subtly exploiting Tatchell's homosexuality.

Although it is unlikely that his sexuality would have been completely ignored (especially during a by-election when the press focus is on just one constituency and a handful of candidates, rather than hundreds as during a general election), Tatchell would probably have received a more positive press if he had been more politically "acceptable" to newspapers. One must also take into account the fact that Tatchell was standing for election, meaning that negative stories about him were potentially much more damaging than for the already elected Roberts and Hampson (*i.e.* the immediacy of the vote meant that the stories would be fresh in the minds of the general public), as well as the fact that he did not have the support of the Labour leadership. These factors destabilized Tatchell, making him extremely vulnerable to negative press coverage. That said, Tatchell was done a great disservice by the press, the tabloids in particular. Criticism of political views is the norm for any politician, but the press focus on Tatchell's (suspected) homosexuality — whether as a method of attacking his politics or as a signal of general disapproval — not only led to intense homophobia and discrimination, but also to readers being given a biased view of Tatchell's beliefs, personality and actions.

The articles are hard to justify; they did not fulfil any public interest criteria and are examples of manufactured press coverage. Tatchell's decision to not "come out" in public (although he was completely "out" in private with his colleagues and he "came out" publicly after the by-election) and his left-wing beliefs, meant that the tabloid press felt able, and even compelled, to constantly mention his sexuality. Of course, the reaction of the press can partly be accounted for in historical terms; although attitudes towards homosexuality were continuing to improve in the early 1980s (before the worst press coverage of HIV/AIDS appeared), and in some parts of the press representations of gay people and issues were becoming more moderate, gay men and women were still frequently discriminated against. And, although various politicians had been "outed" or had their sexuality discussed, no MP had voluntarily "come out" as gay in the press (although Colquhoun did declare that she was gay, it was a response to her press coverage).

## Chris Smith

### *"Coming Out"*

In the aftermath of Tatchell's homophobic defeat it was brave of Chris Smith to come out as gay. To a crowd of supporters he declared "My name's Chris Smith, I'm the Labour MP for Islington South and Finsbury, and I'm gay." Smith's 1984 "self-outing" can be seen as the beginning of a new era for gay politicians, and in some respects, that is certainly true; his declaration — and his homosexuality as a whole — did not receive much press coverage (tabloid and broadsheet), suggesting on first glance that toleration had moved on a step (Frame One), especially in comparison to Tatchell's experiences, even though it was only one year later. However, Smith was in an advantageous position: firstly, by voluntarily "coming out" (out/in being a key binary theme of Frame Three), he pre-empted the press and made a subsequent focus on his sexuality pointless; secondly, "coming out" after being elected to Parliament gave him more stability than if he had stood for election as an "openly" gay candidate; and thirdly, he was seen as more politically acceptable — although as Rayside notes, as a London MP some Labour politicians associated him with the "loony left".

Press coverage of Smith's "self-outing" was free of the hostility and outright homophobia faced by Tatchell and was not even mentioned in the national tabloids, although his local paper, the *Islington Gazette*, allowed him to explain his announcement (Jeffery-Poulter 1991). As for the broadsheets, the *Observer* (COMING OUT, 18 November 1984) recognized the fact that Smith was the only "out" MP, stating in its Pendennis column, "Chris Smith is the only MP who is totally prepared to admit the fact [he is gay]." The *Guardian* (DIARY, 28 November 1984) noted in its diary column that "The Young Liberals have issues a statement commending Islington South MP, Chris Smith, for 'coming out' and calling on Liberals in the constituency for to vote for him next time." Smith did not have to tolerate a focus on his personal and sexual life, *à la* Colquhoun, or cope with the personalization and trivialization experienced by Tatchell just one year earlier. The positive (or perhaps indifferent) press reaction to Smith, and the negative press reaction to Tatchell, perfectly demonstrates the "good" gay/"bad" gay binary theme (Frame Three), and also that the press coverage of gay politicians needs to be read in relation to the "lifestyle" of the individual concerned.

Unlike Tatchell who did not "come out" as gay, and who subsequently had the tabloids knocking at his door, Smith's candour meant that the press had no "sensational" story to put on their front pages. In fact, articles on Smith's homosexuality were rendered pointless. After all, how can a politician be scandalized if there is no scandal (such as a so-called secret life or hypocrisy) to report? As Jeffery-Poulter explains, Smith's actions meant that the press were unable to smear his name. This not only reveals much about the news values of newspapers (tabloids in particular) — the fact that sensationalism is crucial to a good story, and bad news (for an individual) is much more interesting than good news — but it also reveals a great deal about the what the press thinks the public wants: scandal, gossip and a focus on personality rather than politics. The lack of press focus on Smith's "self-outing" also suggests that the "need to know" is a key factor in the "outing" of gay politicians. As his sexuality was already in the public domain, journalists did not have to go to the trouble of "outing" Smith themselves. In other words, curiosity had been satisfied.

The Labour Party's support (or rather, lack of disapproval), a result of his tolerable political beliefs (and possibly his constituency party's more middle-class and liberal membership), and his status as an already elected politician, can also be seen as stabilizing Smith. However, as suggested by Tatchell's press coverage, it seems unlikely that the newspapers would have ignored his sexuality if he had "come out" as gay before or during the campaign. The fact that Smith's sexuality was not scandalous (there was no kiss-and-tell story or evidence of an affair, for example) also contributed to his positive coverage, as did the fact his sexuality was "safe" rather than "dangerous" (another binary theme recognized in Frame Three). As Smith did not (publicly) compromise any sexual "norms" (homosexual ones at least), he was unthreatening and "neutered", tying in with Frame Two, acceptability and public space: his sexuality, while acknowledged in public, was not overt, and thus did not "invade" heterosexual public space.

## Left-wing Associations

Despite the initial indifferent reaction to his sexuality, Smith's later press representation was not wholly positive. Although Smith was not seen as hard-left, he was the subject of tabloid press condemnation when he associated himself with gay or other supposed left-wing causes (Rayside 1998). For example, Smith's trip to the USA to meet with other gay officials was reported by the *London Standard* in 1985 under the headline "MP 'PUT GAY RIGHTS FIRST'" (cited Rayside 1998: 83). The article noted that "Gay MP Chris Smith, who flew to California for a homosexual rights conference last weekend, has been accused of putting Gay Rights before his constituents . . . . Councillor David Hyams, the leader of Islington's Social Democratic opposition said: 'The people of Islington don't want to read in the newspapers that their MP has jetted off to America to tell Gay Rights activists that England will one day have a gay king or lesbian queen'." Although the paper is reporting on the comments of another politician, their publication is important. If the article is read in terms of news values, the story was deemed to be of interest to the public. As with Tatchell, and unlike his earlier coverage, Smith is presented here as being more interested in gay rights than "ordinary" issues, thus crossing the acceptability divide in relation to homosexuality in public space (Frame Two). Certainly, there is no doubt that the "people of Islington" are considered to be heterosexual rather than gay.

In 1986 *The Sun* (cited Rayside 1998: 83) criticized Smith's comments on Page Three girls: "Chris Smith is Labour MP for Islington

South and Finsbury. He is also a self-confessed homosexual . . . He wants to ban Page Three while at the same time go on allowing homosexuals the right to buy magazines containing sado-masochistic porn. So if Mr. Smith had his way the law would allow nasty minded perverts to buy material that would sicken normal people while denying the healthy-minded majority their favourite dose of glamour." The above passage compares "normal", wholesome and glamorous heterosexuality with "abnormal" and dangerous homosexuality. Smith, part of the "abnormal" homosexual minority, is contrasted to the readers of *The Sun*, who are considered part of the "normal" heterosexual majority. Like Tatchell, Smith is categorized as deviant, unconcerned with the preoccupations of "ordinary" people. When Smith suggested that there were other gay MPs, *The Sun* (SIXTY-FIVE MPS ARE POOFTERS [REVEALS ONE WHO IS], 24 November 1987) stated: "Parliament is packed with poofters, a leading gay MP claimed yesterday. As many as 65 homosexuals are camping underground on the front and back benches of the House of Commons." The article was accompanied by a derogatory cartoon showing the House of Commons benches and a male MP in a dress, with a moustache and earrings. As noted by Sanderson, in the 1980s the language used by tabloids became more and more pejorative; words such as "poofter" were used to create a barrier between gay people and society as a whole. Of course, tabloid newspapers took such an approach because they focus on "scandal", are sensationalist and were writing for an assumed heterosexual readership which would echo such opinions. Nevertheless, *The Sun*'s popularity meant that its (potentially very influencing) stance was of concern to many gay activists and groups, including the Campaign for Homosexual Equality, who actually met with the Press Council to discuss the language used to describe homosexuality (Sanderson 1995).

## Single-Issue Politics

Smith was aware of the pejorative manner in which the press could represent him and was therefore keen to ensure that he did not become a single-issue MP. As he stated in an interview with *Gay Times* (1986 cited Rayside 1998: 84): "Obviously I stood up and said what I am and no other politician has done so, and because of that I tend I suppose to be asked to take up issues that relate specifically to lesbians and gays. I want to do that, but I've also consciously tried to take up a lot of other issues as well to make clear to my constituents that I'll fight for all of them, no matter who or what their problems are." Smith was keen to re-state such a view when he became Secretary of State for Culture,

Media and Sport after Labour's 1997 landslide election win, after being part of the Shadow Cabinet under Tony Blair (as Shadow Heritage Secretary then spokesman for social security, then health) and before, part of Labour's Treasury team under John Smith (MP for Lanarkshire North 1970–83 and Monklands East 1983–94 and Labour leader 1992–4). In an article headed "BEING GAY IS SIMPLY ONE ASPECT OF MY LIFE . . . " (*Daily Mail*, 27 October 1998) Smith stated, "The last thing I want to do . . . is to go on an on about my sexuality because it is only one aspect of my life and character." As Prokhovnik (1999) notes, gay men and women are often considered "other" and in opposition to heterosexuality, a dualism which helps to define society, so by "passing" as heterosexual, gay men can be accommodated. In order to be accepted into the political "mainstream" and to ensure a successful political career, Smith needed to be accepted by heterosexual society as a "mainstream" politician; his stated desire to be a politician for all, rather than just gay men and women, thus facilitated his acceptance. Smith's press coverage shows the intricacy of being an "out" gay politician in the 1980s, when it was believed that identifying with "gay issues" too strongly would alienate heterosexual voters.

## "Dangerous" Sexuality

Newspapers attempted, though, to link gay politicians with so called "gay issues" such as HIV/AIDS. Jeffery-Poulter believes *The Times* (LIFE-BLOOD, OR DEATH, 21 November 1984) made an indirect reference to Smith in a leader article on HIV/AIDS: "The infection's origins and means of propagation excites repugnance, moral and physical, at promiscuous male homosexuality. Conduct, which tolerable in private circumstances, has, with the advent of 'gay liberation,' become advertised, even glorified as acceptable public conduct, even *a proud badge for public men to wear* [emphasis added]." By associating Smith's homosexuality with the HIV/AIDS crisis, Smith himself is presented as dangerous and unhealthy. *The Times*'s suggested attempt to link Smith to HIV/AIDS was probably the most negative comment a broadsheet directed towards Smith's homosexuality at the time, and should not be considered illustrative of broadsheet newspapers' attitudes. However, the above passage reveals the fear that gay men sometimes excited in the climate of HIV/AIDS, and the fact that the while less sensationalist generally, broadsheets were still capable of homophobia. As Sanderson (1995: 158) suggests, homophobia can be found in the more serious right-wing press only expressed more "pompously" than in tabloids.

In contrast to the tone of *The Times*'s 1980s article, in early 2005, when Smith revealed that he had been HIV positive for 17 years, the vast majority of the tabloid and broadsheet press approached the news in a straightforward and respectful manner, echoing more relaxed attitudes towards HIV/AIDS (especially when compared to the 1980s), and increased tolerance (Frame One). Yet, some sections of the tabloid press attempted to associate Smith, and thus homosexuality as a whole, with a sense of risk, thus playing upon still existing preconceptions surrounding the illness. The *Daily Mirror* (31 January 2005) was quick to focus on how he caught HIV, with the resulting headline "I HAVEN'T GOT A CLUE WHO GAVE ME HIV", an implicit suggestion that as a "dangerous" gay man, he had had multiple casual sexual partners resulting in his damaged health. As with Tatchell, the correlation between homosexuality and overt sexuality is played upon, and Smith is categorized accordingly. The *Daily Mail* (31 January 2005) took a rather sour tone, suggesting that Smith's admission was possibly a "CYNICAL PLOY BY GREY MAN WHO CRAVES PRAISE?". Hence, HIV/AIDS is presented as a method of gaining political sympathy and privilege. Perhaps the *Daily Mail* took such a tone because Smith had refused to give the paper his story and instead "came out" as having HIV in a self-penned article in *The Times*, thus ruining the *Daily Mail*'s exclusive; it has been suggested that *The Mail on Sunday*, the *Daily Mail*'s sister paper, actually contacted Smith and told him a story was being prepared about his illness, prompting Smith to pre-empt the paper (*Observer*, COMMENT, 6 February 2005). Of course, it should also be borne in mind that the *Daily Mail* will have assumed that its readers shared the negative take. A story on such a topic is hard to justify; although the Press Complaints Commission's Code of Practice allows privacy to be overridden in order to protect public health (PCC 2011), Smith was most certainly *not* a threat to the public's health. More than 20 years since the virus first made the headlines, HIV/AIDS was still being used by some sections of the tabloid press as a political tool.

## Political Activism

While Smith continuously voted for improved rights for gay men and women, and spoke out on these issues in the Commons, his influence was probably greater within the Parliamentary Labour Party itself than in Parliament (Rayside 1998). Smith was most vocal on gay issues during Labour's years in opposition. Indeed, he was one of only a few MPs to speak unequivocally against Clause 28 from the very beginning

(Rayside 1998).[6] Although Smith did not ignore these issues once he became a Secretary of State in 1997, his ministerial position probably limited his ability to speak freely, and he did not vote in every division linked to gay rights in the 1997 and 2001 parliaments.[7] Obviously, as a busy Cabinet minister he would not have been expected to have a perfect attendance record, as shown by the relatively poor voting records of many Cabinet ministers when compared to backbench MPs. It is perhaps more significant, though, that Smith did not vote in every division when he once again became a backbencher.[8] An important point, because as one of the most high profile "out" gay MPs in the Commons, his speeches would most likely have been the subject of media (and activist) interest.

In many ways, Smith's decision to move away from single-issue politics is representative of the Labour Party's attitude to gay rights under Blair, who was keen to ensure that the Labour Party, while extremely supportive of gay rights (as seen by the sweeping legislative changes since 1997, and the fight to lower the age of consent in the midst of intense opposition from right-wing tabloids such as *The Sun*), was not represented in the press as the "pro-gay rights" and thus "anti-family" political party. Such a decision partially elucidates why gay rights legislation was spread-out over the 1997 and 2001 parliaments, rather than every issue being addressed without delay in the first parliament, as desired by many gay rights groups and activists. Aside from the fact that every government has a packed legislative calendar, it was important for the Labour Party to be seen as interested in issues affecting "families", rather than issues affecting so-called "promiscuous" and "dangerous" gay men, images still perpetuated by some parts of the press (of course, in reality, issues which affect families also affect gay people, and vice versa).

## Political Acceptability

The political establishment's acceptance of Smith after his 1984 "outing" was in many ways a landmark victory for gay politicians. Indeed, "private" homosexuality had long been enshrined in British law, and many gay politicians — while privately tolerated — were urged to stay "closeted". As Rayside (1998: 91) writes, "The notion of homosexuality as a 'private' matter is widespread in all countries in the West, but nowhere more institutionalized than in Britain, and nowhere within Britain more deeply entrenched than in the House of Commons. The formula arrived at in the 1960s and culminating in the partial decriminalization of 1967, tolerating sexual deviation when kept within the strict boundaries of public view, remained dominant in parliamentary culture until the early 1990s, and retains powerful currency still." Smith's "self-outing" thus bucked the trend. Naturally, his political acceptability made things much easier for him. After all, not only were his political beliefs unproblematic, he was also a man in a male-dominated institution, as well as being the consummate politician. Perhaps this is another reason why Colquhoun did not receive support from some sections of the Commons. Aside from the fact she was a woman, and therefore already stood out from the pack, she was a colourful politician as well; Smith, in many ways the archetypal career politician, looked and acted the part in a way that Colquhoun never could. Smith was advantaged in another way as well. Unlike the Australia-born Tatchell, who left school at sixteen due to his family's financial problems, Smith had a rather privileged educational background, attending Cambridge and then Harvard universities from where he gained a PhD. Smith thus had the same background and experiences as many of his parliamentary colleagues, and was consequently part of the parliamentary "club".

## The "Outing" Issue

Smith (*The Times*, WHY 'OUTING' IS WRONG, 22 March 1995) wrote in 1995: "I cannot accept that 'outing' in any shape or form is right either tactically or morally . . . It is of course important for people in the public eye to be honest about themselves and their sexuality. Not only is openness better than covert behaviour or pretence; but standing up and saying something about yourself can greatly help and encourage others . . . But this chance to bring confidence to others by being open only comes if the decision has been made voluntarily. If the statement is dragged out by others, it seems there is some cause for shame." Here, succinctly expressed, is the crux of the "outing" issue. If Smith had been forced to "come out", the press would have been able to present his homosexuality as scandalous and shocking, and therefore something that the public needed to be aware of; Smith would have been a "bad", "closeted" gay MP, rather than a "good" and "out" one, binary themes noted in Frame Three. By "coming out" voluntarily, Smith avoided that fate (and the vast majority of his press coverage, apart from the 2005 HIV/AIDS stories, was therefore simple reportage rather than manufacturing). Obviously, as Smith wrote in *The Times*, the benefits of being publicly "open" from the beginning of a political career do not justify "outing" in any way, morally or tactically.

Ironically, in the long term newspapers do not seem to benefit from the "outing" of, or focus on, gay politicians or politicians caught up in a gay "scandal". For, of all of the politicians mentioned so far, the only one to voluntarily give in-depth interviews about his or her personal life, and to allow his or her partner to do the same, is Smith. In 1997, Smith's partner, Dorian Jabri, gave an interview in which he talked about various aspects of their private lives, including how he and Smith met, their commitment to each other, how he "came out" and the prejudice they have faced (*The Times*, WE BOTH THINK IT IS FOREVER, 19 September 1997). It is unlikely that Smith and Jabri would have been quite so forthcoming if the press had mercilessly hounded Smith about his sexuality.

## Harvey Proctor

### Proctor's Story

Proctor's experiences and press representation were enough to dissuade any gay politician from standing up to be counted. His press coverage was very brutal and one of the fiercest and sustained attacks ever seen against a politician, heterosexual or gay. Proctor (MP for Basildon 1979–83 and Billericay 1983–7) received such bad press coverage because, unlike Smith, he did not tick all of the right boxes. In fact, his press representation was almost the opposite of (the majority of) Smith's press representation and his mediated persona was a negative one (Frame Three). So, whereas Smith was politically acceptable, Proctor was seen as controversial and right-wing, whilst Smith was sexually "safe", Proctor was accused of spanking underage male prostitutes, and whilst Smith voluntarily "came out", Proctor was "outed" in a storm of sexual scandal. Undoubtedly, the fact that Proctor's alleged sex life was seen as "exotic" and "dangerous" was the major factor in his downfall. For, his suggested sexual behaviour crossed the ostensible "norms" of homosexual sexual behaviour, let alone heterosexual, if the newspaper reports are to be believed. However, regardless of the fact that Proctor's alleged partners were apparently underage (the age of consent for gay men was still 21 and his partners were said to be 17 and 19) and if so he had therefore committed a crime, his press coverage was still vicious. The tabloid press coverage of Proctor's sex life verged on the obsessive, and the broadsheets, while less fervent, insisted on referring to Proctor's alleged partners as "boys", building on the paedophilic connotations of his tabloid press representation. While manufactured, the underage element of the story mean that Proctor's early press coverage (unlike some later articles) was covered by public interest criteria. However, the methods used by the press to expose Proctor were unethical and can be seem as further proof that the press coverage of Proctor actually turned into a witch-hunt.

In the summer of 1986 the *People* began the attack by claiming that Proctor had engaged in spanking sessions with a young male prostitute. In mid-June the newspaper wrote on its front page: "Tory MP Harvey Proctor admitted yesterday that a young male prostitute had been living at his London flat. But he denies allegations the rent-boy had made to the *People* about kinky sex games, spankings and cane beatings" (SPANKED BOYS IN MP'S FLAT, 15 June 1986). Proctor denied the allegations made against him, but Parris suggests his decision not to sue encouraged the press to search for more stories. Parris describes how the *People* went on to make further claims and actually tracked down one of Proctor's supposed rent-boys — allegedly called "Max" — wired him for sound and then sent him to talk to Proctor, and that the *Daily Mirror* then made the sensationalist claim that on a trip to Morocco Proctor had had a young Moroccan man in his room forced to hide naked under his bed to avoid detection. The press used underhand methods to obtain both stories; apart from being wired for sound, "Max" also assured Proctor that he was over the age of 21 when he was actually 18 and thus underage, and the Moroccan story was extracted from a "friend" of Proctor's, rather than being based on reliable evidence, with the Moroccan "youth" in his mid-twenties according to Proctor, something which certainly makes the story less salacious (Parris 1995). After receiving the *People* "dossier" in 1987, the Metropolitan Police raided Proctor's flat, and in May of the same year decided to prosecute him, resulting in him pleading guilty and admitting to four counts of gross indecency against two underage men. Proctor was charged during a general election campaign and due to the immense pressures he faced as a result, decided not to stand again. He was fined and also ordered to pay costs.

## Loaded Terms

Proctor's press coverage was inexorable, demonstrating, as Baston (2000) recognizes, the antagonism between the press and gay Conservative MPs in the 1980s. As with Tatchell, tabloid newspapers were responsible for the most salacious press coverage, labelling Proctor the "Spanking MP", with frequently made references to "youths", "boys" and similar terms. When following up on the *People* story, for example, *The Sun* (KINKY LOVE ROW MP SLAMS LEFT "LIES", 16 June 1986) wrote "A Tory MP yesterday slammed as 'monstrous' claims that he had a kinky affair with a teenage male prostitute . . . The 18-year-old rent boy told a Sunday newspaper he stayed at Mr Proctor's flat in Fulham, London. He claimed it was the scene of weird sex-games, including spanking and caning sessions involving young men."

As with the majority of Tatchell's broadsheet press coverage, the broadsheets chose to cover Proctor's traumas in a less forthright and lurid manner and instead reported it as a straightforward news item (following up the tabloids' stories, rather than breaking new ones). However, broadsheet newspapers from both sides of the political spectrum often used similar language. The *Guardian* (PROCTOR FACES CHARGES, 8 April 1987) noted that "Mr Proctor . . . was arrested in March after allegations that he had hired boys for sex". *The Times* (PROCTOR QUITS AS TORY CANDIDATE, 17 May 1987) observed that "He [Proctor] is charged with three offences of gross indecency with a boy aged 16 to 17 . . . and one offence involving a youth aged 19." The words "boy" and "youth" are loaded terms, used to link Proctor — and homosexuality in general — to paedophilia. Sanderson (1995: 215) notes that the link is often used to suggest that "given the opportunity, all homosexuals are child-molesters; that homosexuals make inappropriate role models for 'impressionable' young minds; and that homosexuals are 'proselytizing' and 'recruiting' in order to replenish their ranks."

## Defined by Sexuality

MPs who are involved in scandals (whether or not they are sexual ones), are often forever associated with their scandal, something certainly the case with Proctor.

Proctor's public self is defined by his private sexuality; few articles about him do not refer to his supposed sexual tastes, the charges made against him or his personal life in general (such as his relationships). Tatchell is also defined by his sexuality (although, to some extent, he has chosen to be defined in such a manner — since the Bermondsey by-election — what with his rather militant and controversial gay rights campaigns), but Smith is not, at least to the same extent anyway. Certainly, while Smith is known as the first "out" gay MP, he is taken seriously as a politician and commentator — partly because he made it clear from the start he was interested in so-called "mainstream" issues as well as gay rights, but also because he is not "scandalous" and controversial in the way that Tatchell and Proctor are. Ironically, Smith's public declaration also helped to prevent the personal becoming public. So, Proctor's decision to stay "closeted", as justifiable as that may be, flamed the tabloid fires; being gay in itself could be presented as scandalous (because of its "hidden" status), let alone the spanking issue.

The tabloid press continued to label Proctor the "Spanking MP" long after he stood down from Parliament. For instance, when Proctor left politics he opened a shirt shop which various Conservative MPs invested in but failed to declare in the *Register of Members' Interests*. The *People* (30 October 1994) greeted the news with the headline "MR BOTTOM SPANKER AND 10 TOP TORIES SLEAZEGATE; TORY MPS FAIL TO DECLARE SHARES IN HARVEY PROCTOR SHIRT SHOP". The paper went on to state: "HANKY-PANKY AS TOP TORIES KEEP QUIET OVER SHARES IN PERVERT PROCTOR'S BUSINESS . . . THE PEOPLE LIFTS THE SHIRT ON THE NEW SHOCK TORY SCANDAL". In the latter article Proctor is referred to as a "bottom spanking pervert" with a liking for "kinky sex". The article is full of loaded words — "pervert", "spanker" and "kinky" — all used to emphasize just how sordid Proctor apparently is. The expression "lifts the shirt" is outwardly homophobic. As late as 2004 the *Daily Mail* (4 March 2004) reported on Proctor's whereabouts under the headline "QUEEN OF THE CASTLE: NEW LIFE OF SHAMED MP," noting that Proctor "resigned following a scandal that involved rent boys and spanking." While some gay men may use the word "queen" as a form of positive identification (Baker 2002), here it is used disparagingly.

Broadsheet newspapers (from the left and right) also referred to Proctor using these terms long after the initial scandal was over, when Proctor was, after all, a private citizen. When Proctor gave evidence in a libel trial involving his parliamentary successor, Teresa Gorman (MP for Billericay 1987–2001), *The Independent* referred to him as "Mrs Gorman's spanking predecessor" (PALACE OF PLEASURE AND PROFIT . . . , 4 August 1991). By referring to Proctor using words such as "spanking" and "kinky" the press categorizes Proctor as "dangerous" and with sexual habits that meet neither a heterosexual nor homosexual "norm"; the binary themes used to describe him give him a negative mediated persona (Frame Three). The identification of Proctor as a "deviant" homosexual reassures the heterosexual reader that they are "normal" (a classification identified by McIntosh). That tactic did not need to be used with Smith; as an "out" and "good" homosexual with no apparent sexual "kinks" (*i.e.* he was "safe" rather than "dangerous"), Smith was not a threat to the heterosexual reader.

## Invasions of Privacy

In striving to punish Proctor's so-called "deviant" behaviour, some journalists behaved unethically. Proctor has claimed that the press hounded both himself and his mother, by not only camping outside their house, but also by storming in uninvited. The invasions of privacy, along with the secret taping of Proctor's conversation with "Max", raise many questions about the lengths that journalists should be allowed to go to obtain a good story, whether or not it is in the public interest. Without a doubt, it should always be borne in mind that the consequences of "outing" or writing about a gay politician's sexuality can be major ones, and a story long-forgotten by journalists can impact greatly on the life of the subject of the story. For example, in 1993 two men were jailed for causing actual bodily harm against Proctor (they broke his finger) after entering his shop and verbally abusing him about his sexuality. The attack on Proctor (and two of his friends) appears to have been an indirect result of the publicity he received in the late 1980s. In summing up, the judge said: "I am satisfied that both of you went to the shop of Mr Proctor, a man of whom you knew there had been scandal in the past, to cause trouble" (*Daily Mail*, "GAY BASHERS" JAILED FOR ATTACK IN HARVEY PROCTOR SHOP, 7 May 1993).

## Scandal

The reasons for Proctor's intense press coverage correlate with the case studies explored so far. One of the major factors in Proctor's negative portrayal was the fact that he had not publicly "come out" as gay, meaning that the newspapers had a potentially explosive and very scandalous story on their hands. Coupled with his "dangerous" sexuality (Frame Three), that weakened Proctor's position. Importantly, as with Roberts, Proctor's press coverage was not just about sexuality, it was also about scandal. In journalistic terms, scandal (whether hetrosexual or gay) equals a good story and therefore — hopefully — good sales. The 1986/1987 stories were actually preceded by an earlier brush with "scandal" in 1981, when after an argument Proctor's partner spoke to journalists prompting a *News of the World* story about their relationship (Parris 1995). The partner also claimed in a court case that he lived with Proctor, prompting Proctor to publicly reject his comments and distance himself from him (*The Times*, THE "LONER" WHO HIT THE HEADLINES, 2 November 1986). A public interest defence — exposing the hypocrisy of a public figure — could therefore be used to justify Proctor's later intense press coverage. In many respects, a subsequent focus on Proctor's sexuality was almost inevitable, and there is certainly a sense of unfinished business in his press coverage. As with Tatchell, and unlike Smith, Proctor was also damned by the fact that he had already courted controversy with his political views (Baston 2000). The fact that Proctor's alleged sexual partners were apparently underage certainly made his press coverage worse and gave newspapers another public interest justification for the stories. If an MP found himself in Proctor's situation now it would not be as serious legally, due to the lowering of the age of gay consent in 1994 and then 2000. As it happens, Proctor believed his partners *were* of legal age (after all, "Max" assured him he was so). Baston defends Proctor and states that the press's public interest defence was not convincing because he had tried to ensure that his partners were of legal age and he met them in his private home, rather than a public location. While undoubtedly true, it remains the case that Proctor was on the wrong side of the law. That fact, plus the intolerant climate of the 1980s, meant that he did not stand a chance.

## The Parliamentary "Club"

Baston describes how Proctor was not part of the parliamentary "club" and in many respects that is true, particularly in relation to his Conservative colleagues. Certainly, Proctor was not particularly well off, did not attend Oxbridge and was not universally popular. That said, he still had a firm base of friends within the Conservative Party, and while it may not have helped him while he was struggling to keep his seat, it certainly helped him afterwards (for instance, the 16 MPs — from the left and right of the Conservative Party — who invested in his shirt shop). The support which Proctor received from Conservative politicians once he had left Parliament once again demonstrates that — outside of the political arena at least — many Conservative politicians are relaxed about homosexuality. Nevertheless, at the time of Proctor's press coverage, the Conservative Party's (unofficial) rule was "keep it private" (an active demonstration of the acceptability threshold in relation to public space, as discussed in Frame Two, and an acknowledgement of the fact that different "groups" may have different notions of acceptability). As another example, an offer made to the Conservative politician Matthew Parris (MP for West Derbyshire

1979–86) to become a Parliamentary Private Secretary was withdrawn once Parris had made it clear to the Whips that he was gay. As the Chief Whip said to Parris (2002: 260) at the time: "I don't believe in God . . . But I don't shout about it. I don't feel the need to add it to my election address at general elections . . . It's a secret, if you like. It's private. It's between me and my . . . well, I don't believe in Him. See? See my point?"

Parris (1995) suggests in relation to Proctor's standing in the Conservative Party that one of the reasons why he kept the respect of the Party hierarchy was because he could generally be relied upon by the Whips to vote correctly. Nonetheless, even the most supportive political party would have found it difficult to allow Proctor to stay on as an MP in the face of such damaging allegations, especially when the Conservative Government (in spite of the private tolerance of Margaret Thatcher and many other politicians) had made it very clear that improving gay rights was not part of its social agenda and when a general election was fast approaching. The Conservative Party was surely mindful of public attitudes towards gay men and women as well. It is therefore unsurprising that Proctor's constituency party, while initially supportive, accepted Proctor's resignation when he offered it. Parris and Proctor's experiences suggest that while it was possible for Labour MPs to be fully "out" at the time, Conservative politicians could not let their homosexuality be seen *or* heard by the powers that be. Gay Conservative politicians were in a difficult position; their party expected them to "keep it private" but the press could then criticize them for that approach if "outed".

## Voting Record

By voting for the Sexual Offences Act to be extended to Scotland and Northern Ireland, in 1980 and 1982 respectively, Proctor obviously showed his support for the extension of gay rights,[9] something particularly true in the case of the Criminal Justice (Scotland) Bill because while the Government's position was officially one of neutrality, the Government disapproved of the proposal (Jeffery-Poulter 1991). However, Proctor's decision to vote against the Sex Equality Bill[10] (which sought to outlaw discrimination in employment on the grounds of homosexuality, amongst other things) could certainly be interpreted as a vote which disadvantaged gay people. One could of course defend Proctor and state that as a Labour MP introduced the Bill, a vote for it would have been a vote against the Government and thus problematic for his career. But, in 1986 Proctor was one of 43 Conservative MPs who rebelled against the Government's attempt to make it the right of school governors to decide whether or not a parent could withdraw their child from sex education. The rebels (which included Hampson) wanted parents to have the unqualified right to withdraw their children.[11] The rebellion was defeated, but Proctor proved that he was willing to vote against the Government. Proctor's decision to not support the 1983 Bill cannot therefore be explained by the fact he did not feel able to vote against his party. The 1986 rebellion, while not about homosexuality *per se*, was in part a response to the apparent "promotion of homosexuality" in the classroom by Labour run Local Education Authorities (LEAs). So, Proctor's support for the rebellion not only demonstrates that he was willing to vote against the Government, it also suggests that he was willing to vote for a measure that could be seen as presenting homosexuality as morally wrong and potentially damaging to young people (even if he voted against the Bill for unrelated reasons). His press coverage, while unethical in part, could thus technically be justified on grounds of hypocrisy, even if his votes for/against the above Bills were for reasons completely unrelated to sexuality (such as political or tactical).

## The Private/Public Divide

Proctor's negative press representation once again demonstrates that the tabloid press hounds those ("bad") politicians who do not "engage" with their homosexuality (*i.e.* they are not open or relaxed about their sexuality even if they are not "out"). Without a doubt, in the *People*'s view it was unacceptable for Proctor to keep that part of his life private, especially when his sexual life was seen as morally unacceptable; according to such a rationale, his press coverage, while harsh, was justified. The private/public divide relating to homosexuality, as defined by the tabloid press at least, is elucidated by Proctor's experience; while being "closeted" is unacceptable, "active" *sexual* homosexuality is also intolerable. Thus, public homosexuality is perhaps only acceptable if it is unthreatening and almost sexless (Frame Two). Proctor's willingness to vote against the Sex Equality Bill, and his support of the 1986 rebellion, suggest that the cause of gay rights was not the most important thing on his political agenda. While Smith and Proctor approached their sexuality in very different ways, both, to varying degrees, disassociated themselves from homosexuality. Proctor refused to talk about his sexuality at all (believing that his private life was his own personal business), and Smith, while "out", did not want to be seen as a single-issue politician. That approach did not hold much sway with the press. Both Smith and Proctor were aware that being a gay politician in the 1980s was fraught with difficulty, something proved by their troublesome press coverage, with whole recognition (Frame One) some way off.

## Conclusion

In the 1980s it was possible for gay politicians to survive politically once their sexuality had become public or for politicians caught up in a gay scandal to survive politically once their sexuality has been speculated about. However, the identification of HIV/AIDS as a gay "plague" meant that the press (and public) attitude towards homosexuality regressed, affecting the tolerant (or perhaps more appropriately, less hostile) portrayal of gay politicians and homosexuality in general which was beginning to emerge in the early 1980s. The move towards recognition (Frame One of the overarching frame of representation) took a backwards step, with public homosexuality, even if that related to campaigning about gay rights, problematic (Frame Two). Binary themes (Frame Three) were strong in the 1980s, strengthening, in turn, mediated personas — both positive and negative.

While the press takes a dichotomous approach to the representation of gay or "outed" politicians, there is a relational aspect to the binaries (along with the overarching positive/negative mediated personas). A politician may have a stronger negative mediated persona than another. They may also meet the binary themes in a strong or weak fashion (and gradients within). Indeed, the binary themes themselves have been stronger and weaker at different times, depending on socio-political factors. So, while a relational approach is not utilized in the purest sense, within the dichotomous binary themes themselves there are degrees of strength and different possibilities, alongside different combinations of binaries making up negative and positive mediated personas (with some binaries perhaps not even applying to particular politicians). Politicians do not have to meet all of the positive criteria to be presented positively, or all of the negative criteria to be presented negatively. Generally, if they meet more negative binary themes than positive ones then they have a negative mediated persona, and vice versa. Proctor, for example, had a negative mediated persona as he met three out of the four identified negative binaries: he was "in" rather than "out", "bad" rather than "good" (because he was not open and relaxed meaning that the press could not categorize him), and "dangerous" rather than "safe" (because of the link to spanking and atypical sexual behaviour). However, he was "private" in the sense that he did not display his sexuality or engage in public sexual behaviour. Gay or "outed" politicians were therefore generally considered "good" if they were open about their sexuality, but did not "flaunt" it, and engaged in private and safe sexual behaviour, and considered "bad" if they were "closeted" or not open about their sexuality, and engaged in public or "dangerous" sexual behaviour. Newspapers defined or categorized gay or "outed" politicians (in relation to all of the above binary themes), thus reaffirming the heterosexuality — and "normality" — of the press and public. Politicians who did not "engage" with their sexuality were more likely to be hounded about it. As such, the "need to know" is a key factor in the "outing" of a politician.

It is clear that press coverage of gay politicians and politicians caught up in gay "scandals" in the 1980s must be understood in relation to the news values, agendas, and styles of tabloid and broadsheet newspapers. While broadsheet newspapers did discuss the sexuality of politicians, and sometimes used pejorative or problematic terms while doing so, tabloid newspapers tended to be much more vicious in their treatment, using discriminatory language and an often scornful tone. The individual circumstances of each politician must also be considered. In particular: the politics and/or popularity of the politician; the sexual life of the politician; and the lifestyle of the politician. The gender of a politician can also be relevant; it is clear that male politicians in the 1980s suffered because of the link to HIV/AIDS, the false association between male homosexuality and paedophilia and anti-gay legislation which has only ever applied to men. These factors led to the demonization of gay men in general, affecting the representation of male gay politicians or politicians caught up in a gay "scandal". It is difficult to directly compare the representation of male and female gay politicians because there have always been many more male politicians than female politicians. However, linking back to Chapter 5, it is clear that in the 1970s and 1980s the press also engaged with the stereotypes of effeminate male homosexuals and masculine lesbians, a common association (Alley and Dillon 2001; McCreary 1994; McIntosh 1996; A. Taylor 1983), with Tatchell effeminized and Colquhoun masculinized.

Finally, it is important to recognize that heterosexual politicians of course also suffer at the hands of the press, demonized for "unacceptable" sexual behaviour and the apparent resulting threat to the family, in the same way that a gay politician may suffer. However, gay politicians are more of a threat due to the fact that their "indiscretions" are completely outside of heterosexual procreation. Gay or "outed" politicians are therefore at a major disadvantage when caught up in a sexual scandal or story about sexuality: not only can they be criticized for their sexual behaviour in general, they can also be implicitly condemned for the fact they are not heterosexual, something even true of the press coverage of Tatchell, with his support of gay rights a threat to "real" (read heterosexual) issues. *Part Three* explores the issue in detail, emphasizing that even though there was a greater degree of sexual scandal "equality" in later decades, with press representation of gay politicians becoming similar to that of heterosexual politicians, the theme still persisted.

## Notes

1. Hansard House of Commons Debates (vol. 989) 22 July 1980 (Criminal Justice [Scotland] Bill — Homosexual Offences).
2. Hansard House of Commons Debates (vol. 29) 25 October 1982 (Northern Ireland — Homosexual Offences).
3. Hansard House of Commons Debates (vol. 124) 15 December 1987 (Local Government Bill — Prohibition on Promoting Homosexuality by Teaching or by Publishing Material). There were three votes in total: divisions 116–18.
4. Hansard House of Commons debates (vol. 129) 9 March 1988 (Local Government Bill — Prohibition on Promoting Homosexuality by Teaching or by Publishing Material).
5. For example: Hansard House of Commons Debates (vol. 124) 15 December 1987 (Local Government Bill — Prohibition on Promoting Homosexuality by Teaching or by Publishing Material).
6. For example: Hansard House of Commons Debates (vol. 124) 15 December 1987 (Local Government Bill — Prohibition on Promoting Homosexuality by Teaching or by Publishing Material); Hansard House of Commons Debates (vol. 129) 9 March 1988 (Local Government Bill — Prohibition on Promoting Homosexuality by Teaching or by Publishing Material).
7. For example: Hansard House of Commons Debates (vol. 325) 10 February 1999 (Sexual Offences Amendment Bill); Hansard House of Commons Debates (vol. 253) 5 July 2000 (Local Government Bill [Lords] — Prohibition of Promotion of Homosexuality: Bullying).
8. For example: Hansard House of Commons Debates (vol. 373) 29 October 2001 (Adoption and Children Bill — Consideration and Third Reading); Hansard House of Commons Debates (vol. 385) 16 May 2002 (Adoption and Children Bill — Applications for Adoption).
9. Hansard House of Commons Debates (vol. 989) 22 July 1980 (Criminal Justice [Scotland] Bill — Homosexual Offences); Hansard House of Commons Debates (vol. 29) 25 October 1982 (Northern Ireland — Homosexual Offences).
10. Hansard House of Commons Debates (vol. 50) 9 December 1983 (Sex Equality Bill).
11. Hansard House of Commons Debates (vol. 102) 21 October 1986 (Education Bill [Lords] — Local Education Authorities Reserve Power).

# PART THREE

# Exploring "Contemporary" Representation

# 7

# Histories of Homosexuality: The (Slow) Advancement of Gay Equality

"The rejection [of the 1994 attempt to equalize the age of consent by MPs] was a defeat for lesbian and gay activists. But what the activist campaign and even the vote tally on that evening revealed was a significant shift in the balance of forces in the years since the passage of Section 28 of the Local Government Bill, curtailing the 'promotion' of homosexuality." (Rayside 1998: 45)

## All Change?

The 1990s saw significant improvement in attitudes towards homosexuality, demonstrated by the 1994 votes on the equalization of the age of consent for gay men, where a free vote saw 11% of Conservative MPs voting for an equal age of consent, something unthinkable ten years earlier.[1] Although the vote to equalize the age of consent was actually lost, gay issues were on the agenda as never before and gay people achieved even greater visibility. Gay activists welcomed the election of Tony Blair as Labour Prime Minister in 1997, and even though the Government made legislative changes at a steady pace rather than immediately (as wished for by many activists), the changes that were made in the late 1990s and 2000s affected every aspect of private and public life for gay men and women, such as: the ending of the ban on gay people serving in the Armed Forces; the repeal of Clause 28; and the introduction of civil partnerships. However, while newspaper representation of gay people and issues became more liberal post-1990, some tabloid newspapers — even in the 2000s — continued to make explicitly disparaging comments about homosexuality, and gay politicians continued to be "outed", with their sexuality the focus of intense press attention.

This chapter surveys attempts to equalize the age of gay consent in the early to mid-1990s, the sweeping legislative changes made by Labour in later years, the surrounding socio-political climate, and the impact of a more socially liberal Conservative Party in the 2000s, focusing on the periods of 1990–7 and post-1997. In relation to the overarching frame of representation, it is clear that both recognition (Frame One) and public acceptability (Frame Two) edged nearer in the 1990s and 2000s, at times very quickly, but they were not reached completely, even at the end of the first decade of the 2000s. Indeed, opinion polls show that many people still express negative opinions about homosexuality (although the number is decreasing), with negative binary themes and mediated personas (Frame Three) present.

## Homosexuality 1990–1997: The Major Years

### The Age of Consent Campaign

Initially, many gay activists saw John Major's (Prime Minister 1990–7 and MP for Huntingdon 1979–2001) appointment as Prime Minister in 1990 as a welcome and much needed change and a good opportunity for further advancements to be made after the Thatcher years; in Major, the UK finally had a leader with more liberal views on homosexuality (albeit not as liberal as many would like), demonstrated by the sympathetic signals he seemed to send out to the gay community during the 1992 General Election (Sanderson 1995). The lowering of the age of consent for gay men to 18 in 1994 was a huge step forward for gay rights (although a disappointment to many who wanted the age of consent equalized at 16), and was seen by many activists and politicians as the most significant move forward since the Sexual Offences Act of 1967. The presence of European legal rulings encouraged reform in the early 1990s (Rayside 1998), highlighting the ongoing influence of "outside" factors on domestic policy (following on from the impact of Europe on extending the Sexual Offences Act to Northern Ireland in 1982).

The campaign to lower the age of gay consent was fraught with difficulty. The gay rights campaigning organization Stonewall began the first major campaign to lower the age of consent in 1993, launching a legal challenge (*Wilde v. UK*) in the European Court of Human Rights on behalf of three men — Ralph Wilde, Will Parry and Hugo Greenhaulgh — who believed that the age of consent, which was then 21, was a breach of their right to privacy (Stonewall 2006). The

Conservative Government had indicated that it was willing to act on the age of consent issue soon after the 1992 election; after Major's election Conservative ministers privately expressed that the Government was prepared to allow gay-related reforming amendments to the Criminal Justice Bill (which was expected to be debated in late 1993/early 1994) and Major himself told Conservative Members that he was in favour of reducing the age of gay consent to 18, possibly through an amendment to the Bill (Rayside 1998). The Criminal Justice Bill was included in the Queen's Speech of 1993, and soon after the Government indicated that it would not hinder amendments to the Bill. In response to the Government's plans, Stonewall — accompanied by pro-equality MPs of all political colours — began a campaign to lower the age of gay consent to 16. The campaign was led in the House of Commons by Edwina Currie (MP for Derbyshire South 1983–97), a member of TORCHE (the Tory Campaign for Homosexual Equality).

The Conservative Government indicated that a free vote would be allowed on the age of consent, and the Labour Party indicated that it was in favour of setting the age of consent at 16. While many MPs were in favour of equalization, political opposition to the move became more visible as time went on. In early January a group of Conservative Members threatened to vote against the Criminal Justice Bill if the amendment in favour of 16 was passed, and a few days later the then Home Secretary stated that he intended to support 18 as the age of consent, rather than 16 (Rayside 1998). There were two age of consent votes when the issue was discussed in the Commons on 22 February 1994. The first amendment voted on — an attempt to lower the age of consent to 16 — was lost (280 votes to 307). The second amendment — an attempt to lower the age of consent to 18 — was passed (427 votes to 162).[2] The statistics show that in relation to the first vote, the Conservative Party mostly opposed total equality, with 40% voting in effect to keep the age of consent at 21, 84% of the Labour Party voted for equality, and all the Liberal Democrat MPs present in the Commons chamber voted for equality (Rayside 1998). While the lowering of the age of gay consent to 18 was a landmark move, activists were disappointed that the first amendment was lost by only 27 votes. Stonewall continued to campaign for an equal age of consent and launched a second case in the European Court of Human Rights (*Sutherland v. UK*). The Court held that the unequal age of consent was in fact a breach of human rights (Stonewall 2006), but it was not until 2001 that the age of consent for gay men was finally lowered to 16 from 18.

## Political Arguments

The age of consent issue was hotly debated in Parliament, and the types of argument used by politicians when speaking against equalization reflected the arguments of sections of the press. Ellis and Kitzinger (2002: 171–5) note that the House of Commons and Lords debates on the age of consent reflected five main arguments: "(1) Principles of right and wrong take precedence over equality: there can be no 'equality' between normality and abnormality, moral probity and sin . . . (2) Principles of democracy take precedence over equality: the majority of the population opposes any lowering of the age of consent . . . (3) Principles of care and protection take precedence over equality: young men are immature and vulnerable and need the protection of the law . . . (4) Health risks [*i.e.* gay sex is a health risk] . . . (5) Wedges and slippery slopes [*i.e.* the equalization of the age of consent would be the first of many requests for further gay equality]."[3] Although, as Ellis and Kitzinger recognize, arguments for the lowering of the age of gay consent were primarily and initially based on the need for equality, proponents were forced to argue back in relation to the above arguments, meaning that the human rights argument became lost. As these writers note, many parliamentarians quoted medical evidence when opposing the equalization of the age of consent. These arguments were seen as spurious by many; both the Council of the British Medical Association and the National Association of Citizens Advice Bureaux were in favour of 16 as the age of consent.[4]

The impact of HIV/AIDS was also raised by parliamentarians speaking against attempts to equalize the age of gay consent, with some Conservative MPs against a lower age of consent for gay men claiming that it increased the chance of young men catching HIV. One member said (Hansard 1994): "The second factor that is relevant to health is that, according to the Public Health Laboratory included Service, over 75 per cent of all AIDS cases come from male homosexuals. The AIDS dimension cannot be overlooked if we are removing a protective barrier for vulnerable youngsters." However, as pointed out by Stonewall (1993: 4), "All the discussions about the criminal law have taken place prior to the AIDS epidemic." As these arguments suggest, opponents of equalization often did not accept any arguments to the contrary. For many, the issue was not about equal rights *per se* (because homosexuality should not be seen in these terms), but rather morality and propriety. The use of the phrase "vulnerable youngsters" is also significant; the notion of homosexuality equalling paedophilia, with "youngsters" at threat from older gay men, was often present in the debates.

**114**

## 1990s Legislation

Although the battle to lower the age of gay consent dominated the early to mid-1990s, the gay community fought many other battles. In 1991 activists and pro-gay politicians contested the amendment of paragraph 16 of the Children Act, designed to stop gay people from fostering and adopting: the campaign was successful. In 1991 activists also campaigned against Clauses 1, 2, and 25 of the Criminal Justice Bill. Clause 25 gave power to the courts to view "everyday" contact between gay men as sexual offences. Due to immense protest from politicians and activists, the Conservative Government removed three offences liable to harsher punishment: homosexual acts between merchant seamen; procurement; and living on the earnings of male prostitution. The Government claimed that the original aim of the Bill was not to punish gay men by labelling them as sexual criminals, but to introduce heavier sentences for offenders seriously threatening public safety. Another successful campaign was the amendment of the law to recognize male rape as an offence; before then, in legal terms rape could only be committed by a man against a woman. The amendment was introduced and agreed in the Lords and the Government agreed to include it in 1994's Criminal Justice and Public Order Act.

The Armed Forces Bill was also making its way through Parliament in 1991 (while homosexuality was legal, homosexual activity between service men or women was still an offence). The Select Committee scrutinizing the Armed Forces Bill recommended that the legal prosecution of gay troops should end, but gay people should still be banned from serving in the Armed Forces. Labour MPs were at the forefront of the campaign to change the law on gay people serving in the Armed Forces, and were joined in the campaign by many Conservative politicians. The campaign to change the law continued throughout Major's time in office. In 1996, although a Ministry of Defence "homosexual assessment panel" concluded that homosexual activity should no longer be automatic grounds for dismissal (although active homosexual contact should still be banned), the Government refused to relax its rules on gay people serving in the Armed Forces.

## 1990s Political and Public Opinion

The above campaigns indicate that the Major Government, while much more pro-gay than Conservative governments of the past, perhaps saw gay relationships and gay issues as a whole as politically problematic. On the one hand, Major changed the Civil Service rules

in order that homosexuality was no longer necessarily a bar to advancement and, in addition, he welcomed the gay actor Sir Ian McKellen to
10 Downing Street, making him the first Prime Minister to meet a
leading gay activist at the symbolic location. Major's attempts to
appease the gay community pleased liberal broadsheet newspapers
such as *The Independent* (AN OPEN-MINDED PRIME MINISTER,
25 September 1991): "John Major has done a simple and sensible thing
in receiving Sir Ian McKellen at Downing Street . . . The truth of the
matter is that Mr Major will probably have gained a few votes . . . If Mr
Major displays a more tolerant approach, and makes some concessions
to Sir Ian's agenda in the Conservative Party's manifesto, he will bring
back these exiles." In contrast to such liberalness, though, Major
headed a Government which attempted to bar lesbians and gay men
from fostering and adopting. It appears that there was a disparity
between Major's personal liberalness and that of (many of) his MPs,
Party members, and the Conservative supporting press. Indeed, the
Conservative Party's ethos of "family values" was in the midst of being
promoted at the time by Major's "back to basics" campaign (explored
in more detail in Chapter 8). It was still the case gay men and women
were not wholly tolerated, and they certainly had not achieved recognition (Frame One).

Although the Labour Party was a pro-gay organization in the 1990s
(campaigning, for example, to lower the age of gay consent), many
activists believed that the Labour Party was not as outspoken as it
should have been. Of course, a number of Labour MPs were opposed
to particular aspects of equality in contrast to their party's stance (as
many Conservative MPs were pro-equality), the age of consent being
an obvious example. However, in 1996, when an amendment aiming
to lift the ban on gay people serving in the Armed Forces was added to
a defence bill, Blair allowed a free vote, rather than a whipped vote,
something many gay activists saw as problematic. Eight Labour MPs
voted against the amendment, including Labour MPs on the Armed
Forces Select Committee. Rayside (1998: 96) notes that "In a radio
interview the next day, Blair reiterated his belief 'that homosexual
people should not be banned or discharged from the military merely
by reason of the fact they are gay,' but added a qualifying note even
more troublesome than his past statements, saying that any change
would have to be negotiated 'in a way that takes account of the concerns
of the military'." This suggests that while Blair was stronger on gay
rights than previous Labour leaders of the 1990s, he was not immune
to the threat of negative pre-election publicity.

Public attitudes towards homosexuality were more tolerant in the

1990s than previous years. British Social Attitudes data (Britsocat 2011) shows that the number of people who believed that sexual relations between people of the same sex were "always" or "mostly" wrong fell from 68% in 1990 to 55% in 1995.[5] Stonewall (1999) highlights that the percentage of people in favour of equal rights for gay people steadily increased from 1991 to 1995 (1991 — 65%; 1992 — 71%; 1995 — 74%).[6] These figures echo improved political attitudes: while 84% of Labour MPs voted for an equal age of consent in 1994, only 30% were in support in 1990 (Rayside 1998). But, as Rayside also recognizes, there was still public opposition to gay issues at the time, reflecting opposition to equality in Parliament. In fact, surveys show that while a majority of people were in favour of equal treatment, there was still disapproval of homosexuality in other ways. In fact, polling at the time of the 1994 age of consent debates suggested that while the majority of the public supported the principle of equality, only 13 to 16 percent of the public supported 16 as the age of consent (Rayside 1998).[7] "Acceptability" of homosexuality (Frame Two) therefore not only relates to issues of private and public, it also relates to behaviour and active sexuality.

## Gaining Visibility

Gay people actually gained visibility as a result of the negativity shown towards them by some quarters. Without doubt, the gay community was mobilized by attempts to equalize the age of consent and other campaigns, building on the increased visibility gay men and women gained as a result of political struggles in the 1980s. In the 1990s the gay rights campaigning organizations Stonewall and Outrage! gathered momentum and became key figures in the fight for equality. The organizations used different methods to achieve it: Stonewall engaged with the political structures in debate, whereas Outrage!, as a radical, left-wing organization, took to the streets and engaged with the media in an antagonistic fashion. In the early to mid-1990s gay people certainly benefited from more balanced press coverage (in fact, their mediated personas, as discussed in Frame Three of the overarching frame of representation, became more positive), which was in itself a result of the increased visibility of gay people in public spaces and culture (Frame Two) and more positive public attitudes towards homosexuality (Frame One) (Rayside 1998).

In the 1990s liberal broadsheets such as *The Independent* and *Guardian* were now willing to write about gay issues (although Rayside suggests that the *Guardian* only did so in response to claims it had been inattentive in the past). So, London's annual gay pride parade began to receive lots of press coverage, and activist representatives were afforded the respect of the press and given the opportunity to write opinion pieces (Rayside 1998). As Peter Tatchell, head of Outrage!, stated in 1995 (cited Rayside 1998: 59): "Overall the media coverage on gay issues is now much better than it was ten or even five years ago. It's becoming increasingly routine for lesbian and gay spokespeople to be quoted on issues of relevance. Lesbian and gay issues are getting more regularly reported and on the whole reported in a more objective and dispassionate way."

The right-wing broadsheets continued to oppose equality in general terms, but their opposition was balanced by more positive media coverage (Rayside 1998). The tabloid press continued to refer to homosexuality in disparaging terms, but were generally less rabid. Nonetheless, particular tabloid newspapers, such as *The Sun* and *Daily Star*, continued to cause offence to such an extent that regulatory authorities condemned them. In May 1990 the Press Council, the predecessor to the Press Complaints Commission, ruled against *The Sun* and stated that words such as "poof", "poofter" and "woofter" were no longer acceptable (Jeffery-Poulter 1991). *The Sun* (NAME GAME, 14 May 1990) claimed in an editorial that the ruling was an attack on press freedom: "we know a great deal more about how ordinary people think, act and speak. Readers of *The Sun* KNOW and SPEAK and WRITE words like poof and poofter. What is good enough for them is good enough for us. Incidentally, our dictionary defines gay as carefree, merry, brilliant. Does the Press Council approve of homosexuals appropriating such a fine old word?" The managing editor also claimed that the words were in "everyday use" to describe gay people (*The Sun*, RAP FOR THE SUN, 14 May 1990).

In 1991 the Press Complaints Commission criticized the *Daily Star* for "riding roughshod over the sensitivities" of gay people in articles about gay people in the Armed Forces. In addition, the Commission claimed that the *Star*'s articles about the Select Committee of the Armed Forces Bill did not distinguish between comment, conjuncture and fact; the *Daily Star* headed its article "POOFTERS ON PARADE" (*Daily Star*, 24 September 1991). While these headlines were deeply insulting to gay people, they were not representative of the tabloid press as a whole. Press representation of homosexuality was once again becoming more moderate, after the backward steps of the 1980s, and would continue to improve as the twenty-first century approached. However, newspapers, particularly tabloid ones, continued to slip up in the late 1990s and beyond. While sections of the press were becoming more tolerant of homosexuality, full recognition (Frame One) had not been reached.

## Homosexuality Post-1997: The Blair Years and Beyond

*Labour Legislation*

New Labour's election in 1997 heralded a new era for gay legal rights. While some have suggested that Blair was too cautious regarding gay issues in his early years as leader of the Labour Party, both when Leader of the Opposition and Prime Minister (allowing, for example, free votes rather than whipped votes on some key issues, and legislating for improved gay rights over the course of the 1997 and 2001 parliaments, rather than immediately), the Labour Government undoubtedly delivered on gay rights. Between coming to power in 1997 and losing power in 2010 the Party:

- Lowered the age of consent for gay men to 16
- Revised the Criminal Injuries Compensation Scheme to include long-term gay partners as qualifying relatives (fatal cases)
- Amended the immigration rules to allow unmarried gay partners the right to apply for leave to enter/remain in the UK on the basis of their relationship
- Gave same-sex partners of a biological parent the right to request a flexible working pattern
- Gave same-sex couples the right to apply to adopt a child jointly
- Changed laws to ensure that gay people are not discriminated against unfairly on grounds of sexual orientation; for the first time laws relating to sexual offences were the same for both heterosexual and gay people (the offences of buggery and gross indecency were deleted from the statutes)
- Banned workplace discrimination of gay men and women
- Lifted the ban on gay men and women serving in the Armed Forces
- Repealed Clause 28
- Made civil partnerships for same-sex couples legal (giving gay couples the same legal rights as heterosexual married couples)
- Spearheaded social initiatives on combating homophobia.

As with the extension of the Sexual Offences Act to Northern Ireland in 1982, European legal institutions encouraged gay law reform in the late 1990s. In 1997 the European Commission found that the age disparity between the heterosexual and gay ages of consent violated the European Convention of Human Rights, thus pressurizing the Government to equalize the age of consent as soon as possible, and in 1999 the Commission overturned the ban on gay people serving in the Armed Forces, giving the Government little choice but to implement the decision in UK law.

## Political Opinion about Blair's Reforms

Much of the Labour Government's pro-gay legislation was politically controversial, with both the Conservative opposition (in the House of Commons and Lords), and large parts of the press, condemning it. The resistance of the Conservative Party to moves to improve gay rights was very strong in the late 1990s and early 2000s (although, many Conservative politicians voted for equality at various times), particularly in the House of Lords. When the abolition of Clause 28 was debated in 2000, Conservative MPs were under a three-line whip to oppose the move. The Conservative Party also opposed the lowering of the age of gay consent to 16. During the 2000 debate on the issue, the then Conservative Shadow Home Secretary Ann Widdecombe (MP for Maidstone and Weald 1987–2010) presented homosexuality as "other" and an opposition to the norm, stating (Hansard 2000) that: "It is . . . wrong that a young person of sixteen should be free in law to embark on a course of action that might lead to a lifestyle that would separate him, permanently perhaps . . . from the mainstream life of marriage and family."

Rayside ponders the Conservative Party's stance on gay issues in the late 1990s, pointing out that William Hague (MP for Richmond 1989– and Conservative leader 1997–2001) voted for 16 as the age of gay consent in 1994[8] and had been positive towards gay issues on other occasions (he expressed support for gay marriage when campaigning for Party leadership and sent good wishes to gay pride marchers in London). Importantly, though, as Rayside also recognizes, many of the Conservative members who were defeated in Labour's 1997 landslide were pro-equality, leaving the Conservative backbenchers full of traditionalists. The relative lack of outspoken pro-gay Conservative MPs, combined with older, traditional Party members, made any move to the left on gay issues very difficult for the Conservative Party leaders of the past, and Hague's pro-gay stance both before he became leader and during the Conservative leadership campaign of 1997, slowly diminished as he faced political, membership and media pressure. Many

Conservative MPs disagreed with their party's (often negative) stance on gay rights, as many Labour MPs disagreed with their party's (usually positive) stance. However, a split of opinion on the issue was more problematic for the Conservative Party at the time than for Labour, as the Labour Party had worked through its policy changes (under Blair's leadership at least), moving from "old" to "new" Labour, whereas the Conservative Party was still engaging in such a process.

## Political Arguments

While some politicians condemned homosexuality explicitly during Blair's reforms, many used more coded terms and strategies. Burridge (2004) writes that many of the politicians against the repeal of Clause 28 used the verbal technique of "disclaiming", in which they attempted to deactivate claims of homophobia by explicitly stating that they were not anti-gay, thus giving their arguments greater legitimacy. Burridge (2004: 335) goes on to observe that during the debates on Clause 28, many politicians not only attempted to distance themselves from claims of homophobia, they also explicitly stated how tolerant they were: "Not only are there many examples of an assertion of the absence of prejudice on the part of those resisting repeal, many speakers stressed the presence of tolerance, and 'displayed' evidence for their own."

Interestingly, Burridge notes that during the debates on Clause 28 in 2000, many anti-Clause 28 politicians attempted to meet their opposition halfway, even though the majority of pro-Clause 28 politicians refused to do the same, thus giving some legitimacy to anti-repeal claims. As such, Burridge (2004: 338) believes there was "acquiescence to the general climate of disclaiming".

Baker (2004) also discusses discourses of homosexuality in the House of Lords (1998–2000), and suggests that a particular chain of argument was used by some peers to justify opposition to the lowering of the age of male gay consent: first, homosexuality is not an identity, it is an act; second, anal sex is the homosexual sexual norm; and third, anal sex is dangerous and unnatural. Homosexuality as an act — in opposition to the notion of homosexuality as an identity, as suggested by the 1885 Criminal Law Amendment Act — suggests that the sexual defines what it is to be gay. Baker argues that designating homosexuality as an act rather than an identity was an important part of the anti-reform arguments, because it is easier to link criminality to behaviour rather than a social group. As such, the Lords' arguments often moved off the subject of the age of consent, to a more general discussion on the rights and

**121**

wrongs of gay sex *per se*. Baker also states that anti-reform peers frequently used particular terms — anal intercourse, buggery, gross indecency, anal sex and sodomy — and these words suggested that gay sex is wrong and criminal. Linked to this, Baker states that the sexual act most linked with homosexuality (anal sex) was presented as leading to ruin, *e.g.* the infection of blood supplies through donating blood and HIV/AIDS. The suggestion that gay sex can "ruin" boys (the use of the word boys, rather than men, being very important) was strong, and exemplified the false belief that there is a link between homosexuality and paedophilia. Binary themes and negative mediated personas (Frame Three) were therefore heavily present in these debates. Interestingly, Baker (2004: 100) writes that the anti-reformers refer to girls as well as boys: "On the one hand, anti-reform is justified as not homophobic because it will result in danger to girls [*i.e.* girls aged 16 would also be allowed to have anal sex] as well as boys. But on the other, girls aren't seen as being at risk because they are 'more mature' and not 'ruined for life' if 'seduced'." Referring to "girls" (itself an emotive term) could be seen as another way of disclaiming homophobia.

Ellis and Kitzinger argue that although the age of consent debates (both before and after 1997) can be understood in relation to a human rights argument, proponents of change failed to exploit that line of reasoning and instead let anti-reformers set the agenda, thus allowing heteronormativity to remain unchallenged. They also suggest that reformers placed too much emphasis on equality; as equality means different things to different people, the age of consent debates were therefore hijacked by those against change. Epstein *et al.* (2000) state that the age of consent debates in the House of Commons (from 1998) focused around three story-clusters: (1) stories that focused on the predatory nature of gay men; (2) narratives about the age at which sexual preferences become fixed; (3) good/bad gay stories (with the good gay man on the margins, and the bad gay man politically active and visible). As noted by Epstein *et al.* (2000: 19), Sedgwick (1994) has stated that a distinction between "good" and "bad" gays is funda-mental to cultural definitions of homophobia.[9] Indeed, "The stress on sexuality as a private matter functions both as a defence (against homo-phobia) but also as a limitation on open debate and action around sexual inequalities and ways of living." Epstein *et al.* write that in the age of consent debates the "splitting" is not only repeated, it is also strengthened. As they note, a Conservative MP represented the gay-rights campaigning organization Stonewall as "good" and Outrage! as "bad" (Hansard 1998). Stonewall, as an organization which engages with the "mainstream" political process, is presented as superior to the more controversial Outrage! So, in the way that gay people are defined as "good" or "bad" (using Epstein's definition), there is also a distinction made between being gay and heterosexual institutions (Epstein *et al.* 2000).

## Cameron's Conservatives

Although many politicians (and Lords in particular) used pejorative language in relation to homosexuality in the late 1990s, the 1998 age of consent debates highlight that discourses surrounding sexuality have changed over the years. Between 1994 and 1998 a "liberal alliance" emerged, containing both Conservative and Labour members, in place of a hegemonic "moral-traditionalist sexual Right" (Epstein *et al.* 2000: 23). The alliance can be seen as increasing in strength after David Cameron's (Prime Minister 2010– and MP for Witney 2001– ) election as Party leader in 2005, and his attempt to influence his party's attitude towards "moral issues" such as homosexuality. For example, Cameron made it very clear that he opposed allowing Catholic adoption agencies to opt out from discrimination laws (the Equality Act 2006, which came into effect in 2007, does not allow discrimination on the provision of goods, facilities and services on the basis of sexual orientation. The Catholic hierarchy did not want Catholic adoption agencies to have to consider gay couples as adoptive parents and instead wanted the agencies to pass on their details to non-Catholic adoption agencies). It was a radical move, one opposed by many Conservative MPs, including David Davis (MP for Boothferry 1987–97 and Haltemprice and Howden 1997– ), an opponent of Cameron's in the 2005 Conservative Party leadership contest. Cameron also suggested that he wanted to move away from the "traditional" image of a Conservative MP (white, male and middle class) towards a more diverse range of parliamentary candidates, showing once more a desire to appeal to a wider audience, and also paid a well-publicized visit to watch *Brokeback Mountain* in 2006, a film focusing on the hidden love of two gay men in 1960s America, a subtle sign to the press and public that he is a modern and liberal individual, at least in relation to homosexuality. He has also publicly supported gay Conservative MPs when they have "come out", showing that under his leadership it is possible to be an openly gay Conservative MP (suggesting the Conservative mantra of "keep it private" has lost resonance). Recognition (Frame One) and public acceptability (Frame Two) of gay Conservative MPs thus edged closer under Cameron's leadership, at least in relation to attitudes within the Party.

Nonetheless, Cameron's early support for gay rights was qualified by his need to keep more traditional voters and MPs on side, shown by his decision to give a free vote on the Catholic adoption row (unlike the Labour vote which was whipped) and his public support for marriage, when in late 2006 he pushed for tax breaks for married couples and highlighted the importance of marriage when bringing up children. However, Cameron had also previously indicated that gay couples in civil partnerships, if they have children, should receive tax allowances as well. While Cameron's position on issues such as gay adoption is radical when compared to past Conservative leaders, it is perhaps as much about electability as a desire for absolute equality — the need to appeal to traditional voters while attracting new ones from the middle ground. After all, Hague's stance on as gay rights did not win an election, and Cameron was not known as a gay rights campaigner before he became leader. In fact, he voted against gay couples adopting as part of the Adoption and Children Bill.[10]

## Coalition Government

The formation of the Conservative-Liberal Democrat Coalition Government in 2010, with Cameron as Prime Minister and Nick Clegg (Liberal Democrat Leader 2007– and MP for Sheffield Hallam 2005–) as Deputy Prime Minister, led to potential further improvements for gay rights with the publication of a programme of gay rights policies, including tackling homophobic bullying, promoting better recording of hate crimes and removing historical convictions for consensual gay sex from criminal records. A decision to allow civil partnership ceremonies in religious settings followed (a voluntary move, from which religious organizations could withdraw if they objected), along with a consultation on opening up civil marriage for gay couples and the relaxation of blood donor rules, thus allowing gay men to donate blood as long as they have not had sex with another man for one year (and they have not taken part in other behaviour that could be a risk to those receiving blood), ending the policy that gay men are banned from donating blood for life, even if they engage in safe sex, because of fears of HIV/AIDS infection.

These proposals were seen as victories for the Liberal Democrats, suggesting that the proposed changes may not have been possible if the Conservatives were in power alone. Certainly, the Liberal Democrats were many years ahead of Labour on numerous gay rights issues in the 1990s and beyond, with Paddy Ashdown (MP for Yeovil 1983–2001 and leader of the Liberal Democrats from 1988–99), unveiling a policy statement in 1996 promising a massive overhaul of gay legal rights if in power, including: the equalization of the age of consent; changes to sexual offences laws; the repeal of Clause 28; the end to the ban on gay men and women joining the armed forces; the introduction of equal rights in fostering and adoption; and the introduction of anti-discrimination legislation.

The civil partnership proposals lead back to earlier discussion about the politics of recognition/difference versus equality, with some campaigners objecting to the fact that full religious gay marriage was not considered in the consultation. The blood donation ruling is equally striking, with the notion that gay men, if they wish to donate blood, must not be sexually active for one year (anal and oral penetration), even if they use condoms. While it is medically sound that those who participate in unsafe sex, whether heterosexual or homosexual, should not be able to donate blood (for a particular amount of time), the one year abstention only applies to gay men, and not heterosexuals, even if the sex is safe (*i.e.* condoms are used). So, once again, active, sexual homosexuality, is seen as a threat to the heterosexual "norm", with private behaviour judged publicly (Frame Two).

## Post-1997 Public Opinion

Public attitudes towards homosexuality significantly improved over the course of the 1990s, something that continued into the 2000s, which may have impacted on Cameron's move to a more socially liberal (at least when it came to moral issues) agenda. As British Social Attitudes data (Britsocat 2011; Natcen 2010) reveals, in 2007 and 2010 only 36% of people thought that sexual relations between people of the same two sex were "always" or "mostly" wrong, a big decrease compared to previous decades.[11] One relevant factor is age: as younger generations are generally more tolerant than older ones, society theoretically becomes less prejudiced as time goes on, as older generations die and the tolerant attitudes of younger generations impact upon subsequent generations (although, as demonstrated by the fall in approval towards homosexuality in the 1980s, it does not necessarily happen). Public attitudes towards homosexuality also improved because HIV/AIDS became less of a "visible" problem. Without a doubt, in contrast to much of the 1980s when HIV/AIDS was widely seen as only affecting gay people, by the 1990s and 2000s it was widely recognized that HIV/AIDS was of concern to heterosexual people as well (although as the 2011 blood donation ruling shows, there is still a negative association to some degree).

Weeks (2000) suggests that attitudes towards homosexuality (and sexuality as a whole) have shifted for a number of reasons, including: a growing "secularization" of sex: responsibility for behaviour has moved from external institutions such as the church to the individual; a gradual desertion of authoritarian values, linked to a growing sense of individual responsibility; a new explicitness in the way we talk about sex; the liberalization of the legal framework; and a growing recognition of diversity. Crucially, though, while public opinion has become more liberal, many people answering public opinion surveys still have a negative opinion about homosexuality to some extent. So, while it is positive that only 36% of people answering the 2010 British Social Attitudes Survey thought that sexual relations between people of the same two sex were "always" or "mostly" wrong, only 39% of respondents said they were "not wrong at all" (Natcen 2010).[12] It is important to understand this, because gay men and women are still the victims of homophobic crime, bullying and discrimination. In fact, homophobic crime rates in London have increased in recent years, rising by 22% between 2009 (1093 incidents) and 2010 (1336 incidents) (BBC News 2011).

That said, gay men and women have thrived in the more tolerant atmosphere of the late 1990s and beyond, not just in politics — both outside of and inside Parliament (for the first time the Cabinet contained openly gay Cabinet Ministers) — but also in the arts and other areas. As recognized by Hattersley (2004), in relation to the USA, HIV/AIDS actually played a big part: it caused gay culture to enter the mainstream. Interestingly, Hattersley (2004: 34) suggests that the rise of gay culture in mainstream society has contributed to "the gradual extinction of the traditional heterosexual male". As such, it should — theoretically — become "easier" to be gay as time goes on (although as Hattersley notes, it is never "easy" to be gay).

## Contemporary Representation

Just because they are now more visible in the mainstream media, gay men and women are not necessarily conferred "social legitimacy" (Shugart 2003: 87). For example, Shugart believes that gay men, when presented as part of a gay male/heterosexual female partnership in contemporary media, are often framed in a heterosexual context, so homosexuality (male in particular) is thus often defined by, and as less than, heterosexuality. "Shallow" acceptance can be seen in the representation of gay politicians, and gay men and women as a whole, in the (right-wing and/or populist) tabloid press in the 2000s. So, while gay people are often accorded positive press representation, only certain "types" of gay people meet with press approval: those who are "out"; those who have "discreet" sex lives; and those who are not "radical" activists (tying in with Frame Three, binary themes and mediated personas).

The "outing" of various politicians — and other public figures — in the late 1990s and 2000s (discussed in Chapter 8 and 9) shows that sexuality was still an issue of interest to the press. While tabloids were at the forefront of the coverage, broadsheets still discussed it, albeit less salaciously. Indeed, it is still common for gay public figures to "come out" to a newspaper, voluntarily or not. However, while gay public figures may continue to be the focus of press attention, with negative binary themes present, there is almost sexual scandal "equality" in much press coverage, with the "kiss and tell" element of many stories of as much interest as sexuality. Interestingly, when in recent years gay issues have been discussed negatively in the press there has often been a backlash to it. So, when the *Daily Mail*'s Jan Moir wrote an article debunking "the happy-ever-after myth of civil partnerships" (A STRANGE, LONELY AND TROUBLING DEATH, 16 November 2009), there were over 25,000 complaints to the Press Complaints Commission and a furious reaction in other newspapers and on social media, suggesting that for many people recognition (Frame One) and public acceptability (Frame Two) have been reached. However, as the 2010 British Social Attitudes Survey suggests, it is not the case for all. Recognition, therefore, is partial.

## Conclusion

This chapter has demonstrated a move from intolerance to tolerance to partial recognition of homosexuality in the UK, with political, press and public attitudes becoming more liberal over the 1990s and 2000s, but with some set-backs and contrary opinions. The changes observed tie in with attitudes pre-1990, discussed in *Part Two*. Recognition, a "step up" from toleration, suggests that people are entitled to equal rights and respect, rather than a grudging tolerance or acceptance, alongside recognition of their particularity. It is important to identify here that there are different "types" of recognition (and also acceptability) rather than one type, as suggested by the notion that the overarching frame of representation shapes (the character/particularly of) and mirrors (particular moments of) Frames One (recognition) and Two (public acceptability). Indeed, recognition and acceptability can

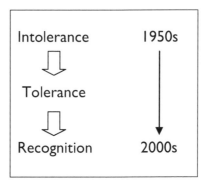

**Figure 7.1**   The progression of tolerance towards recognition.

be thought of as a field of possibilities, the end result of which is influenced by the processes in Frame One and the circularity of the frame of representation as a whole. Also, there is an ongoing debate about what recognition actually involves and its legitimacy as a concept. So, when the move towards recognition is called "partial", the definition and concept referred to is C. Taylor's (1992).[13] It should also be understood that the progression of tolerance towards recognition relates to "stages" of homosexuality (as suggested in figure 2.1 and Frame Two). Therefore, the idea of "partial" recognition, is important. For, while a homosexual *identity* may have been accepted decades ago by many people, the actual act of male to male penetration may not be. So, partial recognition refers to the fact that gay politicians (and gay people generally) are not recognized as wholly unproblematic figures; aspects of their "particularity" can be seen as negative (such as active sexuality, as demonstrated by the arguments utilized by politicians against reform in House of Commons and Lords debates).

Chapter 8 and 9 will demonstrate that the changing representation of gay politicians (and politicians caught up in a gay "scandal") in the UK press, from 1997 to the 2000s, can be understood in terms of the (halting) progression of tolerance towards partial recognition, in which they were tolerated by many people (the press, public and politicians) and were in fact recognized as equal people/political actors in many — but not all — press articles. However, full recognition was not achieved even in the 2000s; gay and "outed" politicians were sometimes depicted in the ("popular" tabloid) press in a derogatory manner, with their sexuality a negative defining feature rather than a positive one, with certain binary themes having to be met before a positive representation was possible. What is very clear by using the frame is that while gay politicians have managed to improve their representation (and mediated personas) over the years (moving *towards* recognition), with gay politicians in the late 2000s often not receiving much press attention at all (suggesting that their sexuality was not of interest) — taking into account the differences between tabloid/broadsheet newspapers and other factors — it is still the case that the press often defines their private sexual acts in terms of the public (Frame Two), with binary themes and mediated personas (Frame Three) linked. The following chapters will explore these ideas in more detail, giving more background to the overarching frame of representation.

## Notes

1. Hansard House of Commons Debates (vol. 238) 21 February 1994 (Criminal Justice and Public Order Bill — Amendment of Law relating to); 11% = 37 MPs.
2. Hansard House of Commons Debates (vol. 238) 21 February 1994 (Criminal Justice and Public Order Bill — Amendment of Law relating to); Hansard House of Commons Debates (vol. 238) 21 February 1994 (Criminal Justice and Public Order Bill — Age at which Homosexual Acts are Lawful).
3. Ellis and Katzinger's analysis is based on Hansard transcripts from 1994. However, the 1998 and 1999 debates on this issue and related newspaper articles from these years are also included as part of the analysis. The article does not specify which periods of time or from which sources the arguments are based, and instead takes an overarching approach.
4. And, as far back as 1976 the Royal College of Psychiatrists (cited British Medical Association 1994: 1) stated that "on the whole we agree that it is now appropriate to make no distinction in the age of consent between heterosexual and homosexual practices."
5. Other options included "sometimes wrong", "rarely wrong" and "not wrong at all". Percentages rounded to whole numbers.
6. Figures based on a NOP poll.
7. As summarized by Rayside, 74% of respondents to a Harris Poll in 1992 favoured an equal age of consent. But, a 1991 Harris poll in which specific ages were mentioned, found that only 15% favoured 16, with 53% favouring 21.
8. Hansard House of Commons Debates (vol. 238) 21 February 1994 (Criminal Justice and Public Order Bill — Amendment of Law relating to).
9. Sedgwick's notion of "good" and "bad" is not to be confused with the "good" and "bad" gay dichotomy aforementioned, although the notion of "bad" gay men being politically active ties in with the notion of unacceptable "visible" homosexuality.

10. Hansard House of Commons Debates (vol. 385) 16 May 2002 (Adoption and Children Bill — Applications for Adoption).
11. Other options included "sometimes wrong", "rarely wrong" and "not wrong at all". Percentages rounded to whole numbers.
12. Percentages rounded to whole numbers.
13. Indeed, this book discusses recognition as part of a media discourse; recognition can be contested in political theory.

# 8

# Scurrilous Politicians, Scandalous Stories: Representation, 1990–1997

"There was an incident which was childish and stupid and naturally I regret it. Whether that is enough to be used to try to destroy a man's career and whole life is of course another matter . . . Whether I am or not [gay] is none of your business. I know you would like me to say yes, or perhaps you would like me to deny it. But I can tell you that no, I am not . . . [the press has] again determined the outcome of an election rather than the common sense and decency of the voters." Alan Amos, Conservative MP for Hexham 1987–92 (*Daily Mail*, SEX SCANDAL MP QUITS; TORY ADMITS A "STUPID ENCOUNTER", 10 March 1992)

## The Introduction of "Sleaze"

In the early to mid-1990s numerous Conservative MPs faced press speculation about their sexuality. While their press coverage was not as ferocious as that experienced by Proctor just a few years earlier, similar language was utilized, as was the false association between homosexuality and paedophilia. The press coverage was political, with the supposed moral crusade of the Conservative Party's "back to basics" campaign giving the press additional justification (at least in the minds of journalists) for the "outings" and speculation: the politicians could be presented as living secret lives *and* as moral and political hypocrites. Politicians such as Alan Amos were unfortunate to be the focus of press attention during a time of supposed Conservative "sleaze". As such, even though Amos denied being gay it did not stop the press from printing salacious details about his private life and alleged homosexual activity.

Analysis of press coverage reveals that the binary themes demonstrated so far continue post-1990. So, even though public opinion

**131**

about homosexuality had became more moderate (Frame One), with public homosexuality more accepted (Frame Two), there was still an underlying consistency in press representation in terms of thematic characterization, in particular, the idea of "positive" and "negative" mediated personas and the binary themes which contribute to them (Frame Three). In fact, the post-1990 case studies show that in relation to the mediated personas of gay politicians or politicians caught up in a gay "scandal", a fifth binary theme can be added to the list: private/public; out/in; good/bad; safe/dangerous; *and clean/dirty*.

## Alan Amos

The first MP to be caught up in a gay "scandal" in the 1990s was Amos in 1992. Amos was caught on Hampstead Heath — presented as a gay "cruising" location in the press — in a car with another man. The police decided that Amos was engaging in compromising behaviour and subsequently arrested and then cautioned him. As cautions are not normally publicized, it may be the case that his arrest was leaked to the press by the police or someone else close to the case (Parris 1995). But, nevertheless, the press could claim to be reporting and reacting to "outside" events, giving justification to their reports. Amos's tabloid press coverage, while not as vindictive and relentless as Proctor's, was still very unsympathetic. For example, the *Daily Star* (AMOS SHOULD STOP BLEATING, 11 March 1992) wrote in an editorial: "He's a teetotaller, opposes abortion and brands smoking a 'dirty, dangerous and anti-social habit.' Hopefully, he is now questioning his judgement in wandering, at dusk, at a place which has been turned into a no-go area for decent families by perverts practising what many people — even smokers — would call another dirty, dangerous and anti-social habit. His downfall must be sad for him. But he shouldn't try and tar us with his own muck." As with the suggestions in Proctor's press coverage, (alleged) homosexuals are presented as a threat to families and children. The word "pervert" is used again, along with "dirty", "dangerous" and "muck", to portray homosexual behaviour as unclean (a new binary of Frame Three). Of course, the fact that Amos was arrested in a public place made his press coverage worse; he could be characterized as "dangerous" and indulging in public sexual behaviour (Frame Three) and as "invading" heterosexual public space (Frame Two). Even so, the choice of words reveals much about the newspaper's attitude towards homosexuality (although the *Daily Star* was of course competing with other tabloid newspapers such as *The*

*Sun* for readers, hence its colloquial and rather over-the-top didactic tone).

As with Proctor and Tatchell before him, the broadsheet press did not join in the moralizing, but instead reported on Amos's tabloid coverage as well as on the general detail of Amos's arrest, in a rather straightforward and non-sensational manner. Many broadsheets did, however, note that Amos was a "bachelor", which is an oft-used euphemism for a gay man. *The Independent*, for instance, referred to Amos as a "teetotal bachelor" (ELECTION 1992: HOW SEX CAST A HEX ON HEXAM, 1 April 1992). Several broadsheet newspapers used Amos's arrest as an opportunity to write articles on "cruising." *The Independent* visited Hampstead Heath and under the headline "OUT IN THE UNDERGROWTH" (15 March 1992) noted: "The scene confirmed that neither the arrest, cautioning and subsequent resignation of Alan Amos, the Conservative MP for Hexham, for committing an act of indecency on Hampstead Heath, nor the bad weather had kept visitors from North London's favourite open-air meeting place for gays." While the article does not condemn gay men, and is instead a rather tolerant exploration of "cruising" on Hampstead Heath, the article does seem to imply that "cruising" is common behaviour for gay men, shown here by the characterization of Hampstead Heath as "North London's favourite open-air meeting place" for gay men.

The fact that Amos was known for campaigning on moral issues contributed to his downfall. As Parris (1995: 283) writes, "we know readers hug themselves with joy when the apparently pious fall." Amos denied that he was gay, and at the time of his caution would only admit to engaging in "stupid" and "childish" behaviour (*Guardian*, TORY MP QUITS AFTER ARREST, 10 March 1992). He stood down from Parliament once it became clear that his constituency party would not back him (Parris 1995). Perhaps, if he was gay, he had happily "come out", becoming a "good" gay man, to use a binary theme of Frame Three, his constituency party would have forgiven him for the alleged lapse in behaviour; public opinion regarding homosexuality was not as unforgiving as in the mid to late 1980s, the time of Proctor's press coverage. As it was, despite the fact he denied being gay, Amos's explanation did not really explain much at all, dissatisfying not just his local party, but also the press. Amos's undoing was also linked to the fact that he was arrested on the eve of a general election, so the timing of his press coverage meant that his party could easily get rid of him.

## David Ashby

At their 1993 party conference, the Conservative Party launched a new policy initiative — "back to basics" — centring on a return to "traditional" Conservative values. Although Prime Minister Major's speech never actually made reference to sexual morality, the speech made reference to how people should behave therefore making the speech appear moralistic (Baston 2000). The speech gave newspapers an excuse to focus on the behaviour of Conservative politicians, with exposure justified on the grounds of hypocrisy. Baston explores the way in which "back to basics" established "sleaze" as a part of British politics, particularly for the Conservative Party (at this time — in recent years the Labour Party has been characterized as "sleazy" too). In fact, use of the word "sleaze" skyrocketed in the early 1990s; as explored by Dunleavy and Weir (1995), while use of the term slowly increased from 1985–93, it escalated from 1993 onwards. The "back to basics" fiasco led to a rush of stories about the personal lives of "sleazy" Conservative politicians, including those of various gay MPs or MPs caught up in a gay "scandal".

David Ashby (Conservative MP for Leicestershire North West 1983–97) was caught up in a bizarre story about whether or not he had shared a bed with another man while on holiday. Although the story amused many journalists — and a great deal of the public — it upset Ashby greatly (Parris 1995). The story appears unfair because, as Baston recognizes, Ashby had never made any homophobic comments in the political arena (although, in 1986, like Proctor, he rebelled against the Government's attempt to make it the right of school governors to decide whether or not a parent could withdraw their child from sex education — a vote which was in part a response to the apparent "promotion of homosexuality").[1] In fact, in 1994 he actually voted for the age of gay consent to be lowered to 16.[2] However, the fact that Ashby's 1992 election address described him as "married with a family and therefore understands the needs of families. He is a man of integrity who believes in traditional moral values" (*The Sunday Times*, WIFE'S FURY OVER ERRANT MP, 9 January 1994) was good enough reason for the press to link him to Tory "sleaze". It was a common justification. Doig and Wilson (1995: 21) note that if a party plays on the notion of morality, "Then they must be prepared, individually and collectively, for the consequences if the apparently private conduct of its MPs is held up to judgement against the party's public stance."

Surprisingly, it was a broadsheet newspaper which first alleged that Ashby was gay. Based on a candid meeting with Ashby's wife, the aforementioned *Sunday Times* article claimed that Ashby had left his wife because of a "friendship with another man", noting that Ashby "attracted attention last year when he negotiated an arrangement with Labour MPs on the [Home Affairs] Committee, whereby he supported an inquiry into party political funding in return for their support for an inquiry into lowering the age of consent for homosexuals." The paper followed that up with the allegation that Ashby had shared a bed with another man while on holiday in Goa. *The Sunday Times* ended up retracting the Goa story, but maintained Ashby was gay and a liar. Ashby sued *The Sunday Times* for libel (with his wife testifying against him) and lost. The original story was pure manufacturing, although his decision to sue for libel meant that later stories were in response to "outside" events. Most of the broadsheets followed up the original story and the court case using, as standard, unobjectionable language, although one or two words or phrases slipped into the broadsheet coverage which could be considered rather stereotypical. Many of the broadsheets called a pub apparently visited by Ashby a "gay haunt", thus characterizing what appeared to be a rather average and un-exciting pub as sleazy and even sexual. As just one example, when reporting on Ashby's libel case, *The Independent* said "the Queens Head [a pub Ashby was seen at] is an unmistakable gay haunt" (ASHBY LOOKED "TOTALLY AT EASE" IN GAY PUB, 15 December 1995).

The tabloid newspapers covered *The Sunday Times* story on Ashby (although less fervently than with Proctor), making use of colloquial language and well-used stereotypes. The *Daily Mail* (30 November 1995) reported on the court case with the headline "LIBEL CASE MP 'WAS SPOTTED IN GAY BAR LOOKING AT YOUNG MEN'" and the *Daily Mirror* (30 November 1995) stated "I SAW MP EYEING YOUNG MEN IN GAY PUB". While not as blatant as in the press coverage of Proctor, a link was still made between homosex-uality and youth. Ashby is also categorized as a predatory (alleged) homosexual, "looking" and "eyeing" up young men. He is "bad" and "dangerous" (Frame Three), even though he denied being gay. These headlines paraphrase what was said in court, and it could therefore be claimed that the newspapers were not actually judging Ashby and were instead summing up the court case. However, news values must always be considered; the newspapers *chose* to publish these headlines and therefore highlight a particular aspect of the case. Both the broadsheet and tabloid newspapers linked Ashby to "sleaze". In a round up of the "back to basics" scandals (including Ashby's) *The Independent* (8 February 1994: 1) wrote "TWO MONTHS OF SEX AND

SLEAZE", neatly summing up everything that Conservative MPs (heterosexual and allegedly gay) had come to stand for in the preceding months.

The fact that a broadsheet newspaper broke the original story about Ashby demonstrates that at the time of "back to basics" there was a frenzied atmosphere surrounding Conservative politicians and "sleaze". *The Sunday Times*'s story was not salacious, but the fact that it was printed at all is very significant: sexual scandal and "sleaze" permeated the political establishment and the press that reported on it. While he survived *The Sunday Times*'s story and the subsequent court case, Ashby's political career died shortly after, with his constituency party deselecting him following his support (during a 1996 Commons Committee on the Housing Bill) for a Labour amendment to the Housing Bill which would have allowed gay couples the right to inherit the tenancy if their partner died. Ashby's constituency association denied that his deselection was homophobic (something asserted by Ashby) and claimed that it had instead come about as a result of his vote against the government and the failed court case. The Chairman of his constituency stated: "Homophobia did not have a bearing on it. It was his court case when he was branded a hypocrite and a liar, and then, finally, when he voted against the Government" (*Press Association*, ASHBY'S ONSLAUGHT ON CONSTITUENCY TORIES, 11 March 1996). Whether or not Ashby was gay (and he denied it during the libel case), the support he gave gay rights in the House of Commons in the 1990s meant that his negative press coverage was hard to justify. Certainly, it would have been easy (and politically sensible) for Ashby to have voted *against* Labour's amendment to the Housing Bill.

## Michael Brown

Michael Brown (Conservative MP for Briggs and Cleethorpes 1979–97) was also caught up in the "back to basics" scandal. In 1994 the *News of the World* revealed that Brown had had a relationship with a 20-year-old man and had taken him on holiday to the Caribbean. While he kept his seat, Brown resigned his Government position immediately, having broken the law; while MPs had by now voted for the age of gay consent to be lowered to 18, the change had not yet taken effect. Brown suffered the typical tabloid headlines. The *News of the World* (8 May 1994) headlined its exposé "TORY WHIP'S GAY SEX TRIANGLE; MP AND MoD MAN BOTH BED UNDERAGE

STUDENT", reducing the relationship to its basest form, as well as highlighting the "youth" of the partner, followed in the inside pages by a double page spread headed "WE EXPOSE THE GAY SHAME OF A GOVERNMENT WHIP, A DEFENCE CHIEF AND A COLLEGE BOY". The *People* (8 May 1994) labelled the story "TORY WHIP QUITS AFTER GAY TOYBOY ALLEGATIONS". *The Sun* (IT'S OK TO BE A MINISTER AND GAY SAYS PM, 10 May 1994) also used the word "boy" when writing about Brown's partner: "John Major has ruled that it is OK for his ministers to be gay. The Premier says they will not be sacked unless they behave irresponsibly — such as cheating on their wives or having affairs with under-age boys." As with Ashby and Proctor before him, a correlation between homosexuality and paedophilia and the corruption of youth was made by the tabloid press. *The Sun* attempted to characterize Brown as a "dangerous" gay man (Frame Three), although the age of Brown's partner lessened the effect, as did the "senior government source" who was quoted by the paper as saying "Michael had to go because the age of consent had not yet been reduced to 18 from 21 . . . Apart from that he did nothing to be ashamed of. The days when a minister could lose his job simply for being gay are gone." In spite of their attempts, Brown's tabloid press coverage was less intense than it was for those politicians "outed" in the 1980s, and he was able to carry on as an MP until he lost his seat in 1997.

The broadsheet press was kinder to Brown (and he is now a well respected broadsheet journalist and political commentator). While the broadsheets covered the story, they did not resort to stereotypical or homophobic language. For many broadsheet newspapers the problem was not that Brown was gay, but that he had technically broken the law and was thus "sleazy". *The Independent* (RULES FOR MPS, GAY OR STRAIGHT, 11 May 1994) believed that "Mr Brown's problem lies not in his sexuality but in having notionally broken the law . . . Unfortunately for MPs, the public expects those who act as legislators not to break the laws that Parliament passes . . . That applies equally to heterosexual MPs . . . What matters . . . is not whether someone is straight or gay, bachelor or married, but how good they are as an MP or minister." So, while the story was manufactured, there was public interest justification.

If Brown had been "outed" as having an underage lover just a few years earlier he may have suffered the same fate as Proctor. As it was, attitudes towards homosexuality had improved to such an extent that it was again possible for gay politicians or politicians caught up in a gay "scandal" to hang on to their seats (even if they were members of the

Conservative Party), showing that the move from intolerance to tolerance (Frame One) had moved on from Proctor's time. Importantly, Brown's colleagues were largely sympathetic to his plight, seeing him as yet another victim of the press (Sanderson 1995), and he was popular with his fellow MPs and was not known for controversial political views (unlike Proctor). Brown also officially "came out" after his tabloid expose (becoming more of a "good" gay man), and therefore managed to gain the respect of tabloid journalists who would have no doubt condemned him if he had refused to "come out" like others. The fact that Brown was known for his pro-gay views also helped him to avoid total political annihilation; he not only voted for the age of consent to be lowered to 16,[3] he also voted against the Conservative whip on Clause 28.[4]

## Jerry Hayes

The final MP to be "outed" in the period was Jerry Hayes (Conservative MP for Harlow 1983–97). On the fifth of January 1997 the *News of the World* claimed that Hayes had had an affair with a man called Paul Stone six years earlier, when Stone was 18 and thus underage. The headline stated: "TORY MP 2–TIMED WIFE WITH UNDERAGE GAY LOVER: INTIMATE LETTERS REVEAL HIS LONGING FOR TEENAGER". As with Proctor and other politicians, a link to paedophilia was made, with the use of "teenager" and "underage" suggesting that Hayes had a relationship with someone very young when Stone was actually 18. In fact, the phrase "his longing for teenager" suggested that Hayes was (allegedly) infatuated with Stone partly because he was "young".

Other tabloid newspapers used similar language. The *Daily Mirror* headlined an interview with Stone's mother "HE BROKE MY BOY'S HEART" (7 January 1997) and the *Sunday Mirror* (5 January 1997) stated: "TORY MP'S PASSION FOR BOY, 18: TORY MP ADMITS LOVE FOR 18-YEAR-OLD BOY". The *Daily* and *Sunday Mirror*, while not right-wing newspapers like *The Sun* and *News of the World*, still understood that the majority of their readers would interpret Hayes's alleged behaviour as unacceptable. Of course, it should also be noted that the *Mirror* newspapers are historically pro-Labour, something especially so in 1997 when a Labour victory appeared a certainty. Conservative sex scandals were thus revelled in, not just for their scandalous (and newsworthy) nature, but also for the political point that could be made. In fact, some Conservative MPs claimed that

Hayes's exposure was orchestrated by Labour Party figures, something denied by the Labour Party, who stated that "Throughout the 'back-to-basics' debacle, the Labour Party never once sought to make any political capital out of the many scandals. We have no intention of starting" (*The Times*, CLIFFORD ANNOUNCES ANTI-TORY VENDETTA, 7 January 1997).

Stone's revelations appeared in the press not because his alleged relationship with Hayes had suddenly been uncovered, but because he decided to sell his story as a "kiss and tell", a mode of revelation traditionally used when female "lovers" expose famous partners (the story can be classed as reportage, rather than manufacturing, because the newspaper reacted to an outside source — although there is an element of manufacturing in "kiss and tell" stories because the newspaper concerned could ignore the seller, hence the blurring of the reporting/manufacturing boundary). The tabloids certainly treated the story in the same manner as a heterosexual "kiss and tell" story, with further revelations about Stone himself published (for example, the tabloids printed photos of him dressed as a woman), as well as subsequent interviews with connected figures. The story was actually very personal, with members of both Stone's and Hayes's families — including Hayes's wife and Stone's parents — giving interviews or comments to the tabloid press. The tabloids characterized Hayes's alleged homosexual behaviour as a threat to his wife. In fact, the *Daily Mirror* (6 January 1997) stated: "JERRY PREACHED SAFE SEX BUT DIDN'T PRACTICE IT WHEN HE WAS CHEATING ON HIS WIFE WITH ME; TORY MP'S GAY LOVER REVEALS NEW SHAME; ALLEGED GAY LOVER OF JERRY HAYES SAYS THEY DID NOT PRACTICE SAFE SEX." The article goes on to mention HIV/AIDS, thus characterizing Hayes as "dangerous" and "unhealthy" (Frame Three). So, Hayes was not only seen as a threat to his wife, he was also a threat to "healthy" heterosexuality.

Although the broadsheet newspapers (on the left and right of the political spectrum) did not treat Stone's professions in such a lurid and censorious style as the tabloids, and also resisted the use of stereotypical language, the alleged "affair" was covered in lots of detail (following the tabloids' lead rather than making new revelations). For example, *The Times* (6 January 1997) stated "SPECTRE OF YOUNG 'ASSISTANT' RETURNS TO HAUNT HAYES". The broadsheet press also reported on the political consequences of the story and how Hayes would fare in the forthcoming general election. Interestingly, the *Guardian* (18 January 1997) interviewed Stone under the headline "OH PAUL, HOW COULD YOU" (his mother's apparent reaction to the story). By interviewing Stone, the *Guardian* moved from factual reporting of the case to the promotion of gossip as valid news, for there was not much point to the article at all — there were no new revelations (apart from the fascinating fact that Stone plucked his eyebrows, itself a suggestion of effeminacy), just musings on the motivations of Stone. If anything, the article is a good example of the growing "tabloidization" (Franklin 1997) of the broadsheet press.

Stone's revelations received lots of press coverage, partly because of the mass of Conservative "sleaze" a few years before, but also because a general election was imminent and politics was high on the media's agenda. Hayes was also damned by the fact that Stone's revelations were so "scandalous". Hayes could be presented as a political and moral hypocrite, "closeted" and as sexually "dangerous", a very newsworthy combination. Hayes denied that he had sex with Stone — and also that he was gay at all — although he did state that his feelings for Stone were confused and becoming "unhealthy" (*The Times*, TORY MP IN "GAY AFFAIR" SCANDAL, 5 January 1997). Still, the letters written by Hayes to Stone, which the *News of the World* based much of its original story on, were rather passionate and could lead the press into thinking that the relationship was sexual. However, even if Hayes was gay and/or had had a relationship with Stone, his press coverage was somewhat unfair. Indeed, in many respects Hayes was not hypocritical; he was a known pro-gay MP, voted for the age of consent to be lowered to 16,[5] and was vice-chairman of the House of Commons AIDS Committee.

Of course, one could equally state that the latter fact justified his coverage; as a safe-sex campaigner, it was hypocritical of him to have (alleged) unprotected sex. Likewise, it should not be forgotten that if Hayes and Stone had had a sexual relationship, that relationship would have been illegal at that time. Nevertheless, in spite of the scandalous nature of Stone's revelations, Hayes kept the support of his constituency party. Even though he lost his seat in the Labour landslide of 1997, it does not appear that the allegations played a major part. Hayes was lucky in that, like Brown before him, he was popular with his colleagues and was not known for controversial political views. The fact that he had a wife who backed him to the hilt (expressing incredulity that he was gay) also contributed to the support he received (*People*, OUR LOVE WILL BEAT GAY LIES; INTERVIEW WITH ALISON HAYES, 12 January 1997).

## Conclusion

On the whole, gay politicians or those caught up in a gay "scandal" at this time were not excommunicated in the brutal manner of Proctor a few years previously: while Brown lost his government post, he stayed an MP; Hayes lost his seat due to the imminent Labour landslide rather than his scandalous press coverage (Brown also lost his seat in the landslide); and Ashby was deselected because of his post-scandal behaviour rather than the press's accusations (at least according to his local party). The only MP who seems to have been forced to resign directly as a result of his scandal is Amos. However, it appears that it was not allegations about his sexuality or behaviour as such that was the major problem, but rather that his explanation for his arrest dissatisfied his local party. While it was not necessarily the case that a gay or "outed" Conservative MP would lose the confidence of their party, "coming out" was still fraught with problems; even if a constituency party was supportive, the tabloid press was still likely to categorize the MP concerned in a stereotypical manner, utilizing negative binary themes and personas (Frame Three).

As a general rule, in the early to mid-1990s tabloid newspapers covered the private lives of gay politicians or politicians caught up in a gay "scandal" using sensationalist and stereotypical language. However, the press coverage of such MPs was not as vicious as in the 1980s, and the moral relevance of sexual stories (*i.e.* judging someone's worth on their actual sex life or sexuality) decreased in the 1990s: what was much more important was whether or not a politician was "truthful". The notion that a politician could be unfit for public office just because they were gay — as suggested in Tatchell's press coverage (*i.e.* the notion that he was only interested in gay issues) — lost resonance, indicating that recognition (Frame One) was moving closer, and public homosexuality (Frame Two) was more acceptable. Instead, politicians such as Brown were presented as unfit for public office because they were deemed "sleazy" and "untrustworthy". However, there was an interesting phenomenon: broadsheet newspapers not only commented on the tabloid press coverage of "outings" or sexual scandals (as they had always done), they began to actively engage with "outings" and scandals as well or even do the "outing" themselves, indicating a "tabloidization" of news, to the detriment of the personal lives of (gay) politicians. So, while tolerance was improving, press coverage could still be negative, with the at-times unnecessary focus on the intimate lives of gay or "outed" politicians suggesting that the presence of gay politicians in public space was still a newsworthy issue.

## Notes

1. Hansard House of Commons Debates (vol. 102) 21 October 1986 (Education Bill [Lords] — Local Education Authorities Reserve Power).
2. Hansard House of Commons Debates (vol. 238) 21 February 1994 (Criminal Justice and Public Order Bill — Amendment of Law relating to).
3. Hansard House of Commons Debates (vol. 238) 21 February 1994 (Criminal Justice and Public Order Bill — Amendment of Law relating to).
4. Hansard House of Commons Debates (vol. 129) 9 March 1988 (Local Government Bill — Prohibition on Promoting Homosexuality by Teaching or by Publishing Material).
5. Hansard House of Commons Debates (vol. 238) 21 February 1994 (Criminal Justice and Public Order Bill — Amendment of Law relating to).

# 9

## Public Life, Public Pressures: Representation Post-1997

"The fact that I'm gay is a personal thing to me . . . I think Chris Smith is a role model for this. I don't think he was ever seen as a single-issue politician." Stephen Twigg, Labour MP for Enfield Southgate 1997–2005 and Liverpool West Derby 2010– (*The Independent*, WIN SOME, LOSE SOME; NIGHT-CLUBBING, EASTENDERS . . . THE NEW MP FOR ENFIELD SOUTHGATE HAS GIVEN UP A LOT, HE TELLS JANIE LAWRENCE. BUT NOT AS MUCH AS MICHAEL PORTILLO, 24 July 1997)

### New Century, New Attitude?

Upon New Labour's election in 1997 it seemed that a new era for gay politicians was beginning. More liberal public and political attitudes suggested that recognition was moving closer (Frame One), and the positive reaction to the election of openly gay Labour politicians and their subsequent promotion to ministerial posts suggested that attitudes towards "public homosexuality" (Frame Two) had improved. However, soon after the 1997 General Election various gay politicians were "outed" by tabloid newspapers with negative binary themes and personas utilized (Frame Three), showing that the sexuality of politicians was still of interest to a large swathe of the press. Broadsheet newspapers, while much more respectful of the private lives of gay politicians than the majority of tabloid newspapers, nevertheless continued to engage with the tabloid coverage, giving the stories even greater publicity. In recent years, representation has become more tolerant and undoubtedly less hysterical, making many of the stories about gay politicians from the late 1990s appear outdated and almost from a different era. But, while in the 2000s "sexual scandal equality" has emerged, with gay politicians and politicians caught up in a gay "scandal" either not receiving much press coverage at all, or the same kind of coverage as "scandalous" heterosexual politicians, tabloid press coverage can still be questionable, echoing the binary themes and negative mediated personas of late 1990s representation.

Storr (2001) believes that the attitude of the tabloid press to the 1998 "outings" revealed a deep-set confusion about sexual values in the late 1990s and beyond. On the one hand, gay politicians engaging in "acceptable behaviour" (*i.e.* gay MPs open about their sexuality and/or part of a couple) were treated respectfully by the press, but MPs who were deemed to be hypocritical (those who were married and/or thought to be lying about their sexuality) were treated in the same disrespectful manner as earlier politicians such as Harvey Proctor. Storr (2001: 124) writes: "there is little indication that British sexual attitudes are undergoing any significant change except in specific and limited contexts. For those who fall outside the bounds of married and/or heterosexual acceptability, the best that one can hope for is that one's sex acts will 'die,' and will enter the 'zone of privacy' by becoming decorporealized. In other words, the condition of tolerance is the desexualization of one's sexual identity. Thus to the extent that Peter Mandelson and Nick Brown . . . won public tolerance, they did so in spite of their sexuality, not because of it." Storr's work certainly fits with the notion of good/bad and safe/dangerous homosexuality discussed here (binaries of Frame Three). While the claim that Mandelson's (Labour MP for Hartlepool 1992–2004) coverage was "gentle" and "ambivalent" and that his sexuality was entering the "zone of privacy" is perhaps over-stated, it is true that Mandelson's coverage unlike, for example, Ron Davies's (Labour MP for Caerphilly 1983–2001), did not suggest that his homosexuality was incompatible with public office, signifying the acceptable/unacceptable behaviour divide.

Importantly, even though the private lives of gay politicians or politicians involved in a gay "scandal" were invaded over and over again in the 1990s and beyond (even the private lives of politicians who voluntarily "came out" as gay), nearly all survived politically. Similar to Proctor and Alan Amos, the politicians who were forced to resign from a political position — Davies, Mandelson, Mark Oaten (Liberal Democrat MP for Winchester 1997–2010) and David Laws (Liberal Democrat MP for Yeovil 2001– ) — were involved in behaviour which had an air of or link to illegality or corruption (although they were not arrested or charged with anything, unlike Proctor and Amos). So, while issues such as the sexual behaviour, lifestyle (whether "in" or "out"), openness, and general popularity of the politician concerned did have an impact on the tone of press coverage, they did not affect whether or not they survived politically. It is now time to explore these key themes in more detail, giving further background to the overarching frame of representation, through which the press coverage of gay politicians can be mapped.

## Stephen Twigg

During the 1997 General Election campaign, Stephen Twigg ran as an openly gay candidate for the London seat of Enfield Southgate, beating the incumbent MP, Michael Portillo (MP for Enfield Southgate 1984–97 and Kensington and Chelsea 1999–2005), in one of the most infamous wins of the election. Twigg's homosexuality was a non-issue to his own party and also to the Conservative Party as a whole (on a public, party level anyway), perhaps because of rumours and gossip surrounding Portillo's own sexuality. Twigg received good national press coverage (both tabloid and broadsheet) during and immediately after the election; the national press did not resort to homophobia (implicit or explicit) and he did not suffer as the still "closeted" Peter Tatchell did in the Bermondsey by-election of 1983. That is not to say that the press did not refer to Twigg's sexuality at all. His sexuality was the focus of much positive press attention, particularly broadsheet, with many post-election articles and interviews focusing on the fact that he was one of only two gay MPs to be fully open about their homosexuality since Chris Smith "came out" in 1984 (in fact, unlike Smith, Twigg "came out" before he was elected).

Twigg received positive press attention for a variety of reasons. Firstly, he had beaten the somewhat unpopular Portillo. Indeed, while a Labour supporting newspaper, the following headline from the *Daily Mirror* (3 May 1997) is representative of the mood of many members of the public, and newspapers, at the time: "WHAT'S THE STORY? MOURNING TORY! WHENEVER YOU NEED CHEERING UP, TAKE A LOOK AT THIS; CUT-OUT-AND-KEEP GENERAL ELECTION CELEBRATION POSTER OF VANQUISHED TORIES". Twigg's openness about his sexuality from the start (which made him a "good" gay MP, to use a binary theme of Frame Three) was also a big factor in the press acceptance of his homosexuality; like Smith before him, he could not be accused of hypocrisy, and because he had pre-empted the press by revealing he was gay, he could not be "outed". The lack of scandal surrounding his sexuality and the "safe-ness" of his sexuality (Frame Three) also contributed to the lack of negative press coverage. The fact that Twigg was a member of a new government and a political party with a fresh approach to sexuality was another reason for his acceptance. As a member of an unsullied, sleaze-free government (at the time), the press was undoubtedly easier on him than if he had "come out" as a member of the supposedly sleazy 1992–7 Conservative Government. Twigg acknowledged in *The Independent* (WIN SOME, LOSE SOME; NIGHT-CLUBBING, EASTENDERS ... THE NEW MP FOR ENFIELD SOUTHGATE HAS GIVEN UP A LOT, HE TELLS JANIE LAWRENCE. BUT NOT AS MUCH AS MICHAEL PORTILLO, 24 July 1997) that his membership of a more liberal political party made it "easier" to be gay: "Although I am by no means claiming that there is no prejudice on our side, on the Tory side there is more prejudice at the grass roots. So some Conservatives might feel it could be politically damaging."

Twigg was always very blasé about his status as an openly gay MP and was keen to show that he was not a single-issue politician. As with Smith, Twigg's ministerial responsibilities probably curtailed his ability to speak on gay rights and he did not vote in every key vote.[1] However, Twigg made it clear that he did not want to become a "crusading" gay politician, noting in the July 1997 *Independent* interview that being gay was "a personal thing". In fact, Twigg has made it very clear that he is opposed to "outing" gay politicians even when the person concerned is making hypocritical statements. In the same *Independent* article, he noted: "It [outing] is just plain wrong, and I know all the arguments about hypocrisy. Obviously I would prefer that people did come out, but nobody has the right to make that choice on someone else's behalf. It's a very personal choice for all of us . . . I don't think that you can put a greater responsibility on someone who happens themselves to be gay. That lets the person who's not gay off the hook. Frankly, what we want is to persuade all MPs to support equality initiatives." While Twigg is obviously keen to support all gay MPs, whether they are "out" or not, part of his statement is problematic; while it is true that gay MPs should not be expected to be of a higher moral standard than any other MP, by making hypocritical statements or voting against gay rights, they are actually holding themselves up to charges of hypocrisy, greater scrutiny and the increased possibility of being "outed".

## Ben Bradshaw

Ben Bradshaw (Labour MP for Exeter 1997– ) was the second gay MP to be open about his homosexuality during the 1997 General Election

PUBLIC LIFE, PUBLIC PRESSURES

campaign and — like Twigg — he won his seat standing as a Labour candidate. The tabloid and broadsheet press were also kind to Bradshaw, even though he was much more ripe for the picking; Bradshaw used to work as a journalist for the BBC, and it emerged a few months before the election that he had been financially maintained by the corporation from September 2004 until the election, during which time he had been campaigning for his parliamentary seat. *The Independent* (THE POLITICS OF THE BBC; BUSY ELECTION-EERING, ON FULL PAY. STANDING FOR LABOUR AND OPENLY GAY. PREPARE FOR THE USUAL FLAK, AND MORE BESIDES, 3 March 1997) pondered why the press was easy on Bradshaw and concluded that society's increased liberalness impacted upon press strategy: "The reticence of the tabloids towards Bradshaw may reflect a growing recognition that attacking minorities can be bad for business, that their readerships are more complex than in the past. This more sophisticated approach was signalled by the *Daily Mail*, for example, when it surprised everyone and championed the family of Stephen Lawrence, the murdered black teenager, against the alleged five white attackers."

Bradshaw believes that the press left him alone during the campaign because he was open about his sexuality (out/in being another binary theme of Frame Three), noting in a comment to the March 1997 *Independent* article, "The tabloids seem more interested in hypocrites. They have not targeted Chris Smith and seem to have little interest in me." If Storr's analysis is applied, due to the fact that Bradshaw was openly and non-scandalously gay, his sexuality entered the "zone of privacy" and was therefore of little interest to the press. Indeed, if Bradshaw's sexuality is understood in relation to Thompson's (2000: 120) theories, it does not transgress "prevailing norms", a defining feature of sexual political scandals. If Bradshaw had "come out" or been "outed" in the mid to late 1980s, his sexuality may have been portrayed as breaking "norms" or "codes", but growing liberalism, and the lack of "dangerousness" surrounding Bradshaw's sexuality, meant that his sexuality was (as Storr would pronounce) "decorporealized". Bradshaw's sexuality was of interest, though, to his Conservative oppo-nent, Dr. Adrian Rogers, who apparently nicknamed him "Bent Ben" and described homosexuality as "sterile, disease-ridden and God-forsaken", going on to name Bradshaw as "a media man, a homosexual . . . he's everything about society that is wrong" (*Guardian*, THE ELECTION: SPOTLIGHT/EXETER: LOVE AND HATE IN A HOLY WAR, 2 April 1997). While it would be unfair to suggest that Rogers was a true representative of the Conservative Party (in fact, he became something of a right-wing caricature and resigned from the Party after being threatened with expulsion for urging people to vote for the UK Independence Party), his candidature does demonstrate the ideological gulf between the Labour and Conservative parties at the time of the 1997 General Election.

Bradshaw (and Twigg) was treated fairly by the press during the 1997 election campaign because he was not considered a political threat. As a loyal centre-ground Blairite (and, later on, an on-message and rather uncontroversial minister), the (predominantly) right-wing tabloid press did not feel the need to mount a campaign against the left, as they did with Tatchell. Nevertheless, Bradshaw was not completely immune from negative publicity surrounding his homosexuality after the election. For example, when he sought concessions for his partner normally reserved for the spouses of heterosexual MPs, tabloid news-papers greeted the news with the headlines "MP'S GAY LOVER TO GET FREE RAIL TRAVEL" (*Daily Mail*, 23 June 1997) and "COMMONS KEY FOR GAY MP PAL" (*Daily Record*, 23 June 1997). While the articles are not homophobic as such, the language used is telling. Bradshaw's partner is referred to as his "lover" in many of the articles, as opposed to "spouse", or even "partner", terms often used to describe heterosexual married partners. While on the surface it may not seem a big issue, and heterosexual *unmarried* partners are also described using the word "lover", the term does explicitly link Bradshaw's relationship to sex, and suggests that the relationship is more frivolous and inconsequential than a "serious" heterosexual marriage. The headlines also suggest that Bradshaw and his partner somehow received undeserved special treatment, and imply that Bradshaw "overstepped the mark". In relation to heterosexual public space (Frame Two), he crossed the line from acceptable to unaccept-able behaviour in relation to his position as a gay man and the way he should act/the expectations he should have. Broadsheet newspapers also reported on the concessions issue. Tellingly, *The Independent*, a liberal newspaper, also used the word "lover" (COMMONS "SPOUSE" PASS FOR GAY MP'S LOVER, 22 June 1997).

Bradshaw, Twigg, and other MPs who "came out" after 1997, were also used by tabloid newspapers — mainly through columnists who have more freedom to be controversial and opinionated — to demon-strate all that was wrong with gay equality and so called "political correctness" as a whole. For example, Simon Heffer asked "DOES MARRIAGE MEAN ANYTHING IN TODAY'S SOCIETY?" (*Daily Mail*, 20 January 1998) in relation to the rail travel issue, and also claimed that society and politics had been "HOODWINKED BY

GAY PROPAGANDA" (*Daily Mail*, 13 June 1998) when two more Labour MPs "came out" before a vote on the age of gay consent. Such articles suggest that late twentieth century tabloid newspapers may not have been as pro-gay as they appeared at first glance: through columnists, true opinions about homosexuality could be expressed (especially in a right-wing newspaper such as the *Daily Mail*). Even so, aside from his minor moments of controversy, the tabloid press did not focus upon the private life of Bradshaw, as he was just too "normal".

## Angela Eagle

Following the example set by Twigg and Bradshaw, three sitting Labour politicians decided to "come out" as gay: Angela Eagle (Labour MP for Wallasey 1992– ); David Borrow (MP for Ribble South 1997–2010); and Gordon Marsden (MP for Blackpool South 1997– ). Eagle became the first lesbian MP to voluntarily "come out" as gay, and also received good press. While she "came out" five years *after* her initial election, her status as the first "openly" lesbian MP, the fact that she was not hypocritical in her lifestyle or politics, and the fact that she was non-scandalous and "safe" (to use a binary theme of Frame Three), meant that all of the press (tabloid and broadsheet, left and right) admired her, rather than condemned her. The *Daily Mirror* (11 September 1997) headed an article about her "self-outing" with "I'M A LESBIAN SAYS LABOUR MINISTER; COURAGE OF MP ANGELA AS SHE COMES OUT; ANGELA EAGLE MP ADMITS TO BEING A LESBIAN." And the *Daily Mail* (11 September 1997) noted in a very respectful and straightforward article, "POLITICIAN GOES PUBLIC WITH BACKING FROM PARTY: THE TIME IS RIGHT TO BE HONEST SAYS LABOUR'S LESBIAN MP." In 2008, when Eagle had a civil partnership with her partner, she also received little media comment, and the comments she did receive were positive ones; *The Mail on Sunday* noted, for example, "TREASURY MINISTER ANGELA TIES THE KNOT WITH GAY PARTNER" (28 September 2008).

Like gay politicians before her, Eagle also made it clear that she did not want to become a spokesperson for gay rights, telling *The Independent* ("I NEED TO GET THINGS SORTED"; ENVIRON-MENT MINISTER ANGELA EAGLE TALKS TO SUZANNE MOORE ABOUT HER DECISION TO COME OUT AS A LESBIAN, ABOUT CHANGING ATTITUDES, AND THE BATTLE TO DO HER JOB AND STILL HAVE A PERSONAL

LIFE, 11 September 1997): "That's just one aspect of what I'm about. I've always supported gay rights to the extent that I believe gay people should have the same civil rights, equal rights, partnership rights and the right to be free from irrational discrimination as everyone else. I've always voted that way whenever such issues arose. Then again, my sister [who is also an MP] feels the same way and she isn't gay." Storr's notion that "the condition of tolerance is the desexualization of one's sexual identity" (2001: 124) applies to Eagle and other gay politicians; to be accepted, they have to limit their identification with gay issues, even if all it involves is a statement to the press. While Eagle did not suffer the same fate as Maureen Colquhoun, and Tony Blair — as well as her constituency party and her fellow MPs — supported her decision to "come out" as gay, her lesbianism did mark her out as different from the supposed "norm". By stating her interest in other issues, Eagle (and other gay MPs who make similar statements) sought to assimilate herself into the political "mainstream".

## David Borrow and Gordon Marsden

Borrow and Marsden "came out" as gay following Eagle's declaration. Like Twigg before him, Marsden made it clear that he was not a single-issue MP in an interview with *The Independent* ("I'M GAY AND I'M HAPPY FOR MY CONSTITUENTS TO KNOW ABOUT IT"; IN THE RUN-UP TO A COMMONS DEBATE ON LOWERING THE HOMOSEXUAL AGE OF CONSENT, ANOTHER MP COMES OUT OF THE CLOSET, 11 June 1998), stating: "I'm a politician first and a gay man second. I am not a single-issue MP. Being gay is part and parcel of what I am, who I am." Most broadsheet and tabloid newspapers declined to make a big deal out of Borrow and Marsden's "self outings" and did not target them for their homosexuality. As with Twigg and Bradshaw, they were non-scandalous, honest, "safe" and "good" gay politicians (Frame Three), reflected by the majority of the tabloid and broadsheet press. However, while the majority of newspapers linked the declarations to a forthcoming vote on the lowering of the age of gay consent — the *Guardian* (11 June 1998) stated "VOTE PROMPTS SECOND MP IN A WEEK TO DECLARE HE IS GAY" — the right-wing *Daily Mail* tabloid newspaper treated their assertions as part of some kind of covert operation aimed at affecting the result of the vote. In an article, which at first glance appears rather positive ("I'M GAY TOO SAYS A SIXTH LABOUR MP"), the *Daily Mail* (11 June 1998) noted: "The 'self outings' are part of a discreet campaign by homosexual MPs in the run up to the Commons vote of the lowering of the age of homosexual consent to 16. Two or three more gay MPs are expected to reveal their sexual orientation before the vote in a fortnight." The *Mail* article also called Borrow and Marsden "avowedly homosexual", suggesting that they were combative activists, emphasizing once again that public homosexuality (Frame Two) was unacceptable in relation to active campaigning (even though the MPs may not have actually been doing that), as well as expressions of sexuality. Of course, it must be borne in mind that the *Daily Mail* is a supporter of right-wing conservatism, and has thus been unimpressed with moves to improve gay rights and homosexuality as a whole.

Simon Heffer, writing in his *Daily Mail* column (HOODWINKED BY GAY PROPAGANDA, 13 June 1998), linked the MPs' "self outings" to schoolboy sex, via the age of consent vote, thus attempting to characterize Borrow and Marsden as sexually "dangerous" (Frame Three): "Two Labour MPs, David Borrow and Gordon Marsden, have announced this week that they are homosexual. They felt the need to do so, apparently, before the Commons votes on legalizing homosexual relations with boys who (thanks also to this Government) are by law too young to buy cigarettes . . . I do, however, worry that the growing acceptability of homosexuality among our legislators will blind them to its unsuitability in certain sections of society — such as immature schoolboys and the armed forces. We are being softened up for reforms in both these areas, with the progressive, metropolitan customs of a small but influential group being pressed upon us." Heffer went on to state that there was the "greater likelihood of boys of 13, 14 or 15 being absorbed into the homosexual world." As Sanderson (1995: 214) asserts, the relationship between gay men and children is "the ace up" the tabloid "sleeve"; the connection is used to suggest that gay men wish to systematically convert young men and boys into homosexuality. While the connexion between homosexuality and paedophilia is not as explicit here as in articles written in the 1980s, Heffer's use of the words "boy", "schoolboy", "immature" and "young" shows that the method is still employed to great effect.

Heffer's words categorize Borrow and Marsden as "other" and present gay men as a threatening group undermining "normal", heterosexual society. While at one point in his column Heffer congratulated Borrow and Marsden for "coming out", it seems very clear that the increased visibility of gay men and woman — and homosexuality as a whole — is seen as very dangerous. Heffer is not representative of the tabloid press as a whole at the time, or even the *Daily Mail*, which he no longer works for (although his presence as a columnist suggested the general ethos of the paper), and his comments were about more than homosexuality, such as the Labour Government's policies and the interests of minority groups taking precedence over the concerns of "ordinary" people. But his work is an example of that of a small, but vocal, group of journalists (present in both tabloid and broadsheet newspapers) presenting homosexuality as an encroaching threat (*i.e.* moving towards heterosexual public space — Frame Two) and gay MPs as symptomatic of all what was wrong with "liberal" Labour policies and moves towards gay equality.

## Ron Davies

### Tabloid and Broadsheet Approaches

After so many MPs had happily "come out" to the press in the late 1990s, with limited negative press representation, the dramatic "outing" of Davies in 1998, and the unusual circumstances surrounding it, impacted greatly. Just after nine o'clock one October night, Davies, who was walking alone on Clapham Common, was invited by a man he had never met to a nearby flat for a meal, which he accepted. Two other people joined them and they all got into Davies's car. After being directed to drive to a nearby estate, a knife was pulled on Davies and he was ordered to hand over his wallet, his phone, his watch and his House of Commons pass. Davies was then forced out of the car, at which point he called the police and gave a full statement. The media immediately suspected Davies of "cruising" for sex, something he emphatically denied. The tabloids got straight to the point and openly suggested that he was seeking gay sex: the *Daily Mirror* (28 October 1998) stated "SHAME OF GAY SEX CABINET MINISTER; RON DAVIES RESIGNS AS WELSH SECRETARY". The broadsheet newspapers used a less dramatic tone, being careful not to state explicitly that Davies was soliciting sex, with the *Guardian* (28 October 1998) writing "MYSTERY MEETING THAT ENDED A CAREER".

As time went on the broadsheets explored Davies's situation in more detail, but generally used respectful language, commenting on, for example, the opinions and language of tabloid newspapers (such as *The Sunday Times*, THEY'LL GET TO THE BOTTOM OF IT, THEY WILL, 1 November 1998). The tabloid newspapers linked Davies's apparent sexual exploits to sleaze, and were thus satisfied that Davies resigned so quickly. The *Daily Mirror* (THE CABINET MUST BE FREE FROM SLEAZE, 28 October 1998) suggested that his actions were in danger of tarnishing the Government: "The best thing that can be said of Ron Davies is that he went quickly. At least that shows that he had no wish to damage or drag down the government with him . . . Tony Blair wants a clean, sleaze-free administration. The speed of Ron Davies' exit shows the Prime Minister will not tolerate anyone breaking his high standards."

Negative words used to describe Davies include "shamed", "disgraced", "foolish" and "bizarre". They suggest that Davies was a guilty, flawed individual who had engaged in some kind of disreputable behaviour (even though none of the newspapers actually had any proof of what Davies was doing in the park). Clapham Common itself was frequently labelled a "gay sex haunt", "murky" and "notorious", thus directly linking Davies with unseemly, dangerous behaviour. Davies was quickly categorized as "other" by the press; like Proctor before him, his alleged liking for sex not considered to be the (heterosexual or homosexual) norm defined him as "dangerous" (Frame Three), in opposition to heterosexuality. As Storr (2001: 119) notes: "Davies' alleged transgressions were aggressively corporealized. Tabloid allegations were not just of homosexuality in the abstract, but of specific acts which were clearly located outside the zone of privacy both by their homosexuality . . . and by their non-domestic setting".

## Unacceptable Behaviour

As Storr suggests, Davies's alleged public sexual acts and sexuality as a whole were unacceptable in heterosexual society (Frame Two). As with Field and Harvey *et al.*, his lack of openness about his supposed sexuality, coupled with the unexplained circumstances surrounding the incident, meant that Davies could not be slotted into a neat, safe sexual category. As Michael Brown (*The Independent*, THE GOOD GAYS AND THE BAD GAYS, 9 November 1998) suggests, he was "bad" rather than "good", fulfilling that binary theme of Frame Three. Davies's sexuality was presented as crossing the line between acceptable and unacceptable behaviour. Rubin (1992) writes that according to hierarchies of sexual values, "normal" sexuality should be heterosexual and reproductive, and any sexual acts which violate that can therefore be regarded as "abnormal". While, as Rubin remarks, some forms of homosexuality are in the process of crossing the acceptable/unacceptable line, this relates to coupled and monogamous homosexuality; Davies was therefore presented as abnormal or "dangerous" by much of the tabloid press.

The unusualness of Davies's supposed sexual behaviour was condemned by the tabloids (even the Labour supporting *Daily Mirror*); while tabloid newspapers would by now accept "good" gay politicians (although the tabloid press was not particularly in favour of "campaigning" gay politicians), any "extreme" behaviour which suggested that a politician had an "active" rather than "neutered" sexual life was too much for them to take. The tabloid newspapers also revelled in Davies's predicament because it was the first major "gay scandal" of Blair's time in power, and his private life was seen as particularly scandalous. His press coverage can be read in relation to Thompson's (2000: 120) definition of sexual scandal, in which it is not the legality/illegality of actions which are important, but rather that the "norms" which are transgressed have a degree of "moral bindingness". Interestingly, Thompson (2000: 120) states that the activities concerned do not have to be considered "transgressions" by everyone, but instead need to have "a sufficient degree of moral bindingness" in order that public expressions of disapproval are made. Davies's alleged transgressions met these criteria unquestionably.

## "Dangerous" and "Dirty" Sexuality

Newspapers even linked Davies with a so-called "gay sex disease". Following on from the original *Mail on Sunday* story, the *People* (1 November 1998) exclaimed: "SHAMED MP HAS GAY SEX DISEASE; RON DAVIES PICKED UP HEPATITIS B SAYS EX-WIFE". The article went on to state that "Shamed MP Ron Davies caught the deadly gay sex disease hepatitis B, his ex-wife sensationally claimed last night . . . It is primarily caught by gay men through sex and intravenous drug users . . . She [Davies's wife] sent him for medical help when he turned up at her home looking gaunt . . . Last night Dr James Le Fanu said: 'biologically, the hepatitis B virus closely resembles the HIV virus'." By linking Davies to "gay sex disease" and even HIV, the *People* is further categorizing him as "dangerous" and even "dirty" (Frame Three). By categorizing gay men alongside drug users, the article slots Davies into one of the "categories of blame" identified by Sanderson in relation to HIV/AIDS (homosexuals, drug abusers, prostitutes), and it is Davies's own fault he allegedly has the disease. Storr (2001: 118) notes that the link with HIV/AIDS in the above article is a clever use of precedent: "the casual reader of the headline will certainly have assumed [the gay disease] to be HIV. Thus the tabloids in particular condemned Davies in terms more familiar from previous 'gay scandals'." There is no public interest reason for the *People* article to be published and it could be considered unethical. As Clause 3 (i) of the Press Complaints Commission Code of Practice (PCC 2011) states, "Everyone is entitled to respect for his or her private and family life, home, health and correspondence, including digital communications. Editors will be expected to justify intrusions into any individual's private life without consent."

## Defined by (Bi)Sexuality

The *Mail on Sunday* and *People* articles further intruded into Davies's private life and went into lots of detail about his first marriage, revealing how many times he and his first wife had sex, the fact that he allegedly liked to visit Turkish baths, and that he supposedly has a low sperm count. Through the articles, Davies's public life became defined by his private self. He has never been allowed to forget the incident and his political career did not recover. The intrusion into Davies's private life (particularly the *Mail on Sunday* and *People* revelations) is even more problematic when one looks at his voting record on gay issues. Davies could not be accused of hypocrisy in the way he voted; his pre-1997 voting record was strong[2] and while his post-1997 record was less impressive[3] (post-scandal), he did vote in the key 1998 division on the age of gay consent.[4] So, the articles are not only against the public interest, they are blatant manufacturing (unlike his original exposé, which can be regarded as reportage and in the public interest).

Davies's subsequent behaviour did not help his cause, and the media accused him of "cruising" for sex on two further occasions (1999 and 2003), one accompanied by apparent photographic proof (*News of the World*, 13 June 1999). The second incident prompted Davies to "come out" as bisexual (*Observer*, "I'M BISEXUAL" SAYS DAVIES AFTER NEW ACCUSATION, 13 June 1999), something many commentators saw as proof that he *had* been "cruising" for gay sex on Clapham Common. Guidry (1999) notes that the assumption that sexual orientation is either hetero or homosexual (dichotomous) contributes to the marginalization of bisexual people. Thus, Davies's bisexuality can be seen as more of a threat to the "norm" than homosexuality; homosexuality, while seen as "abnormal", is at least a fully recognized "other". In fact, even after his admission of bisexuality, the press still frequently groups Davies with other gay politicians with no mention of his bisexuality. While "gay" is often used to signify "non-heterosexual", rather than to deliberately exclude bisexuality *per se*, the

**155**

lack of reference suggests the strength of the hetero/homosexual dichotomy and even the invisibility of bisexuality.

The 1998 scandal forced Davies to resign as Welsh Secretary and forgo the opportunity to be the first First Secretary of the new Welsh Assembly. He stood down from Parliament in 2001 and became Welsh Assembly member for Caerphilly, a post he resigned when the third incident became front-page news. The Labour Party was relatively supportive of Davies after the 1998 scandal (Davies became the Welsh Assembly economic development chief). However, the continuing embarrassment Davies brought Labour meant that the Party could no longer support him. Davies's case shows that while the press would accept non-heterosexual MPs and ministers, any "extreme" behaviour — behaviour perceived as a threat to the "norm" — was too much for the press to take. Mandelson's "outing" just a few weeks later showed that the Labour Party did not object to Davies's bisexuality in itself; it was the circumstances of his "outing" that were the problem, alongside his way of managing the event.


## Peter Mandelson

### *"Outing" by Television*

In the midst of Davies's scurrilous press coverage, Mandelson's homosexuality became the focus of intense media speculation. His press coverage is important because it is representative of a period during which gay politicians were at the forefront of journalistic attention. In fact, his press coverage reached fever pitch, and was probably the most intense of any gay politician or "gay scandal" since Proctor ten years earlier. At a time when homosexuality had supposedly become less contentious (signalling tolerance, if not the move towards recognition — Frame One), Mandelson's press was astonishingly profuse. At the time of the "outing" Mandelson was a very influential figure in British politics; he was a confidant to Blair, one of the masterminds of the 1997 General Election and the New Labour project as a whole, Trade and Industry Secretary, and a controversial political figure whom much of the press loved to hate (partly due to the fact that he was a proponent of "spin" and had therefore spent many years dealing with the media). His sexuality was also an open secret in the political and media worlds (Macintyre 2000), putting him in a vulnerable position.

Mandelson was "outed" on the BBC2 current affairs programme *Newsnight*. While discussing Davies's case on the programme,

Matthew Parris, by now a political journalist, stated in an interview "there are at least two gay members of the Cabinet." His interviewer, Jeremy Paxman, asked "Are there two gay members of the Cabinet?" to which Parris replied "Well, Chris Smith is openly gay and I think Peter Mandelson is certainly gay." The following day Mandelson was confronted by journalists and photographers on his doorstep, all eager to enliven his press coverage. Most tabloid newspapers covered the story, although the coverage was not, in the first instance, that sensational. For instance, *The Sun* (ABOUT PETER; THE SUN SAYS, 28 October 1998), a newspaper which had in the past printed problematic articles about gay politicians, other public figures, and gay men and women as a whole, stated: "*The Sun* has a few thoughts about these incredible events. Firstly, Mandelson's outing — coupled with the Ron Davies affair — will prove to be a major turning point in British politics. Secondly, there is a massive difference between Davies's shenanigans on Clapham Common and Mandelson's homosexuality. *The Sun* knows that Mandelson has struggled with this issue for many years. He knew biographers were about to spill the beans anyway. So last night's furore was a controversy waiting to happen. The fact is: Mandelson is gay. He also has a brilliant mind. He is also a talented politician. And it is also true that times have changed. The British people will not turn on Mandelson because he is gay. And they will sympathise with him for the way in which he was 'exposed.' We say to Mandelson: tell the truth. You will win respect for your honesty."

Of course, the volte-face by *The Sun* may have been an attempt to appeal to Blair via Mandelson. Some newspapers actually turned on Parris for "outing" Mandelson (he was in fact sacked as a *Sun* columnist). The *Daily Mirror* (29 October 1998) stated "FURY AT TORY'S OUTING OF MANDELSON", managing to display its pro-gay credentials and political allegiance at the same time. *The Times* decided not to publish anything at all on Mandelson's initial "outing". The paper's then editor, Peter Stothard, justified his decision in a *Guardian* interview (ETHICS MAN; WHEN MATTHEW PARRIS "OUTED" PETER MANDELSON ON NEWSNIGHT, IT CREATED CONFUSION IN NEWSROOMS ACROSS THE COUNTRY. HOW SHOULD THE MEDIA DEAL WITH SUCH A DELICATE ISSUE, 2 November 1998) saying, "It wasn't a story . . . Mandelson has had more outings than Saga Holidays. Even though it came from our own wise and distinguished columnist, we didn't consider it to be a sufficiently new story to warrant space." The newspapers which did comment on the *Newsnight* incident treated the news that Mandelson was gay as if it had never before been the subject of press speculation, even though Mandelson had been "outed" on numerous occasions, from as early as 1987, with the *Daily Mirror* stating "MANDELSON IS GAY, SAYS FORMER MP" (28 October 1998). The story was such big news in 1998 because Mandelson had become one of the most powerful men in the country (Macintyre 2000).

## The Need to Know

The initial positive reaction to Mandelson's "outing" faded just a few days after the *Newsnight* incident. As Macintyre notes, the BBC, sensitive to the possibility that Mandelson was offended, and the thin line between the public interest and private intrusion, issued a memo stating that Mandelson's sexuality should not be referred to on any programme (thus highlighting the different approaches of the press and television towards the publicizing of private lives). While a great deal of the newspapers' anger was directed at the BBC, Mandelson lost much of the sympathy he had received, with Mandelson's friendship with the then Director General of the BBC, John Birt, making it seem as if he was getting special treatment (Macintyre 2000). The *Observer* (1 November 1998) claimed there was "OUTRAGE AT BBC BAN ON CABINET SEX GOSSIP" and *The Mail on Sunday* (1 November 1998) stated "ANGER AT BBC GAG ON MINISTER'S SEX LIFE". The BBC defended the memo, noting that it is only policy to comment on a politician's sexuality if it is relevant to public policy.

Mandelson further enraged the press by refusing to state his sexuality. Even though he has been photographed with his male partner Reinaldo Avila da Silva on numerous occasions, cooperated with Macintyre's friendly biography which mentioned his homosexuality, and later on thanked Avila in the acknowledgements of his autobiography (published in 2010), he has never actually said "I am gay" to the press. It can be argued that there is no need for Mandelson to state whether or not he is gay, or for the press to write about his sexuality, due to the fact that no public interest criteria have so far applied. However, Mandelson's reticence on the subject has definitely affected the press coverage his sexuality has received. Unlike Smith, Bradshaw, Twigg *et al.*, Mandelson has not given journalists what they want; his refusal to publicly and definitely "come out" means that the press has found it difficult to define or label him, and therefore homosexuality and heterosexuality, as sharply as it would like to. He is thus a "bad" gay man, to use a binary theme from Frame Three (although not as bad as Proctor, for example, showing the graduated nature of the binaries). In fact, even though Mandelson discusses his partner in his autobiography, he was criticized by some journalists for not doing it enough, with the lack of focus on his sexuality in the book presented as strange. The *Observer*'s Andrew Rawnsley (THE COURTIER WHO WANTED TO BE KING, 18 July 2010), said "There are pictures of him with the New Labour 'family', but not a single snap of Peter and his partner, Reinaldo. I guess this is down to his complicated feelings about his sexuality and privacy. At the time when he was rising to prominence, there was still enormous prejudice at the expense of gay politicians. It is, though, frankly bizarre that his partner of many years is never introduced as such and receives just four passing references compared with five for his dog, Bobby." It does not seem to occur to Rawnsley that Mandelson's partner may not want to be the focus of publicity.

While the press representation of gay men and women at this time was much less vicious than compared to the mid-1980s, and the representation of deviancy was therefore more implicit than explicit, there was certainly a case of "them" ("abnormal" homosexuals) and "us" ("normal" heterosexuals, *i.e.* the newspaper and its readers) in some (tabloid) newspaper discussion of Mandelson. So, recognition (Frame One) was not achieved. For example, while stating that "The old-fashioned era of gay bashing is over" *The Sun* (ABOUT PETER; THE SUN SAYS, 28 October 1998) noted that, "As Richard Littlejohn [then a *Sun* columnist] — never a man to sport a limp wrist — says . . . being gay should not be a cause for shame." *The Sun* stereotypes gay men as effeminate in order to define what Littlejohn, a heterosexual, is not. Although professing to accept Mandelson's sexuality, *The Sun* got into trouble over another Littlejohn column. Littlejohn (*The Sun*, MANDY, MANDY, MANDY, OUT! OUT! OUT!, 30 October 1998) stated: "The truth is that there is a virtual freemasonry of homosexuals operating at the highest levels in politics . . . This, like Peter Mandelson's sexual preferences, is well known to those who work and mix in these circles. It is not common knowledge to everyone else. Which is why I believe Matthew Parris was right to out Mandy on Newsnight. This Government is committed to furthering the homosexual agenda. It has given top priority to reducing the age at which schoolboys can be buggered legally to 16, in the face of public opinion. If MPs and Cabinet ministers have a vested interest in furthering this agenda, we should be told." By that reasoning, every male MP would have an avid interest in the female age of consent. Would Littlejohn demand a public register of heterosexual MPs if a debate ever took place on that topic? Yet, he clearly uses the public interest defence for Mandelson's "outing", as did many journalists at the time.

## Stereotyping Sexuality

Mandelson's initial 1998 press coverage can be classed as reportage, rather than manufacturing, because newspapers were reacting to outside events (his "outing" on television). However, much of his later press coverage was either pure manufacturing or his sexuality was brought up when it was not relevant. In fact, it is clear that Mandelson has often been defined by his sexuality, particularly in tabloid newspapers. For example, Mandelson is often referred to using exaggerated, ostentatious terms such as "exotic". The *Daily Mirror* (23 December 1998) headlined Mandelson's 1998 ministerial resignation with "RISE AND STALL OF MR EXOTIC" and the *Daily Mail* (MANDELSON HOME LOAN BOMBSHELL; THE PRINCE OF DARKNESS AND A HOUSE DEAL THAT DIDN'T ADD UP, 22 December 1998) described him thus: "Peter Mandelson is one of the most brilliant, exotic and mysterious figures the Labour movement has produced. A flamboyant former television producer . . . His glittering success triggered a mixture of admiration and envy among New Labour MPs through his closeness to Tony Blair, his condescending attitude to colleagues and his liking for the highlife." The adjectives serve to categorize Mandelson as an unusual, "showy" gay man, thus promoting a gay stereotype. While Mandelson did once describe himself as "exotic" (*Daily Express*, WEALTHY FRIENDS OF AN "EXOTIC CREATURE", 24 January 2001), seemingly legitimizing the use of the word, it is doubtful that he was referring to his sexuality at the time; there is no doubt that when the *Daily Mail* uses "exotic", combined with "flamboyant", that reference is being made to the fact that Mandelson is gay. In more recent years he has been referred to as a "dandy" by both *The Times* (HOW MANDY THE DANDY WENT ALL HI-DI-HI ON THE DANCEFLOOR, 25 July 2010) and *The Mirror* (DANDY, MANDY, 22 January 2010), showing that such characterization still takes place.

On occasion, Mandelson has been referred to using stronger, even homophobic, terms. While he may not have been purposely making a derogatory comment about his sexuality, *The Spectator*'s Rod Liddle used the word "mincing" to describe Mandelson: "What we have to remember, as we are fed all the spin — most recently from the revolting Peter Mandelson, that mincing embodiment of sanctimony and obfuscation — are the following indisputable facts" (A DESPICABLE AND COWARDLY DIVERSION, 26 July 2003). The suggestions of effeminacy — an assumption often made by heterosexuals about homosexuals (McIntosh 1996) — were at their strongest when

**160**

Mandelson held his seat at the 2001 General Election. Mandelson's loud, enthusiastic election speech caused Peter McKay from the *Daily Mail* to state "Peter Mandelson's extraordinary 'I'm no quitter!' victory speech after he recaptured Hartlepool was the political equivalent of Gloria Gaynor's disco anthem I Will Survive. His enemies and those who prefer a quiet life want Mr Mandelson to disappear and open a ballroom dancing academy with Reinaldo, perhaps, or lead a Home Rule for Hartlepool movement. But having got a taste of him in Gloria Gaynor mode, wouldn't you prefer him to kick up merry hell about getting back into government?" (MANDY, THE GLORIA GAYNOR OF HARTLEPOOL, 11 June 2001). The term "Mandy" is a label and a stereotype, used to suggest effeminacy. Quite why Mandelson would open a ballroom dancing academy is unclear, as is the association with Gloria Gaynor; the only firm link between Mandelson and the *Mail*'s imagery is the fact that ballroom dancing and Gloria Gaynor are stereotypes frequently associated with gay men.

Littlejohn has also used problematic words and phrases when writing about Mandelson, and his articles (particularly when he wrote for *The Sun*) were often accompanied by sketches showing Mandelson dressed in outdated stereotypical gay clothing such as leather chaps, or side-by-side with his partner. For example, one column in *The Sun* (LATER TONIGHT ON THE BAY BEE C, 19 May 2000) showed a drawing of Mandelson dressed as Carman Miranda, with Reinaldo showering him with money. While Littlejohn's *Sun* coverage should not be taken as typical of the tabloid press, the fact that Littlejohn was able to describe Mandelson as "Iago played by Kenneth Williams . . . a mixture of mincing, obsequiousness and fake menace" (*The Sun*, HOW CAN THIS SLEAZY CREEP REPRESENT US?, 27 July 2004) and write with regard to Mandelson's purchase of a dog that "it has confirmed what we always suspected. Mandy's best friend is a little woofter" (*The Sun*, WHEN IT COMES TO REARING CHILDREN, GAYS AREN'T EQUAL, 17 December 1999), shows that Mandelson's public life has been defined by his private sexuality, something which has continued in recent years, with Mandelson's elevation to the House of Lords and reinstatement to the Cabinet as Business Secretary (from 2008 to 2010). In fact, in 2010 Littlejohn referred to "Lord Mandelson and the Lady Reinaldo" in a *Mail* column (A VERY BRITISH ROYAL WEDDING, 19 November 2010), and in early 2007 he penned a fake telephone call between Mandelson and Avila using plenty of innuendo and suggestions of effeminacy (*Daily Mail*, WHO DO YOU THINK YOU'RE TALKING TO — RORY BREMNER, 27 February 2007). Of course, in many ways Littlejohn is an anachronism. As always, though, news values must be considered. Indeed, his inclusion as a columnist in *The Sun* and *Mail* newspapers reveals something about the news values of those tabloids at the time the articles were published and the opinions the papers expected their readers to have. Perhaps it is the case that Littlejohn expressed what those newspapers would like to express in the main news pages, but could not.

Incredibly, Mandelson was called a "poofter" by a columnist in one tabloid newspaper as recently as 2001. The *Daily Star* (OUT AND OUT LIAR, 25 January 2001) stated: "Do you seriously give a monkey's about who Peter Mandelson sleeps with every night? Thought not. Yet somehow petulant Pete has reportedly convinced himself that his ousting is all a vicious plot by journalists because he's gay. Yeah, right. Like it's nothing to do with him being a lying, cheating scuzzball who only cares about himself and his ambition. Actually, thinking about it, the raving poofter might have a point. Because if it was just to do with him being a lying, cheating scuzzball etc etc then we wouldn't have any politicians left at all, would we?" Not only does the newspaper define Mandelson by his sexuality in a very crude way (while berating Mandelson for apparently doing the same thing himself), the use of the term would be regarded by many people as offensive. While the *Daily Star* is more "downmarket" than *The Sun*, the term's use is still surprising (even if the writer is trying to be "ironic"). If a newspaper used a derogatory term about a black or Jewish person, for example, condemnation from other newspapers and politicians would likely be fierce (with the "irony" excuse not tolerated).

## Mandelson's Partner

The press representation of Mandelson's partner highlights the fact that Mandelson is often defined by his sexuality, as well as the blatant manufacturing that the press have engaged in. After Mandelson's 1998 "outing", the *Sunday Express* became the first newspaper to write about Avila under the headline "BRAZILIAN STUDENT WHO IS MANDELSON'S CLOSE FRIEND" (1 November 1998). Not only was the article manufactured, it was not in the public interest. When Mandelson heard that the paper was planning to run a story on his partner, he tried to have the article removed (he telephoned the editor-in-chief of the paper, as well as the head of the Press Complaints Commission) and after negotiation the article was moved from the front-page to page seven (Macintyre 2000). The editor of the *Sunday*

*Express* was eventually fired. While the newspaper denied that the editor was sacked because of the article, an internal investigation revealed that the story had not been investigated legitimately; photographs were taken of Avila against his will and an airbrush was used to erase the hand that he had raised to block the camera lens (Macintyre 2000).

Between Avila's initial publicity in late 1998 and Mandelson's second resignation in January 2001 (he first resigned from the Cabinet in December 1998 before being reinstated in October 1999), Avila managed to escape excessive, intrusive press attention; he was the subject of a few relatively positive articles and occasionally photographed (the *Sunday Mirror* [30 April 2000] photographed Mandelson and Avila in Venice and published an article headed "JUST ONE PORTFOLIO; MANDY AND REINALDO SOAK UP BEAUTIFUL SIGHTS OF VENICE"). The coverage was not all good (for example, Littlejohn begun to question Avila's immigration status), although negative publicity was minimal. However, Mandelson's 2001 resignation opened a floodgate; his fall from grace and the diminishment of his power meant that journalists felt free to write about his personal life with relish. In the majority of articles written about Mandelson at the time of his second resignation, Avila was mentioned and often pictured, something not confined to the tabloids; broadsheet newspapers also referred to Avila, although they generally took a less intrusive tone. Many tabloid newspapers followed Littlejohn's lead and queried Avila's immigration status. The *Daily Star* (25 January 2001) asked "HAS YER BOYFRIEND GOT A PASS-PORT MANDY?" and went on to state: "As Peter Mandelson resigned AGAIN in disgrace, last night mystery surrounded the citizenship status of his gay Brazilian lover . . . key questions remain: Does Reinaldo, 28, have a British passport? If so, how did he qualify for it? And — crucially — did Peter Mandelson pull any strings on his behalf?" Although there has never been any proof that Avila is in Britain unfairly, the press claimed that their queries were legitimate because it was in theory possible that Avila (a Brazilian national until he received British citizenship in 2005) had only been allowed to stay in the country because of Mandelson's influence.

Even so, other articles about Avila, both at the time of Mandelson's second resignation and after, cannot be considered to meet any public interest criteria at all. Articles have been published about Avila's family, friends and alleged past partners, details of where he studied, and allegations that he and Mandelson were on the verge of ending their relationship. The articles relate Mandelson and Avila's private relationship to Mandelson's public life. For example, Mandelson's appointment as a European Commissioner in 2004 prompted speculation on the effect that it would have on his relationship and whether he and Avila would have to take part in a civil partnership in order for Mandelson to receive a spouse allowance (*Sunday Telegraph*, MARRIAGE MAY PAY FOR MANDELSON, 1 August 2004). His partner was also the focus of press attention in 2008, after Mandelson was made a Lord (*Daily Mail*, LIFE IS SWEET FOR "MR AND MRS MANDELSON", 4 October 2008). While the partners of heterosexual MPs are obviously the focus of much press attention, the focus on Avila post-Mandelson's 2001 resignation has been mostly negative (used to demonstrate a political point or to speculate on the state of Mandelson's private life) rather than constructive (*i.e.* using Avila to positively promote Mandelson's political career).

Avila's original Brazilian nationality further strengthened the characterization of Mandelson as an exotic gay man. Twinned with this, journalists love to mention Mandelson's supposed love of designer clothes and furniture, his famous friends and his smart appearance. *The Scotsman* (25 January 2001), for instance, suggested that Mandelson was a "SMART-SUITED MACHIAVALLI WHO TRIED TO IMPRESS ONE MILLIONAIRE TOO MANY". While Mandelson is not categorized as "dangerous" in the way that Proctor was in 1987, his younger partner (Avila is nineteen years younger than Mandelson) pushes him closer to that category than politicians without a (publicized) partner altogether, or with less "glamorous" partners. Storr believes that coverage of Mandelson's sexuality in 1998 was "gentle" and "ambivalent" (2001: 118) and that his sexuality entered the "zone of privacy", but the fact that his sexuality made the front — or prominent pages — of most newspapers, and Avila became the focus of intense press speculation, particularly after Mandelson's 2001 resignation, suggests that it is not the case at all. While Davies was explicitly presented as "dangerous" due to the supposed "abnormal" nature of his lifestyle, Mandelson's "exoticness", coupled with his refusal to officially "come out" to the press, means that the press coverage of his sexuality has been mostly unfriendly (especially once the BBC published its infamous memo and it became clear that Mandelson would not say that he is gay). Davies and Mandelson's cases neatly show the acceptable/unacceptable divide; Mandelson's sexuality, while considered "exotic", was not seen as a bar to ministerial office, unlike Davies's alleged "immoral" and "dangerous" behaviour, which meant he was not fit for the cabinet.

The manner in which Mandelson and Avila have sometimes been

portrayed by sections of the tabloid press can be shown through an examination of a front-page article from *The Sun* (MANDY GAY LOVER SHOCK, 26 January 2001). The article was written when Mandelson resigned his Government post in January 2001 over the Hinduja passport affair, when he was accused of helping the Hinduja brothers (Indian businessmen) to get British passports in return for sponsorship of the Millennium Dome.[5] The article continued inside the newspaper, with more pictures of Mandelson's partner and more personal detail, such as where he and Mandelson met and the name and details of Avila's alleged previous partner, Howell James. *The Sun* justified the detail because James was in charge of the Hindujas' PR at the time of Mandelson's resignation. In the form of an accompanying commentary the paper (FIND TRUTH BEFORE POLL, 26 January 2001) stated: "Now we learn that Mandelson's Brazilian boyfriend had a two-year fling with the man who has just taken over the Hinduja PR operations . . . That probe must now be extended to include Howell James' links with ministers, if any."

The public interest is presented as a reason for the article's publication, because *The Sun* seemed to think that Avila had somehow compromised the political process (although it is never openly stated how) by allegedly being in a relationship with James before his relationship with Mandelson. While the article does not go as far as to explicitly state that Mandelson and Avila are outside the realm of civilized society, it is clear that *The Sun* tries to portray Mandelson and Avila's relationship as morally questionable and politically and sexually scandalous. The article tries to make their relationship appear more controversial than it actually is (there has never been any proof of wrongdoing on Avila's behalf) in order to punish Mandelson for his alleged political wrongdoings. The words "toyboy", "fling", "affair" and "gay lover" are used to sexualize Mandelson and Avila's relationship and to portray gay relationships as inconsequential. In terms of news values the article satisfies all of Galtung and Ruge's (1973) rules, discussed in Chapter 1: The meaning of the event was quickly arrived at (1); the event was at the right threshold — *i.e.* it was worth reporting (2); the event was relatively simple to understand (3); the event was UK based (4); most of the media desired the chance to humiliate Mandelson (5); the event was unexpected (6); there was the chance to cover the story for a long time (7); the story was different to many other stories being covered at the time (8); Mandelson is from an elite nation (9); Mandelson is an elite person (10); the event was highly personalized (11); the event was a negative story (12). The article also fulfils Hartley's (1995) "map" concept; in it society can be seen as: fragmented (Mandelson is part of the political sphere); hierarchical (Mandelson is an "important" person); consisting of individuals in charge of their own destiny (Mandelson is responsible for his own problems); consensual (society is united — against the "scandalous" Mandelson).

Mandelson would probably have received the same kind of press coverage if he had had a female partner who had allegedly had a relationship with the person responsible for the Hindujas' public relations operation. As such, there is almost sexual scandal "equality". *Almost*, because gay sexual scandal stories are inherently more "scandalous" than heterosexual sexual scandal stories, for the simple fact that homosexuality is often portrayed by the (tabloid) press and thought of by the public (even in the twenty-first century) as unusual and even aberrant, demonstrated by the kinds of words used by many tabloid newspapers to describe Mandelson over the years. Thus, *The Sun*'s article is not only newsworthy because of the suggestion of political scandal; it is newsworthy because Mandelson's partner is male. The fact that Mandelson and Avila's privacy was invaded is not important, at least to *The Sun*: the story was newsworthy and was therefore published.

## Pre-1998 "Outings"

Mandelson had been "outed" many times before — although the press treated the 1998 "news" that he was gay as something previously unknown — something that undoubtedly contributed to the fuss surrounding his 1998 "outing". After all, if Mandelson had "come out" as gay after his first "outing" in 1987, then his homosexuality would have been old news. That said, there is no reason why Mandelson needed to "come out" after any of his public "outings", or at all, especially as he has always been completely open in his private life and with his colleagues, and has never acted or voted hypocritically. Plus, the press could still have made a fuss about his younger partner or particular aspects of his private life even if he had "come out".

His previous "outings" demonstrate the changing press coverage of gay politicians very well. In 1987 the *News of the World* carried a front-page story about Mandelson's relationship (which ended in the late 1980s) with Peter Ashby and Ashby's child, whom they were both helping to raise. At the time Mandelson was the Labour Party's Director of Communications. The front-page stated "KINNOCK'S NO 1 MAN IN GAY SENSATION" with a subheading of "HE PLAYS UNCLE TO BOY, AGE 7, IN BIZARRE TRIANGLE", followed by "MY LOVE FOR GAY LABOUR BOSS" on pages two and three (17 May 1987). The language used was designed to damage

Mandelson's reputation and career. Kay Carberry, the mother of Ashby's child, was questioned about their relationship and stated, presumably in response to a question asked by the paper: "I'm not worried about Joe catching AIDS off them. After all, they have a long, stable relationship and are unlikely to catch the disease." The link to AIDS was designed to characterize Mandelson as "other" and "dirty" (Frame Three) and suggested that Mandelson — and homosexuality as a whole — were dangers to heterosexual family life and to children in particular.

The article also claimed that "his appointment is bound to be seen as an embarrassment on the eve of the general election. The Tories will make gay rights education in schools in loony Left boroughs a key election issue." The paper went on to state in a leader column (THE HIDDEN MENACE): "Pity Kinnock, too, over our exclusive revelation today about the life-style of his right-hand man. Publicly, Kinnock tries to distance himself from the loonies and the gays. Can he not see that proximity to the likes of Peter Mandelson is bound to bring embarrassment?" Mandelson was therefore characterized as a threat to all that was "normal" and grouped in the same category as the "loony left", echoing the press coverage received by Tatchell in 1983. As a backroom assistant, there was absolutely no public interest reason for Mandelson's sexuality or his relationship to be written about, and because he was not yet an MP, the press could not even claim to be informing constituents about the person representing them, a weak justification at the best of times.

Mandelson's next "outing" came in 1995 when Mandelson, Ashby and Ashby's son were mentioned in a political autobiography. In response, *The Sun* (23 August 1995) wrote "GOULD 'OUTS' BLAIR'S RIGHT HAND MAN; MANDELSON LABELLED GAY", with the article claiming that Mandelson, who had "never publicly discussed his sexuality", had been "sensationally exposed". Rather strange headlines, considering Mandelson was first "outed" by *The Sun*'s sister paper the *News of the World* many years previously. Other journalists from 1995 to 1998 mentioned Mandelson's homosexuality, although the stories were few and far between. In May 1998, for example, the *London Evening Standard* stated "he is gay" in an article about Mandelson (WHY WE SHOULD LEARN TO LOVE PETER, 6 May 1998). It was as if the previous "outings" had never happened. Mandelson's lack of candour meant that the press could represent his homosexuality as "scandalous" news. After all, it was extremely unlikely that readers would remember that Mandelson is gay, or even who he was.

## Popularity

Mandelson's sexuality is of interest to the press for reasons other than his fame, his power, the fact that he has not officially "come out" and the issue's newsworthiness. Certainly, for much of his career Mandelson has been unpopular with many of his colleagues and many journalists, much of the unpopularity stemming from his dealings with the press when he was Labour's Director of Communications (see Macintyre 2000). So, unlike Twigg, Bradshaw *et al.*, the press has always been inclined to write negative stories about him, with the negativity surrounding his sexuality influenced by his unpopularity (*i.e.* it can be used to score points against him) rather than his actual sexuality being the focus of the papers' detestation. It is definitely not the case that Mandelson's voting record gives just cause for negative press surrounding his sexuality, as his voting record on gay rights is strong.[6] Mandelson is in a strange position; he does not hide his sexuality, and has in fact acknowledged his partner and his 1998 "outing" in his autobiography, yet because he has not said those three words to the press — "I am gay" — he is treated as not being fully "out". Mandelson's negative press coverage demonstrates that politicians who are fully "out" are much better able to manage (or "spin") their press coverage than ones who are "in" (even if they are "in" only in the minds of journalists), suggesting that politicians themselves are aware of the binary themes (Frame Three) in play.

## Active Sexuality

The public seemed relatively blasé about Mandelson's sexuality, and opinion polls carried out in 1998 suggested that the public did not care about gay MPs as a whole. As Storr notes, a self-selecting telephone poll in the *Daily Mirror* found that approximately two-thirds of its readers did not want to know about the sexuality of their MPs (*Daily Mirror*, A VOTE FOR TOLERANCE; YOU DECIDE 3-2 AGAINST KNOWING MPS' SEXUALITY IN RECORD MIRROR POLL, 11 November 1998). However, the opinion polls also revealed that there was more opposition to the lowering of the age of consent for gay men, suggesting that the public is less tolerant of gay sex acts ("active" homosexuality) than homosexuality in itself (Storr 2001). Indeed, a *Guardian* opinion poll (run by ICM) found that only 26% of people were for the lowering of the age of consent, as opposed to 69% against (10 November 1998), perhaps suggesting why Davies was so roundly condemned: his sexuality was presented as active and overt.

Storr (2001: 122) believes that such data backs up Mandelson's decision to not "come out" as gay: "In insisting that they 'did not want to know' about the sexuality of MPs, respondents to the opinion polls effectively endorsed the strategy adopted by Mandelson and perhaps even Davies, both of whom steadfastly refused throughout the allegations in October and November 1998 to come out as gay or bisexual." It certainly suggests that to succeed politically gay MPs need to push their "active" sexuality to one side. So, while MPs should not hide or lie about their sexuality, they should not be seen as being sexually "active" either (*i.e.* they should not cross the acceptability threshold of Frame Two). Ultimately, Mandelson's refusal to "come out" did not affect his actual political career; his ministerial career floundered due to alleged personal financial impropriety and suggestions that he speeded up a passport application, rather than any kind of sexual scandal. It has, though, left the press unsatisfied, meaning his negative mediated persona continues.

## Nick Brown

### A Forced Confession

The intense focus on gay politicians in late 1998 continued when Nick Brown (Labour MP for Newcastle upon Tyne East 1983–97 and 2010– and Newcastle upon Tyne East and Wallsend 1997–2010) was "outed" just a few days after Mandelson. An ex-partner of Brown's, in his mid-twenties, tried to sell a story to the *News of the World* in which he alleged that Brown paid him for sex on numerous occasions. Brown pre-empted the "kiss and tell" story and instead "came out" to the newspaper, revealing that while the relationship did take place, he never paid the man for sex. The front-page of the *News of the World* (8 November 1998) declared "MINISTER CONFESSES GAY FLING TO BLAIR; EXCLUSIVE" and went on to state: "Nick Brown's 2-year affair. Prime Minister is standing by him. It follows lover's kiss'n'tell threat." The newspaper aimed to present Brown's "confession" and his sexuality as "scandalous". The words "fling", "affair" and "kiss'n'tell" suggest that the relationship was frivolous, although a two-year relationship seems anything but inconsequential. The word "confesses" suggests that Brown was living a surreptitious life, a theme expanded on by the newspaper (I AM DEEPLY EMBARRASSED ABOUT THIS; EXCLUSIVE, 8 November 1998) later on: "Mr Brown, who is agriculture minister and was formerly Chief Whip, decided to make his admission to put an end to the rumour mill about his private life at Westminster. Commons insiders say he has been tormented all week over his secret life. The man has made a series of lurid and fanciful allegations which Mr Brown totally denies and which the News of the World has not been able to substantiate in any way." The passage begs the question, if the allegations were so "fanciful", why did the newspaper force Brown to "come out"?

Although the original article can be classed as reporting rather than manufacturing because the paper was reacting to a "kiss and tell", there were no valid public interest criteria applicable; the article would only be justified under the Press Complaints Commission's Code of Practice if it was "detecting or exposing crime or serious impropriety" (PCC 2011), and if the allegations were "fanciful", than it was not the case. The use of the words "secret life" help to categorize Brown as duplicitous and homosexuality as something to be ashamed of. It did not seem to occur to the *News of the World* that, like Mandelson, Brown could have been "out" to many people in his private life.

### Tabloid and Broadsheet Coverage

Other newspapers, both tabloid and broadsheet, were supportive of Brown, although as Storr notes, there was some interest in the allegations of sex for sale. Although they did not withhold the details of the story, broadsheet newspapers reported Brown's embarrassment in a straightforward and non-sensational manner. For instance, *The Times* (10 November 1998) said "BROWN TAKES NO ACTION OVER 'OUTING'". Tabloid newspapers covered the *News of the World*'s story in all its detail, although the vast majority refrained from using problematic terms. However, the *Daily Mail* (DIS-PROPORTIONATE REPRESENTATION, 9 November 1998), a Conservative supporting newspaper, took the opportunity to criticize the Labour Government and homosexuality as a whole, suggesting that the "emergence" of another gay MP somehow impinged upon family values: "Like white rabbits from a conjurer's hat, gay Ministers continue to materialize from this New Labour Government before the bemused gaze of the public. Metropolitan commentators may smile indulgently, but many of the great mass of voters, who put their trust in New Labour with its reassuring espousal of family values, may take a less relaxing view."

The *Daily Mirror* (VOICE OF THE MIRROR: JUDGE HIM ON MERIT, NOT ON HIS SEXUALITY, 9 November 1998), in its support of Brown, highlighted the fact that homosexuals who are "militant" who engage in "dangerous sex" or who are "bad" rather than "good" (binaries of Frame Three) are not acceptable public figures: *"The Mirror* has no sympathy at all with militant gays who want to 'out' those who would rather keep their situation to themselves . . . His [Brown's] situation is very different from that of Ron Davies . . . He [Davies] had to get out because he was trawling the park for sex, apparently lied to the police and still refuses to be honest about what he was up to." Unlike Davies, Brown had "come out" straight away when questioned about his sexuality, and suggestions of illegality, while of interest, were unfounded. Furthermore, in contrast to Mandelson (who was very unpopular in much of the press), the press had no particular axe to grind against Brown. Brown's response to the article — total honesty and obvious embarrassment — also counted in his favour; he was very upset by the *News of the World*'s story and other politicians and journalists responded to that.

Although the majority of the tabloid press was respectful of Brown, one newspaper misread the public, political and journalistic mood. *The Sun* (TELL US THE TRUTH TONY, 9 November 1998), sister paper of the *News of the World*, claimed on its front-page "Are we being run by a gay Mafia?". The newspaper went on to state: "his [Blair's] Government is going to get itself into MASSIVE trouble if it doesn't tell us the whole truth. Is Britain being run by a gay Mafia of politicians, lawyers, Palace courtiers and TV bigwigs? The revelation that a FOURTH member of the Blair Cabinet, Nick Brown, is gay has set alarms ringing. Not because people despise gays, or fear them, or wish to pillory them, but the public has a right to know how many homosexuals occupy positions of high power. Their sexuality is not the problem. The worry is their membership of a closed world of men with a mutual self-interest." *The Sun* also asked gay MPs, "SO YOU WANT TO COME OUT? COME ON" (9 November 1998) and enquired: "Are you a gay MP who'd like to come out? *The Sun* has set up a hotline on 0171 782 4105 for ministers and MPs who are secretly homosexual. Don't worry about the cost, we'll ring you back."

The idea of hidden self-interest was also used against Mandelson in relation to his political position and the favours he could possibly do his partner, and was roundly condemned by other newspapers, as was the idea that gay MPs were a figure of legitimate fun, epitomized by *The Sun*'s articles. *The Independent* (13 November 1998) stated: "YOU COULDN'T MAKE IT UP; THE SUN SAYS: 'HANDS OFF OUR GAYS.' THEN IT SAYS: 'IS THERE A GAY MAFIA?' IS DAVID YELLAND THE MOST VOLATILE TABLOID EDITOR IN BRITAIN? WE THINK YOU SHOULD BE TOLD". The *Guardian*

(14 November, 1998) exclaimed: "SQUIRMING SUN SETS RECORD STRAIGHT IN FURORE OVER GAYS; WILL WOODWARD ON A FAMOUSLY FEARLESS TABLOID IN FULL RETREAT FROM HOMOPHOBIA AS POLLS SHOW IT OUT OF STEP WITH POPULAR MOOD". *The Sun* was actually forced to apologize for its articles and made it known that gay men and women would never again be "outed" unless there was overwhelming public interest in the story. However, as shown in relation to Clive Betts's press coverage (Labour MP for Sheffield Attercliffe 1992–2010 and Sheffield South East 2010– ), explored later in Chapter 9, *The Sun* did not keep its promise. The then editor of *The Sun*, David Yelland, went on to tell the *Guardian* (WAPPING TALES, 14 June 2004): "I had been at a think tank in Dublin; came back on Sunday about 4 p.m. and we didn't have a splash. I was talked into running this leader. I'm not blaming anybody, because the decision was my responsibility. But I learned fairly quickly that the buck really did stop with the editor and you have to be strong enough to resist people around you." The notion of using private lives as a "splash" emphasizes that the newspaper approached "outings" in an impersonal and business-like manner; the private lives of gay (and heterosexual) politicians could be invaded if a "good story" was in the offing.

### Public Acceptability?

Brown was backed by Blair and other political parties did not make capital out of his misfortune either. The political establishment's acceptance of Brown mirrored the public's growing acceptance of homosexuality. As Storr highlights, an opinion poll commissioned by the *Guardian* and run by ICM (before Brown's "outing") found 52% of interviewees thought that being openly gay was compatible with being in the Cabinet, compared to 33% who considered it incompatible (10 November 1998). Storr (2001: 121) notes that Brown received public support despite the fact that he had no known partner, suggesting: "not only are monogamous gay couples entering the 'dead' zone of privacy, but other forms of 'bad' sexuality may also be 'dying' — in declaring that they 'do not want to know' about their MPs' sexuality, for example *Mirror* readers could be seen as resituating all of their MPs, heterosexual or otherwise, in the abstract realm of the 'dead' sexuality rather than the corporealized realm of the 'live'." While it may be the case for the public, it does not appear to always be the case for the press; Mandelson, a gay politician with a long-term partner, has had his privacy invaded more than any other gay politician in recent times.

So, for a gay politician's sexuality to be of no interest to the press, certain conditions have to be met, and Mandelson did not meet them. The case studies so far suggest that Brown's political (and public) acceptance would have been less forthcoming if he had lied about his sexuality or about the way he lived his life, and/or been hypocritical, and this was not the case with Brown; while he was not known as a gay rights campaigner, he had a strong voting record on gay rights, even when he was a minister.[7] In relation to the binary themes of Frame Three, Brown's swift acknowledgement of his homosexuality pushed his press representation towards the "good", unlike Davies, whose refusal to address his sexuality at the time of his initial press coverage made him "bad". Brown was in danger of being categorized as a "dangerous" gay man, due to the sex for sale allegations, but he managed to escape such a categorization as a result of his swift admission, the lack of proof and the support he had from large sections of the press (particularly as a result of *The Sun*'s controversial coverage).

## Michael Portillo

Michael Portillo's 1999 admission of "homosexual experiences as a young person" in an interview with *The Times* (HE'S BACK, 9 September 1999) not only affected his standing in the Conservative Party, it also damaged his leadership ambitions (particularly when combined with his contentious pre-1997 politics and his controversial shift to the left post-1997; all of these things combined served to portray Portillo as an opportunist, someone who would change his politics and outlook simply to achieve power, however unfair such a characterization might be). Rumours that Portillo was gay or bisexual had been circulating for years, but had never been proved, making Portillo's disclosure a big news story even though he was in a seemingly happy, long-term heterosexual marriage, and did not actually say he was gay. The press reaction to his declaration was initially positive, following on from the good reaction to the "self-outings" of Twigg *et al.*, although many of the tabloid newspapers related Portillo's "experiences" directly to gay sex (even though he never actually admitted to having sex with anyone). For instance, the *Daily Mirror* headed an article: "PORTILLO: I HAD GAY SEX" (9 September 1999).

The acceptance and support of some newspapers seemed to be dependent on the fact that Portillo's homosexual experiences were apparently rooted in the past. However, the news that Portillo's gay experiences may have continued once he left university — an alleged ex-partner claimed their relationship lasted for eight years, after meeting at university (*The Mail on Sunday*, PORTILLO'S FORMER HOMOSEXUAL LOVER TELLS OF THEIR EIGHT-YEAR AFFAIR, 12 September 1999) — damaged his acceptance. The revelation that this — and a second — alleged ex-partner had AIDS (both men actually died soon after they made their revelations) also damaged him; the *Daily Mirror* (PORTILLO'S GAY EX HAS AIDS, 31 October 1999) noted "Mr Portillo will be very embarrassed by the revelation." Much of the press seemed unwilling to accept that Portillo's marriage was a happy one, and that his wife was aware of and accepting of his past gay experiences (the *News of the World* [12 September 1999] reported "HE CHEATED WITH MAN"), indicating the narrow view of the family present in some sections of the press.

Portillo's gay past was used against him when he stood for the Conservative Party leadership in 2001. His disclosure, plus the fact that he and his wife do not have any children, was used to suggest that he was not quite right for the post. In fact, Portillo's childless "status" was used as a coded reference to his past homosexual experiences. In a *Daily Mail* article headed "WHAT FAMILY LIFE HAS TAUGHT THE MAN WHO WANTS TO BE THE TORIES' TONY BLAIR" (15 July 2001), Iain Duncan Smith (MP for Chingford 1992–7 and Chingford and Woodford 1997– and Conservative leader 2001–3), Portillo's competitor and the eventual winner of the leadership contest, explained how family life has shaped his views. The author of the article noted: "He [Duncan Smith] was born in Scotland, went to a private school, is sporty, had no interest in politics in his youth, has two sons and two daughters, a stable marriage, family connections with the stage and a lifelong passion for Italy. It could almost be a description of the qualities that helped to propel Tony Blair into Downing Street. And it is also a description of the man who hopes to defeat him as the next election."

The references to family life and children in the article are used to suggest that the heterosexual Duncan Smith has the qualities needed to be a successful political leader, with the comparison to Blair, a seemingly happily married father of four, strengthening the notion that fatherhood equals superior leadership. As with Blair, Duncan Smith's "family man" image is not the reason he succeeded, but it can be seen as giving him an extra edge, helping to make him a more attractive candidate in the eyes of a newspaper like the *Daily Mail*. Does such a focus negatively affect the political process? Can a gay MP (or a heterosexual MP) without children fully compete on the "family-friendly" playing field? It may be that politicians themselves give too much stock to the importance of presenting a "family friendly" image. However, it seems that in Portillo's case, acceptability (Frame Two) only stretched so far, with his earlier association with gay sex and HIV/AIDS as presented by some newspapers, and the resulting negative binary themes (dangerous, unclean sexuality, binaries of Frame Three), not helping.

It must also be borne in mind that Portillo's lack of success (by only one vote) was also related to the fact that he was a fairly unpopular politician; not only did his party think that he had latterly become too liberal, many gay rights campaigners thought that his previous right-wing views and votes and speeches (for example, when Defence Secretary he supported the policy that gay people should be banned from serving in the Armed Forces) made him a hypocrite. As the *Daily Record* (PORTILLO ON WAY BACK WITH EURO WARNING, 3 November 1999) noted, when he stood for re-election in 1999, protesters, including Tatchell, demonstrated outside the election count, citing his hypocrisy as the reason. In fact, the majority of his pre-1997 votes on gay rights (when the Conservative Party was in power) were against liberalization.[8] Even post-1997, when Portillo had appar-ently become more liberal, he was absent for various votes on gay rights.[9] Of course, he may have been absent in order to avoid having to choose between voting either with his party or for gay rights when, for instance, the Party instructed its MPs to vote against liberalization. Yet, Portillo was prepared to vote against gay rights post-1997 (*e.g.* 2000's Local Government Bill [Lords] — Prohibition on Promotion of Homosexuality: Bullying, when he voted with his party).[10] And, he was also willing to vote against his party if needed (*e.g.* 2002's Adoption and Children Bill — Suitability of Adopters, when he voted against the Party whip and even spoke out against the wisdom of it in the preceding House of Commons debate).[11] Portillo's somewhat confused voting pattern is symptomatic of the Conservative Party's confused position on gay rights in the past.

## Alan Duncan

### *A New Conservative Attitude?*

In mid-2002, after deciding that he should no longer have to hide his homosexuality, Alan Duncan (MP for Rutland and Melton 1992–) became the first serving Conservative MP to voluntarily "come out" as gay. The reaction of the press — tabloid and broadsheet newspapers from both sides of the political divide — was very positive, particularly when compared to Portillo's press coverage a few years earlier; virtually every newspaper reported the story in a straightforward and non-judgemental manner (the main news pages at least, as opposed to the more independent columnists), the broadsheets in particular. The broadsheets used Duncan's "self-outing" to discuss wider issues such as the Conservative Party and homosexuality, in particular how Party members would react to Duncan's announcement (for instance, *The Times* [29 July 2002] noted "SENIOR TORY'S GAY REVELATION TO TEST PARTY"). This could be seen as evidence that recognition (Frame One) was edging closer. In fact, many broadsheet newspapers saw Duncan's proclamation as proof of a newfound *public* tolerance in the Conservative Party (*i.e.* "keeping it private" was no longer necessary). Certainly, the Conservative Party hierarchy praised Duncan for "coming out", both publicly and privately; Iain Duncan Smith, then leader, praised Duncan's honesty and offered his "personal support" (*London Evening Standard*, COMING OUT EARNS ALAN DUNCAN SUPPORT OF LEADER AND JOB HINT, 29 July 2002).

While some Party members were unhappy about Duncan's announcement, they were not excessively vocal. Those members that were outspoken tended to take issue with Duncan speaking publicly about his homosexuality, rather than his homosexuality *per se* (suggesting that for the more the traditional Conservative members, "keeping it private" was still important). As Norman Tebbit (MP for Epping 1970–4 and Chingford 1974–92) wrote in *The Spectator* (WHO CARES WHAT ALAN DUNCAN DOES UNDER HIS DUVET? WHAT THE TORIES NEED IS POLITICAL CLOUT, 3 August 2002): "The great mass of us have no desire to emulate Mr Duncan's activities under his duvet; we do not think it our business exactly what he does do there; we do not wish to join in; we just wish profoundly that he would not bore us with his sexual problems. We would prefer him to get on with finding answers to our problems of healthcare, crime, pensions, excessive taxation, uncontrolled mass immigration, traffic congestion, lousy schools, environmental pollution and more." Matthew Parris, writing in *The Times* (NOT IN FRONT OF THE VOTERS, 30 July 2002), stated that Duncan's political and press acceptance proved that such a response was losing resonance: "that he [Duncan] was able as a frontbencher even to contemplate such honesty speaks volumes about the [Party's] change. For Tories, the changed approach has not been to homosexuality, but to openness. Homosexuality has never been a problem for top Tories — any more than adultery . . . But there was a code among us, and it was under-stood: 'Not in front of the constituents.' So you didn't campaign for reform of the law, you didn't advocate social change in public and you didn't talk about yourself."

There were one or two examples of tabloid press insensitivity in the reporting of Duncan's declaration. The *Daily Star* used Duncan's "self-outing" to urge all gay politicians to "come out", and for politi-cians in general to be more honest about their private lives. The paper stated in a leader article headed "A GAY TORY SHOWS WAY" (30 July 2002): "Should we care that a politician is gay? . . . But politicians are always sticking their noses into OUR private lives. They constantly bang on about whether we should get married, how old we must be to have sex, and who we can have that sex with. So it's only fair to know where they're coming from when they get all high and mighty. MPs have to state financial interests — why not personal interest too? Make them state if they're gay, having an affair, on their third wife, trapped in a loveless relationship or into a bit of bondage." According to the *Daily Star*, politicians should not only be judged on their politics, they should also be judged on the way they live their lives in order to expose hypocrisy and the possibility of hidden interest. Seaton (2003) states that one of the media's defences is that democracy depends on the scrutiny of public power and how it can be used to further private ends. While that may be the case in theory, in practice the press often goes further than it should (in relation to Press Complaints Commission criteria). Interestingly, the above quote from the *Daily Star* equates homosexuality with other apparent "immoral" activities such as extra-marital sex, thus suggesting that homosexuality as a whole is morally wrong. However, while troubling, that type of comment was not common or representative of the (tabloid) press as a whole.

This was further shown in 2008, when Duncan announced that he was having a civil partnership ceremony with his male partner. The press reaction — tabloid and broadsheet — to his announcement, and the ceremony itself, was very upbeat; the events were either not covered at all, or if they were, the coverage was very positive, without the use of negative binary themes or stereotyping, with Duncan's civil part-nership emphasizing his positive mediated persona. As *The Sun* (26 July 2008) put it, "TRUE BLUE LOVE TORY". In fact, Duncan was interviewed in *The Sunday Times* (MY BIG FAT GAY TORY WEDDING, 9 March 2008) and the *Daily Telegraph* ("I'M AN MP WHO HAPPENS TO BE GAY"; ALAN DUNCAN IS THE FIRST LEADING TORY TO ENTER INTO A CIVIL PARTNERSHIP. HE TELLS NEIL TWEEDIE HOW IT CAME ABOUT, 5 March

2008) about the forthcoming ceremony. Both interviews took the opportunity to discuss wider issues such as the Conservative Party and gay rights, but otherwise were very straightforward.

## Kissing and Telling

The biggest disappointment for Duncan in relation to his press coverage was a "kiss and tell" story in *The Mail on Sunday* (4 August 2002) a few days after the original story broke. In an article headed "MY SECRET GAY KISSES AND CUDDLES WITH ALAN DUNCAN IN COMMONS", a supposed ex-partner of Duncan's expanded on their relationship and declared: "I suppose I was surprised when he cuddled me in the kitchen and, after going upstairs to show me the rest of the house, we ended up in bed. I'm quite a shy and considered person and I don't usually take things so fast. But Alan is not backward in coming forward and I didn't reject his advances." The article was not in the public interest at all, although it can be classified as reportage rather than manufacturing (like most of the articles on Duncan's sexuality), because the paper was reacting to someone's decision to sell their story. The article categorized Duncan as a seductive, sexually active gay man who would not commit to a younger partner portrayed as "betrayed", "bitter" and "seduced". Duncan's categorization as a "predatory" gay man further emphasizes the idea that gay relationships are entirely about sex, and the notion that all gay men want to seduce younger men (something expanded upon by Sanderson 1995). As with Mandelson, the presence of "a young gay lover half his [Duncan's] age", added to the article's sensationalism. But, unlike Mandelson, whose representation leans towards the "bad" (due to his refusal to be as open as the press would like), Duncan can be considered a "good" gay MP; he may have once been "in" (to the press), but his later openness actually negates that. Duncan's status as the first openly gay Conservative Member of Parliament, and the lack of real sexual scandal surrounding his press coverage (after all, the "kiss and tell" did not reveal anything particularly shocking, just the details of a rather ordinary relationship), also makes Duncan a "good" gay MP.

There was a distinct lack of gossip about Duncan's sexuality before his "self-outing", meaning that the press did not approach his private life in a hysterical, fervent manner. The fact that Duncan "came out" voluntarily was also a factor in his positive representation. Duncan's predominantly positive press coverage (most newspapers did not follow up the "kiss and tell" story) was also a consequence of his political acceptability; Duncan was not particularly controversial (although he was involved in a minor financial scandal in 1994) or hypocritical, and was in fact one of the few Conservative MPs to vote to lower the age of consent for gay men to sixteen in 1994,[12] and a regular speaker in House of Commons debates on gay issues. Duncan did give in to the Party whip though in relation to the Adoption and Children Bill; in 2001 and 2002 Duncan voted with his party and thus technically against gay rights (the Conservatives were attempting to prevent unmarried couples, heterosexual and gay, from adopting children).[13] It could be said that the vote was less about letting gay couples adopt, than about letting *unmarried* couples adopt (something claimed by the Conservative Party leadership). However, Duncan was absent for another vote on the Adoption and Children Bill in 2002,[14] thus managing to avoid voting in a way that could be considered problematic.

## Duncan's Political Ambitions

Although Duncan's "self-outing" was predominantly well received, it may have had an impact on his political ambitions, as with Portillo's confession of past gay experiences. In 2005 Duncan considered standing for the leadership of the Conservative Party — a result of Michael Howard's (Conservative MP for Folkestone and Hythe 1983–2010 and Conservative leader 2003–5) decision to stand down as Party leader — but quickly pulled out of the race once he realized he did not have the political or media support that he needed. While Duncan was never a serious candidate when compared to someone like David Cameron, his homosexuality appears to have affected his support. Duncan hinted that was so in the *Guardian* (THE TORY TABLIBAN MUST BE ROOTED OUT: THE CONSERVATIVES NEED A LEADER WHO CAN MODERNISE THE PARTY AND TACKLE ITS MORALISING WING: IT WON'T BE ME, 18 July 2005) when he announced his decision to withdraw from the leadership race: "Our achilles heel, though, has been our social attitude. Censorious judgmentalism from the moralizing wing, which treats half our own countrymen as enemies, must be rooted out. We should take JS Mill as our lodestar, and allow people to live as they choose until they actually harm someone. If the Tory Taliban can't get that, they'll condemn us all to oblivion. Thank heavens for the new intake of MPs who do." While his comment was not representative of the tabloid media, Paul Routledge in the *Daily Mirror* (VOTE IS SUCH BAD NOSE FOR DAVIS, 22 July 2005) responded to Duncan's decision by saying that he had "flounced out" of the leadership race, thus undermining Duncan's political status, effeminizing him, and resorting to a gay stereotype. Parris's claim that "there has been a change in the stratosphere among Conservatives" (*The Times*, NOT IN FRONT OF THE VOTERS, 30 July 2002) seems overly optimistic in relation to Duncan's experiences; while Duncan was able to "come out", the notion of a gay Conservative Party leader was perhaps a step too far at the time.

## Clive Betts

In early 2003 *The Sun* newspaper claimed that Betts was in a relationship with an alleged part-time rent-boy from Brazil, whom he also employed in his Commons office. In a front-page article headed "GAY MP AND THE RENT BOY; SECURITY SCANDAL" (26 February 2003) the newspaper claimed that "A top Labour MP has hired a Brazilian rent boy to work in the House of Commons. Smitten Clive Betts, 53, employed lover Jose Gasparo, 20, as a research assistant. But the move has sparked major security fears because Betts met the man just two months ago when he worked in a seedy escort agency in London . . . Betts now wants Gasparo to get a Commons pass — but security chiefs fear the rent boy could pass on sensitive information to other clients." Betts's press coverage is especially interesting because it is often suggested that homosexuals are a particular risk to security. In fact, Herek (1990) notes (in relation to US Government security clearances) that there are three frequently raised objections to granting gay people security clearance: first, gay people are more likely than heterosexual people to have psychological problems; second, gay people are more susceptible to being blackmailed; and third, gay people are less likely to be trustworthy and rule abiding. Thus, as a suggested gay man, Gasparo was deemed particularly risky, especially given the fact that he purportedly worked in the sex industry.

When writing about the "massage parlour" Gasparo allegedly worked at, *The Sun* used the words "seedy", "sordid", "reeking" and "sweat" (SEX FOR SALE AT SORDID PARLOUR, 26 February 2003). While similar words are used in relation to heterosexual sexual scandals (particularly those involving prostitutes), their use in the article — alongside "rent boys", "gay escort" and "half-naked men" — highlights the "dirtiness" of Betts's homosexuality (clean/dirty being a binary theme of Frame Three). Other male sex workers are referred to as "boys" thus suggesting a subtle link between homosexuality and paedophilia. Generally, though, *The Sun*'s press coverage was in typical tabloid style, illustrating that the newspaper now reported heterosexual and homosexual sexual scandals in a very similar manner. For example, the "SEX FOR SALE" article even declared that the reporter visiting the parlour "made his excuses and left" when offered sexual services, a well-used heterosexual "kiss and tell" phrase (as just one of many examples, a reporter for the *People* "made his excuses and left" when investigating a council worker who allegedly also worked as a prostitute [HARLOT OF NOISE, 13 January 2008]). To use another binary theme of Frame Three, *The Sun* categorized Betts as a "dangerous" gay MP; the link to prostitution and massage parlours ensured that his sexuality could not be considered "acceptable" (in heterosexual public space — Frame Two — or indeed in any space). Coincidentally, Betts did "come out" to his local newspaper a few days before the article in *The Sun* appeared, but denied it was an attempt to pre-empt his "scandal". Betts's public acknowledgment of his homosexuality may have meant that the press could now define him (and thus itself in opposition to him), but Betts's lack of previous candour, the allegations surrounding prostitution, and the fact that the admission may have been forced, counteracted it, making him far from a "good" gay MP in *The Sun*'s eyes (Frame Three).

Other tabloid newspapers covered the story, although with less zeal than *The Sun*. Many echoed the security-risk fears, and also used similar, evocative words, particularly the right-wing *Daily Mail* (BETTS FACES CALLS TO RESIGN OVER CLAIMS THAT HE MISLED VOTERS; BRAZILIAN RENT BOY CLAIMS BETTS PAID HIM 70 POUNDS FOR SEX, 28 February 2003). The *Daily Mirror*, while less sensationalist, was not sympathetic; Betts was listed in its "TERRIBLE TEN" MPs, all of whom had brought "ridicule on themselves" (17 June 2003). Sections of the tabloid press not only condemned Betts because he was deemed a threat to security, but also because the story became more and more "muddied" as time went on, causing Betts's honesty to be questioned (*Daily Mail*, THE MP AND THE RENTBOY — WHO'S LYING?, 28 February 2003). In fact, as suggested by the title of the first *Daily Mail* article, Gasparo later claimed that Betts had in fact paid him for sex, suggesting that Betts lied about first meeting him at a social event. Broadsheet newspapers also covered Betts's predicament, although as with previous sexual scandals and "outings", reported it in a straightforward manner. Betts's "outing" and the justification given for the story were not universally popular; more "liberal" broadsheet newspapers such as the *Guardian* suggested that "security" was "an old excuse for what otherwise appear to be intrusive stories" (SUN'S OUTING OF MP ADDS TO PUSH

FOR PRESS CONTROLS, 27 February 2003). Indeed, *The Sun*'s earlier claim that gay men and women would never again be "outed" unless there was overwhelming public interest in the story does not hold up when scrutinized; House of Commons pass holders are subject to strict scrutiny designed to weed out potential security risks, and it was claimed that Betts had abandoned the application for a pass for Gasparo before the story even broke.

In response to the *Guardian*'s claims, many tabloid newspapers claimed that it was not Betts's homosexuality that was the problem, but his "sleaziness". The *People* (VOICE OF THE PEOPLE: A SQUALID AFFAIR, 2 March 2003) stated: "Talking of political correctness, the outpouring of it which followed the gay revelations about Labour MP Clive Betts was truly stomach-turning. Newspapers who criticized the MP for hiring a male prostitute as his Commons researcher were accused of homophobia and targeting Betts because he is gay. Yet if Mr Betts was heterosexual and the Brazilian rent-boy had been a South American vice girl the affair would be equally scandalous. It is not the gender of a lover half Mr Betts's age which makes this sorry business so seedy, squalid and sordid. It's the fact that he was prepared to lavish taxpayers' money on a disgusting piece of low life who charges for sex." That is not quite true. While Betts was condemned by much of the press for his foolishness rather than his sexuality, his homosexuality made the stakes much higher. So, his transgressions could not only be portrayed as "sleazy", but also — on a more implicit level — as a threat to the "norm" (*i.e.* heterosexuality and family life). While not a gay rights campaigner, Betts consistently voted in a pro-gay manner.[15] Betts's lack of hypocrisy and pro-gay voting record further illustrates the problematic nature of his press coverage; while many newspapers claimed that there was justification for his "outing", much of the tabloid press coverage was unnecessarily prurient and can be considered manufacturing. Despite his negative press coverage, and the fact he was eventually found guilty of breaching the MPs' code of conduct by agreeing to copy a doctored document which Gasparo hoped would allow him to extend his stay in Britain, and for damaging public confidence in the integrity of Parliament by applying for a security pass for Gasparo, Betts has since carried on as a successful backbench MP.

## Chris Bryant

### *Valley of "Shame"*

When Bryant (Labour MP for Rhondda Valley 2001– ) stood as an openly gay candidate at the 2001 General Election he seemed to have everything going for him: he was uncontroversial politically and sexually; his openness meant that the press could not "out" him against his will; and, following on from the public's acceptance of Twigg, Bradshaw *et al.*, he knew that public and press knowledge of his sexuality would not hold him back politically. Bryant's selection as a candidate in the solidly working class Rhondda Valley showed how far gay politicians had come over the preceding decades; local Party members were more upset that Bryant had once been a member of the Conservative Party than the fact he was gay. However, in late 2003 Bryant was embarrassed when the press published a picture of him wearing just a pair of Y-front underpants taken from the gay dating site *Gaydar*. Along with the picture, it was suggested that Bryant had sent a series of sexually explicit messages to a man he met on the website who he then arranged to meet. The tabloid press revelled in Bryant's embarrassment. Alongside the photograph of Bryant in his underwear, headlines read "PANTS MP IN VALLEY OF SHAME" (*Daily Star*, 1 December 2003) and "BLAIR ALLY IN GAY WEBSITE STORM" (*Daily Mail*, 1 December 2003).

Words used to describe the emails include "graphic", "obscene", "disgusting" and "lewd", highlighting the sexual nature of the messages, and the fact that the sex itself (whether or not it actually took place) should be thought of as "dirty" (Frame Three). *The Mail on Sunday* (POSING IN HIS Y-FRONTS FOR A WEBSITE CALLED GAYDAR, THE MP WHO HELPED SCRAP BAN ON GAY SEX IN PUBLIC, 30 November 2003) pointed out that many of the messages were "unprintable in a family newspaper, even with asterisks", placing Bryant in direct opposition to "sanitary" heterosexual family life (his sexual behaviour had crossed the acceptability threshold — Frame Two). Bryant is categorized as a sexually active gay man and, to make matters worse, that sex (or the arrangements surrounding the sex) was "unconventional" and "dangerous". Unlike Twigg, Bradshaw *et al.*, who are somewhat desexualized (although not completely, because as gay men there is an assumption made about their sexual lives which underpins representation, namely that penetration is the default sexual act between gay men, as suggested in recent House of Lords debates about homosexuality [Baker 2004]), and like Proctor, whose "unusual" sex life appeared on the front-page of every newspaper, Bryant's overt sexuality — which does not appear to meet the (heterosexual or homosexual) "norm" — made him "dangerous" (Frame Three). Bryant's public self became defined by his private sexuality and did not enter the "zone of privacy" defined by Storr. While homosexuality has become more publicly visible in recent years, Bryant's homosexuality was the unacceptable face of it. As Richardson (2004) notes, many of the equal rights gained by gay people in recent years relate to sexual coupledom, thus leading to a desexualizing of gay people; gay people must therefore conform to an idea of sexual citizenship that pushes the idea of sexuality being private within a normative public (*i.e.* gay sexual relationships should be modelled in relation to heteronormative ones). Bryant did not meet these criteria.

Some tabloid newspapers linked the furore with the Government's sexual offences legislation, suggesting that Bryant had some kind of hidden agenda; the *Daily Mail* article stated that "[the revelations] raised questions about his role in forcing through controversial Government legislation which scrapped a ban on gay men using parks and public lavatories to 'cruise' for sex." The *Daily Mail* also questioned whether Bryant could be left open to blackmail, noting that he "gave the man his full address and mobile phone number, possibly leaving himself open to the threat of blackmail." As Weeks (1981a) notes, the link between homosexuals and blackmail dates back as far as the Cold War and McCarthyism. While it is true that someone in receipt of such emails could have blackmailed Bryant, it had nothing to do with the situation in itself; a politician (whether heterosexual of homosexual) could just as easily be threatened by a partner met in a more conventional manner. Still, the notion of possible blackmail, combined with the suggestion of a hidden agenda, gave the paper a public interest justification for publishing the story, even though the stories were completely manufactured.

## Nonchalance?

As with many post-1997 gay politicians, the broadsheet press was predominantly respectful of Bryant, with some sympathetic (*Guardian*, ACTIVISTS TO DECIDE ON GAY WEBSITE MP, 4 December 2003), perhaps encouraged by Bryant's no-nonsense response to the situation. Like the tabloid newspapers, many broadsheet newspapers commented on the fact that Bryant was wearing Y-fronts (often using columnists to discuss the issue). However, unlike the tabloids, broadsheet newspapers took a light-hearted tone when discussing or mentioning Bryant's choice of underwear. For instance, *The Sunday Times* (7 December 2003) stated "BLAIR'S ATTACK POODLE SAYS PANTS TO THE LOT OF YOU", highlighting and making fun of Bryant's attire simultaneously. Many broadsheet newspapers used Bryant's predicament to discuss wider issues, such as his political future, Welsh politics and gay online-dating. *The Independent on Sunday* (7 December 2003), for example, wrote an in-depth article about the *Gaydar* website captioned "FOCUS: WHY THE REST OF THE WORLD IS WATCHING". It could be argued that the broadsheet press uses "nonchalance" as a cover for discussing the private lives of gay MPs and other public figures. Nonetheless, the broadsheet press's general indifference was perhaps more in keeping with the public mood than that of the tabloids. While many members of the public quoted by the tabloids found Bryant's suggested behaviour unacceptable (otherwise, why would the comments be considered newsworthy?), Bryant's Y-fronts (presented as an unfashionable choice) seemed to be of most interest to those people quoted (*Daily Mail*, HOW GAY IS MY VALLEY, 4 December 2003), hence the papers labelling Bryant the "pants MP".

The Labour Party echoed the broadsheets' lack of concern about Bryant's behaviour. In fact, the Labour hierarchy declined to condemn Bryant publicly, stating that the matter was a private one. Bryant was supported by his party because he was "on-message" politically, free from hypocrisy, "out" as gay and thus a "good" gay man, and — before the *Gaydar* incident — non-threatening sexually (*i.e.* "safe" rather than "dangerous", to use a binary of Frame Three). While Bryant lost credibility after the *Gaydar* episode, and sections of the tabloid press presented him as "dangerous", he stayed an MP with no serious pressure on him to quit (pressure which would have been more likely in the late 1980s/early 1990s, showing that the press/public *were* more tolerant, even if whole recognition had not been met — Frame One) and continued to support gay issues without much media comment. In fact, Bryant — both before and after his controversy — continuously voted for gay rights in the House of Commons.[16] Bryant's strong voting and campaigning record emphasizes the flimsiness of a public interest excuse for his media exposure: Bryant was an "out", single, young gay man living his life free of hypocrisy and illegality.

# Mark Oaten

## *Scandal!*

In early 2006, the Liberal Democrat's Mark Oaten was reported by the *News of the World* as having had affairs with rent-boys, sourced via the gay dating website *Gaydar*, while married with a young family. The newspaper (LIB-DEM RENT BOY SCANDAL, 22 January 2006) said "he paid rent boys for kinky sex" and (MP SEX SHOCKER, 22 January 2006) "British Liberal Democrat leadership challenger Mark Oaten has been leading a sordid secret double life — sneaking off from Parliament to pay rent boys for three-in-a-bed sex . . . One young male prostitute told us: 'Oaten was a regular punter for six months. He loved gay sex and humiliation'." As a result of the exposé, Oaten resigned his front-bench opposition post and withdrew from the Liberal Democrat leadership contest. He was clearly given a negative mediated persona and categorized using negative binary themes (Frame Three): the sexual acts he was supposed to have engaged in were seen as "dirty" and "dangerous", his sexuality was at the forefront of the story with an air of "publicness" about it (the *Gaydar* allegations), his sexuality was difficult to pin down (he did not admit to being gay) making him "bad", and he was therefore seen as being "in" rather than "out" (regardless of whether or not he was gay). Once again the youthfulness of his alleged partner was highlighted, via use of the word "young", echoing earlier case studies.

The *Daily Express* (23 January 2006) headlined an article "LIB DEMS IN CRISIS OVER GAY SEX SHAME". While the article may have been referring to the alleged affair as being shameful, rather than gay sex *per se*, such a connotation is certainly suggested in the headline, even if unintentionally. The *Daily Mail* (DEVOTED FATHER AND THE £80 AN HOUR RENT BOY, 23 January 2006) found it strange that someone as "ordinary" as Oaten could possibly be gay or have experimented with gay sex: "Days ago Oaten was displaying his family to the world with real pride as he threw his hat into the ring for the Lib-Dem leadership . . . 'It never occurred to anybody that he could be gay,' said one of his fellow Lib-Dem MPs yesterday. 'I just don't see it. He's an ordinary bloke, quite sociable in his way, working his way up in the party. We knew he was ambitious his summer and Christmas drinks parties for friends and journalists made that clear enough. But gay? Rent boys? Never'." The safe/dangerous binary (Frame Three) is very clear in Oaten's case, with his alleged behaviour stepping over the acceptability threshold, with Stephen Glover in the *Daily Mail* (26

January 2006) asking "EVEN FOR THE LIBDEMS, IS THIS A DEPRAVITY TOO FAR?" The question refers to the sort of sexual activity Oaten was suspected of (of which Glover writes, "It seems to me that what he did was so depraved that it is absolutely in the public interest that we should know about it.") rather than gay sexual behaviour in itself, but the notion of some sexual acts, even when legal, being more acceptable than others, is clear.

Broadsheets reported the story in a straightforward manner, although made sure to include all of the details. For example, *The Sunday Times* (LIB DEM CONTENDER OATEN RESIGNS OVER RENT BOY CLAIM, 22 January 2006) noted that "According to the News of the World, the relationship with the rent boy lasted through 2004 and into 2005 with a long series of secret meetings. The newspaper claimed Oaten had regularly paid £80 a time for sex with the man, but on one occasion had a sex session with him and another male prostitute for £140." Various broadsheets discussed sex scandal politicians more generally and what drove Oaten to apparently take risks with his personal and therefore political life, such as the *Daily Telegraph* (23 January 2006) who asked "WHAT POSSESSED HIM TO TAKE SUCH A RISK?". Bruce Anderson in *The Independent* (THE JUDICIARY MUST PROTECT THE PRIVATE LIVES OF PUBLIC FIGURES FROM PRESS INTRUSION, 23 January 2006) was very sympathetic, claiming that he could not "see that Mark Oaten has done anything very wrong. Nor can I see why his sexual peccadillo should destroy his career. But it probably will. Although we need a law of privacy to restrain the red tops' bestial behaviour, many more careers will be shattered and many more families reduced to misery before one is passed." Oaten could certainly not be accused of behaving hypocritically in relation to his voting record, even if some accused him of being hypocritical in relation to his personal life (being married while allegedly cheating).[17]

## A Tainted Reputation

Oaten decided to remain an MP, until stepping down in 2010, embarking on a somewhat confessional relationship with the press, describing in *The Times* (OUT OF CONTROL, 7 May 2006) how, along with his unhappiness at work, his baldness was the catalyst for his behaviour: "I doubt that, on its own, my dissatisfaction with politics would have prompted me to act as I did, but it coincided with something of a mid-life crisis. I was turning 40 and I really felt that I was losing my youth. The problem was undoubtedly compounded by my dramatic loss of hair in my late thirties. This really knocked me for six. I started to look noticeably older." His explanation was widely mocked in the press, although some articles were sympathetic about the possible impact of hair loss. In an unusual twist, the confessional approach extended to Oaten's wife, who told *Hello* magazine (April 2006) in a five page interview that she and her husband were receiving therapy. In 2009, while still an MP, Oaten published a book titled *Screwing Up*, detailing his experiences, revealing that he was sexually abused as a child. In it he admits visiting a male prostitute, but denies having sexual intercourse.

In common with "scandalous" politicians before him, Oaten is forever identified with his story. Many articles about him years later refer to rent-boys and baldness. For instance, when it was revealed that he would become Chief Executive of the International Fur Trade Federation, the *Daily Mirror* (FUR JOB FURY, 23 March 2011) noted he "quit after cheating on his wife with a rent boy." And, in an article about MPs expenses, *The Sunday Times* (LOOPHOLE GAVE MPS' SPOUSES EURO-BREAKS, 4 April 2010) wrote "Among the MPs to have charged a spouse's ticket to the taxpayer is Mark Oaten, the disgraced Liberal Democrat MP for Winchester, who is standing down at the general election following his involvement in a rent boy scandal." His earlier brush with "scandal" is irrelevant to those stories, but it is still highlighted. However, while he will forever be discussed in relation to his negative press coverage, it is important to recognize that the coverage was and is not explicitly homophobic (for example, utilizing discriminatory words), in the manner of many earlier politicians. That said, his behaviour is still deemed unacceptable, suggesting that his alleged acts were unsuitable ones whether they took place in private or public (Frame Two). That would almost certainly have been the case if he had been accused of seeing female prostitutes (giving some of the binary themes of Frame Three a universal aspect), but the idea that it was a shock that someone like him — "ordinary", a father — could possibly be gay or have engaged in gay sexual acts, suggests that recognition (Frame One) has not been reached completely; the homosexual aspect of the scandal adds an extra edge to Oaten's press coverage, and recognition would only be reached when that is not the case.

## Simon Hughes

*Revisiting the Past*

Just a few days after Oaten received his negative press coverage, Simon Hughes (Liberal Democrat MP for Bermondsey 1983, Southwark and Bermondsey 1983–97, North Southwark and Bermondsey 1997–2010 and Bermondsey and Old Southwark 2010– ), also standing for leadership of the Liberal Democrats, was also the focus of intense press speculation about his sexuality. Hughes was "outed" by *The Sun* after the paper told him that they had proof of his use of a gay chat service. The news was deemed particularly interesting by much of the press because it was Hughes who stood against Tatchell in the 1983 Bermondsey by-election, an election described by *Gay News* as "THE MOST HOMOPHOBIC BY-ELECTION OF OUR TIMES" (3 March 1983), during which the Liberals were accused of courting anti-gay feeling (Rayside 1998). As with Oaten, the stories were manufactured, although *The Sun* could claim the story was in the public interest as it exposed apparent hypocrisy. Hughes's case was not helped by the fact he denied being gay in the wake of Oaten's scandal, telling *The Independent* (SIMON HUGHES: "I HAVEN'T BEEN AS SUCCESSFUL AS I WOULD HAVE LIKED", 16 January 2006) "No, I'm not [gay] . . . But it absolutely should not matter if I was." While it is true he is not gay, the fact he did not address his *bisexuality* was seen as disingenuous by many newspapers.

*The Sun* (26 January 2006) headed its front-page article: "A SECOND LIMP-DEM CONFESSES: I'M GAY TOO". The homophobic nature of "Limp" Dem is very clear. Hughes told the paper, "I am perfectly willing to say that I have had both homosexual and heterosexual relationships in the past. I hope that does not disqualify me from doing a good job in public life and I propose to carry on doing that with the usual enthusiasm and determination." In relation to his statement, *The Sun*'s headline is a good example of how the press categorizes non-heterosexual politicians as either homosexual or heterosexual (a strict binary approach): as with Davies's earlier press coverage, Hughes's bisexuality is pushed to one side, even though he made it very clear that he had had relationships with women as well as men. In terms of the acceptability scale (see figure 2.1), bisexuality — as a sexuality, as well as in relation to acts/expressions — would be below the acceptability threshold (Frame Two), as it is not even acknowledged in much of Hughes's press coverage, let alone discussed. Hughes's previous lack of candour meant that he was "bad", with the chat line element nudging him towards "dangerous" as well (Frame Three). However, the fact he very quickly addressed his sexuality meant that his press coverage was not as hostile as it could have been, making his negative mediated persona much less severe than Oaten's.

## Truth and Lies

Other tabloids followed up the story, focusing on the fact that Hughes apparently "lied" about his sexuality (he was "in" rather than "out", to use another binary of Frame Three), also categorizing Hughes as gay and ignoring his bisexuality. The *Daily Express* said on the 26th January 2006, "I'M GAY TOO: SHOCK ADMISSION BY HUGHES", the *Evening Standard* "YES BUT NO BUT I'M GAY AFTER ALL, SAYS HUGHES; LIB DEM HOPEFUL ADMITS HOMO-SEXUAL AFFAIRS AFTER TWO DENIALS", and the *Daily Mail* "I AM GAY, SAYS LIB DEM HOPEFUL SIMON HUGHES". While in the minority, a few columnists made questionable comments, such as the *Daily Mirror*'s Paul Routledge (HUGHES HE THINK HE'S KIDDING, 27 January 2006) who said "I do not think the elec-torate is yet ready to put a gay into Number Ten, and that is the basis on which any party leader must be chosen . . . And I'm a bit worried about Ming Campbell [another candidate], the leadership front-runner. Didn't he spend much of his youth chasing young men round a track with a stick in his hand?" Again, "youth", and all its connota-tions, is mentioned. Lowri Turner, in the *Western Mail* (HOWEVER MUCH I LOVE MY GAY FRIENDS, I DON'T WANT THEM RUNNING THE COUNTRY, 27 January 2006), claimed that "Frankly, I don't trust a man who says he swings both ways, unless he is a spotty teenager who hasn't sorted himself out yet . . . Those who claim to be bisexual are simply trying to fudge the truth." She also said that gay men do not make good leaders or prime ministers because "Their lifestyles are too divorced from the norm. They are not better or worse, but they are different." So, not only is bisexuality pushed to one side, it is completely denied as a valid sexuality, with the notion of the "norm" firmly established as heterosexual.

Unsurprisingly, the broadsheets took a straightforward approach, also discussing Hughes's supposed "lie" as well as the ramifications for the Liberal Democrat leadership contest, with *The Times* (27 January 2006) concluding "BETTER OUT THAN IN" and *The Independent* on the same day "ANOTHER DAY, ANOTHER LIB DEM DISASTER; HUGHES ADMITS HE LIED ABOUT HIS SEXU-ALITY". The *Guardian*'s Philip Hensher (OUT AND PROUD?, 27

January 2006) questioned whether the Liberal Democrats should have a leader who was not upfront about their sexuality, writing: "Hughes is right: the fact of someone being homosexual should not debar them from holding high political office. But it ought to be someone who regards their homosexuality just as a heterosexual regards their sexuality: unremarkable, uninteresting to strangers, not worth talking about and, for many reasons, not worth thinking about concealing or lying about." That sounds a lot like recognition (Frame One), but it would be difficult for Hughes or any non-heterosexual politician to take such an approach unless the press did too. Indeed, many newspapers criticized Hughes for not being "open" and answering questions about his sexuality honestly, but was it a question he should ever have been asked in the first place? If recognition means that marginalized groups are entitled to equal rights and respect rather than a grudging or reluctant tolerance, alongside recognition of their own particularity, then the sexuality of a gay or bisexual politician should be something which is recognized, but not treated as unusual or of extra importance. It just *is*.

## After Effects

Likes many MPs before him, Hughes made it clear that he did not want to be seen as a single-issue politician. In an article for *The Independent* (SIMON HUGHES: IN HIS OWN WORDS, 28 January 2006) he wrote: "We really have got to have a society where people don't presume things or label us as this sort of MP or that, whether it's gay or bisexual. I want to be labelled a human rights activist, a campaigner for justice, a fighter for the poor." He also wrote that it was not his intention to lie about his sexuality, but he was in fact "trying to reinforce that barrier around my private life. It is not dishonest to protect your privacy. What I said wasn't morally wrong. It was not factually wrong." That statement did not hold much weight, however, with many newspapers. While Hughes did not win the leadership election, he was made Deputy Leader of the Liberal Democrats in 2010. He was possibly saved by the fact he had a strong voting record on gay rights[18] and after his exposure held his head high and carried on in as normal a manner as possible. His appointment as Deputy Leader gave him the status as the only (openly) gay or bisexual leader or deputy leader of any Westminster political party, now or in the past. Of course, politicians such as Mandelson have been more powerful, even though they have not had an official leadership position, but Hughes's elevation is important, if only for the relative lack of press coverage he received when appointed. It could be a clear sign that as we enter the second decade of the 2000s, whole recognition (Frame One) moves ever closer — or, a result of the lack of importance of Hughes's role in the political and party landscape as a whole.

## Gregory Barker

In late 2006 Barker (MP for Bexhill and Battle 2001– ) was reported by the *Daily Mirror* (26 October 2006) as having left his wife for another man. The headline read "IT'S SUCH A SHOCK . . . BUT MEN THINK THEY CAN GET AWAY WITH IT THESE DAYS — MOTHER-IN-LAW GEORGINA: EXCLUSIVE TOP TORY DUMPS WIFE FOR MAN". The article pointed out that Barker had voted against various pro-gay bills in Parliament,[19] hinting he was a hypocrite (although a "Tory official" quoted in the article pointed out that he was following the party line when voting, and he did in fact vote *for* civil partnerships), meaning that the article, while manufactured, can be seen as meeting the Press Complaints Commission's public interest criteria: "Preventing the public from being misled by an action or statement of an individual or organisation" (PCC 2011).

Other tabloids covered the issue, with the *Evening Standard* (26 October 2006) writing "TORY MP AND A GAY AFFAIR WITH HIS INTERIOR DESIGNER" and the *Daily Record* on the same date "TORY QUITS FAMILY FOR GAY LOVER; MP VOTED AGAINST HOMOSEXUAL RIGHTS". Various tabloids went into more detail about Barker's alleged male partner, with the *Daily Mirror* (28 October 2006) going on to write "THE GAY LOVER; EXCLUSIVE SEX SCANDAL MP'S SECRET BOYFRIEND". The *Daily Mail* and *Mail on Sunday* seemed particularly interested in the supposed partner, with one lengthy article in the former titled "THE GAY TORY MP AND THE DECORATOR; CAMERON ALLY'S MALE LOVER IS A HIGHLIFE SOCIALITE WHO USED TO WORK FOR VISCOUNT LINLEY" (27 October 2006). The main threads of discussion in many of the articles were Barker's "hypocritical" voting record, as well as the notion that by leaving his wife he had therefore left his family. The latter point highlights that newspapers can have a narrow view of what makes a family, because whether in a relationship with his wife or not, he is still the father of his children and they are his family. Two articles used the word "camp" in relation to Barker, with Fraser Nelson in the *News of the Word* (SCANDAL . . . AS USUAL, 29 October 2006) writing "camp Greg Barker", and Paul Routledge in the *Daily Mirror* (27 October 2006) heading an article

"ALL BRIGHT PINK AT CAMP DAVID". The notion that gay men are effeminate is a well trodden path, but the articles were not representative of press coverage as a whole.

Some broadsheets did cover the story, with the *Daily Telegraph* (28 October 2006) writing a rather gossipy story about Barker's alleged partner, under the headline "MP'S GAY LOVER IS HIGH-LIVING STAR OF THE PARTY CIRCUIT INTERIOR DESIGNER WAS A GOSSIP-COLUMN FAVOURITE EVEN BEFORE AFFAIR WITH TORY SPOKESMAN WAS MADE PUBLIC". *The Times* (26 October) went very low-key, writing a 42-word article titled "MP LEAVES WIFE", following it up with a longer article the next day ("TORY LEADER STANDS BY HIS CLOSE ALLY OVER GAY AFFAIR") which discussed what happened but which also went into detail about the Conservative Party's approach to gay rights under Cameron, noting that the Conservative leader was aware of the situation before it reached the press. Generally, though, the broadsheets did not spend much time on the issue — if any — although *The Independent on Sunday* (6 May 2007) did list him in its "PINK LIST 2007", a list of the most influential gay people in Britain.

Barker's case certainly shows how the sexuality of politicians has become less and less important as time has passed; he did not stand down as an MP or have his career affected in a negative way as a result of his press coverage, and in May 2010 he was appointed Minister of State for Energy and Climate Change. It was still the case, though, that his sexuality was of prurient interest, giving the stories about him a more sensationalist edge, suggesting that recognition (Frame One) was not achieved at the time. Barker's mediated persona (Frame Three) leant towards the positive, helped by the fact his sexual life was private with no "unseemly" elements, plus the fact he had not lied about his sexuality beforehand. However, because of the voting record issue his mediated persona was not wholly positive, showing their graduated nature. Nonetheless, Barker was presented as "good" (because he seemed comfortable with himself and did not create a fuss) and "safe" (because his sex life was unthreatening and private). So, while press representation had improved, certain categories still had to be met for positive representation to be possible.

## David Laws

David Laws has the ignominy of being Westminster's shortest serving cabinet minister, resigning after just 16 days as Chief Secretary to the

Treasury. The Liberal Democrat was caught up in an expenses scandal, accused by the *Daily Telegraph* of claiming expenses for rent paid to his secret gay partner when it was against parliamentary rules. Laws claimed the reason he had claimed expenses in such a way was to keep the details of his sexuality private (he was not publicly "out" at the time). The *Daily Telegraph* (TREASURY CHIEF, HIS SECRET LOVER AND A £40,000 CLAIM, 29 May 2010) did not intend to disclose Laws's sexuality, but Laws himself disclosed it in a statement to the paper pre-publication, so mentioning it was fair reportage.

The vast majority of Laws's press coverage, both tabloid and broadsheet, was sympathetic about his personal situation, but clear that the issue was not about sexuality, but about expenses. The *People* (LESSON OF LAWS, 30 May 2010) wrote in an editorial: "David Laws' sexuality is not the issue. There is no shame in being gay in Britain today even if the Treasury Secretary did not feel he could be open with his own family and friends. The issue is his use of public money. And paying it to a partner against guidelines laid down by Parliament." *The Mail on Sunday* (A MAN BEHAVING BADLY IS DOING THE RIGHT THING) commented on the same date that "His relationship with James Lundie is not at issue. The problem is that Mr Lundie was both his boyfriend and his landlord, and that he paid his rent with public money. It would have been just as wrong had the relationship been heterosexual." And, the *Observer* wrote: "SORRY, THIS ISN'T ABOUT SEXUALITY. IT'S ABOUT MONEY". One tabloid did step back in time though in relation to the approach it took towards Laws's sexuality. *The Sun* (LAWS EXIT "WON'T WRECK COALITION"; BRITS' VERDICT ON EX-TREASURY CHIEF, 1 June 2010), echoed earlier press coverage by conducting an opinion poll where one of the questions was "Should gay people be cabinet ministers". *The Sun*'s approach was roundly condemned in other newspapers and by gay rights organizations, but the fact that such a poll was conducted, in 2010, shows that the sexuality of politicians is still seen as a contentious issue by some journalists.

Laws's voting record on gay rights is extremely strong,[20] despite his past reticence about his own sexuality, but, even so, his mediated persona (Frame Three) leant towards the negative rather than positive: the fact he was seen as hiding his sexuality (he was "in") and uncomfortable and reticent ("bad"), carried more weight than the positive aspects to his character as a gay man. Even though his press coverage was not about his sexuality, *per se*, the fact that it received so much comment shows that the sexuality of politicians is still a newsworthy topic (even if its newsworthiness has decreased over the years, and to receive really bad coverage particular criteria — including negative binaries — have to be met). Many newspapers covering Laws's story suggested that his sexuality was irrelevant, but perhaps the opposite was the case; his sexuality fed the story, giving it an extra, gossipy dimension, using his public responsibilities to discuss his private sexuality, and vice versa. Anyone reading his press coverage would get the impression that recognition (Frame One) and (public) acceptability (Frame Two) had been reached, and Laws was a fool for not realizing. But, it seems Laws did not think it was the case.

## William Hague

After the 2010 General Election, Hague — previously Conservative Party leader — was appointed Foreign Secretary to the newly formed coalition government. His appointment was soured, however, by gossip about his private life in the autumn of that year, when newspapers followed up on internet-based rumours about his newly appointed male special advisor, whose appointment was deemed strange (Hague now had more special advisers than previous foreign secretaries and the aide had no prior experience in the Foreign Office). Of note is the *Daily Mail*'s article about the appointment, with photos of Hague and his aide walking down a street together in casual clothes (ANOTHER HAGUE SPECIAL ADVISER, 22 August 2010). The press coverage culminated in a *Telegraph* story headed "CABINET MINISTER MAY ACT OVER FALSE CLAIMS OF GAY AFFAIRS" (27 August 2010), in which an unnamed minister was said to be prepared to take legal action if claims he is gay appeared in the mainstream media. All of the speculation prompted the married and heterosexual Hague to release a statement declaring that his aide was not appointed because of an improper relationship between them and he has never had a relationship with a man. He also stated that his marriage was fine and he and his wife had tried multiple times to conceive, without success.

While the articles about Hague were certainly manufactured at first, his statement gave later articles validity. The statement was well covered in both tabloid and broadsheet newspapers. The *Daily Mail* (28 August 2010) said "OUR BABY AGONY", the *Daily Mirror* (1 September 2010) "HAGUE: MY OUTRAGE AT MALE AIDE HOTEL SLUR" (Hague and the aide had shared a twin hotel room during the general election campaign), *The Times* (1 September 2010) "HAGUE DENIES ONLINE RUMOURS OF RELATIONSHIP

WITH ADVISER" and *The Sun* (2 September 2010) "HAGUE FURY: I'M NOT GAY". As with Laws, much of the media coverage questioned Hague's poor political judgement, but there were some troublesome elements to it. Many newspapers highlight his aide's "youthfulness" (he was 25 at the time): the *Mirror* (SILLY BILLY: GAY SEX CLAIMS FIGHT FOR SURVIVAL, 3 September 2010) called him a "young aide", and the *Telegraph* (6 September 2010) noted that "HAGUE TOOK HIS YOUNG ADVISER ON TRIPS BEFORE HE HAD GIVEN HIM JOB". The *Daily Record* (2 September 2010) went as far as to say "HAGUE'S BEDROOM BOY QUITS; FOREIGN SECRETARY'S ASTONISHING STATE-MENT". The link between homosexuality and youth is a frequently made one, as previous case studies have shown. There is also an inference in many articles that being thought of as gay is a slur and something to be upset about; when juxtaposed with Hague's point about trying for a family with his wife, it is not difficult to come to the conclusion that heterosexuality is presented as a welcome "norm" and homosexuality as a disappointing "other". Hague's mediated persona (Frame Three) was a negative one; he was seen as over-anxious and uncomfortable ("bad") and the hints of "youth" gave him a dangerous air, however unfairly.

Hague's tactics were questioned, particularly mentioning his wife and their failure to conceive in his statement to the press. Rumours about his sexuality were not new and he had denied being gay in the past, so it was clearly a frustrating, false allegation for him. But, by denying homosexuality so forcefully (in conjunction with a poor voting record on gay rights, apart from voting to lower the age of consent in 1994[21] and voting for civil partnerships in 2004[22]), it bought the story to the foreground, making it even more of a big deal. As with Laws, the fascination with his sexuality suggests that whole recognition (Frame One) was not present — if it was, the sexuality aspect of the article would not be of particular importance — and public homosexuality (Frame Two) is also problematic. The *Guardian* (WILLIAM HAGUE: PRIVATE LIFE, PUBLIC JUDGEMENTS, 3 September 2010) summed it up well in a leader column: "It has to be said that something is awry when rumours about a politician's sexuality leave him feeling forced to publicise the miscarriages his wife has suffered . . . Homosexuality is not the bar to office that it once was, and yet gay politicians face a distinctive pressure to declare themselves as such. While suggestions that the foreign secretary is anything other than straight are no more than gossip, in a truly tolerant society there would be nothing to gossip about."

## Crispin Blunt and Nigel Evans

The press coverage received by Laws and Hague was intense, almost overwhelmingly so. While not explicitly homophobic, the fact that Laws's sexuality and the gossip surrounding Hague's sexuality received so much press coverage suggests that homosexuality in politics is still an issue of fascination. As such, whole recognition (Frame One) is not yet met. However, Laws and Hague were caught in the midst of wider, political dramas, and sexuality was just one element of their press coverage. Contemporary politicians who "come out" without added political drama, or gossip, or sensationalism, do not receive as much press coverage, demonstrated by the experiences of two Conservative MPs — Crispin Blunt (MP for Reigate 1997– ) and Nigel Evans (MP for Ribble Valley 1992– ) — who in the same year "came out" voluntarily. In August 2010 Blunt took the unusual step of releasing a statement from his office which said: "Crispin Blunt wishes to make it known that he has separated from his wife Victoria. He decided to come to terms with his homosexuality and explained the position to his family." Evans "came out" in December, in an interview with *The Mail on Sunday*. Coverage of their statements, and sexuality, was therefore fair reportage.

*The Sun* (28 August 2010) reported Blunt's announcement with "I'M GAY TORY IN WIFE SPLIT" and the *Daily Mirror* on the same day "PRISONS CHIEF: I'M GAY; DAD OF TWO LEAVES HIS WIFE". The biggest issue for both tabloid and broadsheet newspapers was Blunt's ministerial record (as prisons minister, he was at the time under pressure because of some of his controversial political decisions and announcements), rather than his sexuality, although some newspapers such as the *Daily Express* (TORY MINISTER LEAVES WIFE SAYING "I'M GAY", 28 August 2010) noted his problematic voting record (while he voted for civil partnerships,[23] he voted against lowering the age of consent for gay men to sixteen[24]). Evans's announcement also received little interest, although the *Daily Mail* (18 December 2010) was quick to point out that he'd voted against gay rights in the past, (such as the equalization of the age of consent in 1998[25]): "COMING OUT, THE TORY MP WHO VOTED AGAINST EQUAL RIGHTS FOR GAYS". His interview in *The Mail on Sunday* (GROWING UP IN SOUTH WALES, IT WAS HARD ENOUGH BEING A TORY, LET ALONE BEING GAY. IT WASN'T SO MUCH THE ONLY GAY IN THE VILLAGE AS THE ONLY TORY IN SWANSEA, 19 December 2010) was notable for the fact he claimed a Labour MP had threatened to "out" him (showing, if true, that sexuality can still be a politician weapon), as well as for his understanding of the changes in the Conservative Party and politics as a whole: "I suppressed it. In those days you kept it quiet. It was more or less impossible to enter politics in either party as an openly gay person. When Margaret Thatcher was asked about homosexuals in the party she said, 'Oh, we don't talk about those sort of things.' It was all swept under the carpet. But it has all changed. First we had people coming out as gay MPs, and now openly gay people are being elected to Parliament. It is so much better." His comments are an apt description of how recognition (Frame One) and acceptability (Frame Two) have improved over the last few decades.

Despite their voting records, both Blunt and Evans had positive mediated personas (Frame Three): they were "good", "safe", "clean", "private" and now "out". The lack of press attention they received was clearly linked to the more relaxed position of the Conservative Party under Cameron, as well as more liberal attitudes of the press and public, backed up by the fact that there are other contemporary Conservative (and other party) MPs known to be gay, but who have not received much press comment, if any (and who are not discussed here). However, the move towards a more "equal" representation of sexuality does not necessarily mean that full recognition has finally been achieved. What is important is that Blunt and Evans met positive criteria: it is that which is essential if positive media coverage is to be received. If there is a hint of "dirt", "danger" or "public" sexual activity, for example, then a gay or "outed" politician will be pushed towards the negative. Of course, the extent of negativity in 2010 is much less severe than in 1980 or even 1990, once again showing the graduated nature of mediated personas and binaries, and perhaps how gay "scandal" is becoming similar to heterosexual "scandal" (although some binaries, such as out/in and good/bad apply only, or more strongly, to gay politicians). The fact that the sexuality of Blunt and Evans was still deemed a newsworthy topic (by the press, but also the politicians themselves), however limited that may have been compared to the press coverage of earlier politicians, also signals that whole recognition is not met. But, the fact that MPs who are not "outed" or "scandalous" or do not have a problematic voting record, receive even less press coverage in modern political life, suggests that huge strides have been made and whole recognition may be edging closer (Frame One).

## Conclusion

Building on the previous case study chapters, it is clear that the changing representation of gay politicians (and politicians caught up in a gay "scandal") in the UK press can be understood, discussed and mapped using three interconnected frames within an overarching frame of representation:

1 The move towards recognition
2 Acceptability/time (in relation to "heterosexual public space")
3 Mediated personas as "constructed reality" (of which binary themes are part).

So, gay politicians — or their mediated personas — are represented in newspapers using binary themes, the use of which is fairly consistent, although certain themes may be stronger at particular times (*e.g.* the notion of being "closeted" or "in" was particularly contentious in the late 1990s) and for particular politicians (Frame Three). The binaries are influenced by public opinion towards homosexuality — the move towards recognition (Frame One) — and the acceptability of public homosexuality (Frame Two). The case studies show that while representation has become more liberal, the overarching frame of representation persists.

The representation of gay politicians and politicians caught up in a gay "scandal" in UK newspapers (broadsheet and tabloid) has undoubtedly improved from 1997 to the current day, with gay MPs welcomed by much of the press, suggesting a move from intolerance to tolerance to partial recognition (Frame One). But, even in the twenty-first century, gay politicians often find themselves at the mercy of a powerfully heteronormative, often discriminatory, sensationalist tabloid press. That is why the move towards recognition is partial; they are generally accepted, but only bar "bad" acts and the meeting of certain criteria. As suggested by Sanderson (1995), "unusualness" stands out (whether it relates to sexual acts or homosexuality as a whole). The move towards more liberal press coverage has been gradual, with setbacks (indicating the halting aspect of the process). Indeed, while representations of gay politicians and politicians caught up in a gay scandal in the late 1990s and 2000s were an improvement on those of the early 1990s, gay politicians were still "outed" by tabloids, with their private lives used to define public responsibilities.

From the late 1990s onwards, many gay politicians have decided to voluntarily "come out", which the majority of the press has responded to positively, illustrating a more relaxed attitude toward homosexuality (press and public). However, while homosexuality in itself is no longer a scandal (in the way that it was up until the 1980s), the sexuality of politicians can still be seen by the press as a newsworthy and somewhat controversial topic, suggesting that gay politicians are still discriminated against, even if it is on a more implicit level; through characterization and negative binary themes (Frame Three), and references to the personal (a gay politician is often defined as such above anything else), their problematical status may be made clear. Interestingly, many gay politicians seek to point out that they are not single-issue politicians, thus recognizing that being seen as a "gay politician" can be problematic. In fact, many gay MPs seem to reject being set up as "surrogate" representatives, described by Mansbridge (2003) as when politicians from minority groups represent people from outside of their constituency (so, a gay politician could represent gay people from across the country, rather than just their electoral constituents).

The case studies have revealed that sexual behaviour which is not considered to be the (heterosexual or homosexual) norm intensifies the press coverage of gay politicians and politicians caught up in a gay "scandal", and often leads to vilification; their mediated personas (Frame Three) are more strongly negative (highlighting the fact that mediated personas are graduated within the positive/negative categories, as are the binary themes themselves). The safe/dangerous binary theme suggests that gay politicians who are part of a couple and/or who are engaging in "acceptable" sexual behaviour are considered worthy of press approval. Otherwise, they are considered a threat to the "norm" (the family and heterosexuality), suggesting in turn that the press in general has a narrow view of families and partnerships. The lifestyle of a politician (*i.e.* whether they are voluntarily "out" as gay, or [seemingly happily] acknowledge their homosexuality once "outed") is another important factor in press coverage. If gay politicians are seen as being comfortable in their own skin then the press tends to be much more respectful towards them; a sensational story, as well as a public interest defence (*i.e.* exposing hypocrisy), is not possible. Gay politicians who are open and relaxed can be considered "good" gay MPs; they can be safely pigeonholed and are therefore not a threat to heterosexual society. Further, "good" gay MPs in publicly recognized relationships, such as Bradshaw, can be considered good citizens; through their "normal" relationship, they assert their citizenship rights (Richardson 2004). They are also careful not to cross the acceptability threshold in relation to heterosexual public space (Frame Two).

The fact that the press is more negative towards those politicians who refuse to engage with their sexuality, are uncomfortable or hypocritical ("bad" politicians), but is easier with those who are open and/or confident ("good" politicians) (Frame Three), reveals much about the way the press works. First of all, it reveals that the press (tabloid newspapers in particular) has a distinct view of what should be private and what should be public; total disclosure is the only acceptable option for gay politicians (if they want to receive a wholly positive press), ideally voluntarily, or, if they are "outed", soon after. That said, there is such a thing as too much information; sexual details must be kept private (unless a tabloid newspaper decides to publicize them in a "kiss and tell"), as must any kind of apparent "antagonistic" campaigning activity. Secondly, the high expectations that the press has for gay politicians (and, indeed, any politician or public figure) with regard to openness (and "acceptable" behaviour too), actually contributes to sexual scandals; politicians are ordinary people with ordinary fears, foibles and private lives, who will make mistakes, and to expect otherwise is preposterous. Another reason for the press focus on "bad" gay and "outed" politicians is that the stories are generally more interesting. Certainly, the case studies are not just about sexuality; they all contain an element of scandal and often hypocrisy, all of which make the stories better "value".

Most of the above politicians were able to resume their political careers after their "outings" and/or scandals. If gay, it seems the key to being left alone post-public life is to "come clean" as soon as possible. Interestingly, in recent years gay politicians such as Bryant, Duncan and Barker have received the same sort of press coverage politicians caught up in heterosexual sexual scandals have received, which suggests that while particular stereotypes are often still utilized in the 2000s, explicit homophobia (*e.g.* use of particular words) is much less common; it is often the "kiss and tell" aspect of a gay sexual scandal story which is utilized, rather than its homosexuality. The case studies show that it has always been more common for the press to react to a story such as a "kiss and tell" or another kind of incident such as a politician being arrested for "cruising" (reporting) than to actually "out" a politician just for the sake of it (manufacturing). So, there is almost sexual scandal "equality". However, because homosexuality is often portrayed by the press as different from the "norm", even as "other", stories involving homosexuality often have an extra (negative) edge to them, hence the use of the word "almost".

## Notes

1. For example: Hansard House of Commons Debates (vol. 373) 24 October 2001 (Relationships — Civil Registration); Hansard House of Commons Debates (vol. 373) 29 October 2001 (Adoption and Children Bill — Consideration and Third Reading); Hansard House of Commons Debates (vol. 386) 20 May 2002 (Adoption and Children Bill — General Interpretation, etc.).

2. For example, Davies voted in the following key debates: Hansard House of Commons Debates (vol. 50) 9 December 1983 (Sex Equality Bill); Hansard House of Commons Debates (vol. 124) 15 December 1987 (Local Government Bill — Prohibition on Promoting Homosexuality by Teaching or by Publishing Material) (divisions 116–18); Hansard House of Commons debates (vol. 129) 9 March 1988 (Local Government Bill — Prohibition on Promoting Homosexuality by Teaching or by Publishing Material); Hansard House of Commons Debates (vol. 238) 21 February 1994 (Criminal Justice and Public Order Bill — Amendment of Law relating to).

3. For example, he was absent for the following key debates: Hansard House of Commons Debates (vol. 325) 10 February 1999 (Sexual Offences Amendment Bill); Hansard House of Commons Debates (vol. 253) 5 July 2000 (Local Government Bill [Lords] — Prohibition of Promotion of Homosexuality: Bullying).

4. Hansard House of Commons Debates (vol. 314) 22 June 1998 (Crime and Disorder Bill [Lords] — Reduction in Age at which Certain Sexual Acts are Lawful).

5. An official Government enquiry later found Mandelson not guilty, although much of the media implied that the enquiry was a "whitewash".

6. For example, he voted in the following key debates: Hansard House of Commons Debates (vol. 238) 21 February 1994 (Criminal Justice and Public Order Bill — Amendment of Law relating to); Hansard House of Commons Debates (vol. 238) 21 February 1994 (Criminal Justice and Public Order Bill — Age at which Homosexual Acts are Lawful); Hansard House of Commons Debates (vol. 314) 22 June 1998 (Crime and Disorder Bill [Lords] — Reduction in Age at which Certain Sexual Acts are Lawful).

7. For example, he voted in the following key debates: Hansard House of Commons Debates (vol. 238) 21 February 1994 (Criminal Justice and Public Order Bill — Amendment of Law relating to); Hansard House of Commons Debates (vol. 238) 21 February 1994 (Criminal Justice and Public Order Bill — Age at which Homosexual Acts are Lawful); Hansard House of Commons Debates (vol. 314) 22 June 1998 (Crime and Disorder Bill [Lords] — Reduction in Age at which Certain Sexual Acts are Lawful).

8. For example: Hansard House of Commons debates (vol. 129) 9 March 1988 (Local Government Bill — Prohibition on Promoting Homosexuality by Teaching or by Publishing Material); Hansard House of Commons Debates (vol. 238) 21 February 1994 (Criminal Justice and Public Order Bill — Amendment of Law relating to).

9. For example: Hansard House of Commons Debates (vol. 373) 29 October 2001 (Adoption and Children Bill — Consideration and Third Reading); Hansard House of Commons Debates (vol. 386) 20 May 2002 (Adoption and Children Bill — General Interpretation, etc.); Hansard House of Commons Debates (vol. 401) 10 March 2003 (Local Government Bill — Repeal of Section 2A of Local Government Act 1986) (divisions 108 and 109).

10. Hansard House of Commons Debates (vol. 253) 5 July 2000 (Local Government Bill [Lords] –Prohibition of Promotion of Homosexuality: Bullying).

11. Hansard House of Commons Debates (vol. 392) 4 November 2002 (Adoption and Children Bill –Suitability of Adopters).

12. Hansard House of Commons Debates (vol. 238) 21 February 1994 (Criminal Justice and Public Order Bill — Amendment of Law relating to).

13. Hansard House of Commons Debates (vol. 373) 29 October 2001 (Adoption and Children Bill — Consideration and Third Reading); Hansard House of Commons Debates (vol. 386) 20 May 2002 (Adoption and Children Bill — General Interpretation, etc.).

14. Hansard House of Commons Debates (vol. 392) 4 November 2002 (Adoption and Children Bill –Suitability of Adopters).

15. For example, he voted in the following key debates: Hansard House of Commons Debates (vol. 238) 21 February 1994 (Criminal Justice and Public Order Bill — Amendment of Law relating to); Hansard House of Commons Debates (vol. 325) 10 February 1999 (Sexual Offences Amendment Bill); Hansard House of Commons Debates (vol. 401) 10 March 2003 (Local Government Bill — Repeal of Section 2A of Local Government Act 1986) (divisions 108 and 109).

16. For example, he voted in the following key debates: Hansard House of Commons Debates (vol. 373) 29 October 2001 (Adoption and Children Bill — Consideration and Third Reading); Hansard House of Commons Debates (vol. 386) 20 May 2002 (Adoption and Children Bill — General Interpretation, etc.); Hansard House of Commons Debates (vol. 401) 10 March 2003 (Local Government Bill — Repeal of Section 2A of Local Government Act 1986) (divisions 108 and 109).

17. For example, he voted in the following key debates: Hansard House of Commons Debates (vol. 314) 22 June 1998 (Crime and Disorder Bill [Lords] — Reduction in Age at which Certain Sexual Acts are Lawful); Hansard House of Commons Debates (vol. 325) 10 February 1999 (Sexual Offences Amendment Bill); Hansard House of Commons Debates (vol. 386) 20 May 2002 (Adoption and Children Bill — General Interpretation, etc.).

18. For example, he voted in the following key debates: Hansard House of Commons Debates (vol. 238) 21 February 1994 (Criminal Justice and Public Order Bill — Amendment of Law relating to); Hansard House of Commons Debates (vol. 238) 21 February 1994 (Criminal Justice and

Public Order Bill — Age at which Homosexual Acts are Lawful); Hansard House of Commons Debates (vol. 314) 22 June 1998 (Crime and Disorder Bill [Lords] — Reduction in Age at which Certain Sexual Acts are Lawful); Hansard House of Commons Debates (vol. 325) 10 February 1999 (Sexual Offences Amendment Bill).

19. For example, he did not vote "pro-gay" in the following key debates: Hansard House of Commons Debates (vol. 373) 29 October 2001 (Adoption and Children Bill — Consideration and Third Reading); Hansard House of Commons Debates (vol. 386) 20 May 2002 (Adoption and Children Bill — General Interpretation, etc.); Hansard House of Commons Debates (vol. 401) 10 March 2003 (Local Government Bill — Repeal of Section 2A of Local Government Act 1986) (divisions 108).

20. For example, he voted in the following key debates: Hansard House of Commons Debates (vol. 373) 29 October 2001 (Adoption and Children Bill — Consideration and Third Reading); Hansard House of Commons Debates (vol. 386) 20 May 2002 (Adoption and Children Bill — General Interpretation, etc.); Hansard House of Commons Debates (vol. 401) 10 March 2003 (Local Government Bill — Repeal of Section 2A of Local Government Act 1986) (divisions 108 and 109).

21. Hansard House of Commons Debates (vol. 238) 21 February 1994 (Criminal Justice and Public Order Bill — Amendment of Law relating to); Hansard House of Commons Debates (vol. 238) 21 February 1994 (Criminal Justice and Public Order Bill — Age at which Homosexual Acts are Lawful).

22. Hansard House of Commons Debates (vol. 426) 9 November 2004 (Civil Partnerships Bill [Lords] — Third Reading).

23. Hansard House of Commons Debates (vol. 426) 9 November 2004 (Civil Partnerships Bill [Lords] — Third Reading).

24. Hansard House of Commons Debates (vol. 314) 22 June 1998 (Crime and Disorder Bill [Lords] — Reduction in Age at which Certain Sexual Acts are Lawful).

25. Hansard House of Commons Debates (vol. 314) 22 June 1998 (Crime and Disorder Bill [Lords] — Reduction in Age at which Certain Sexual Acts are Lawful).

# Conclusion

"The importance of recognition is now universally acknowledged in one form or another; on an intimate plane, we are all aware of how identity can be formed or malformed through the course of our contact with significant others. On the social plane, we have a continuing politics of equal recognition." (C. Taylor 1992: 36)

## Summing Up

*Sex, Lies and Politics: Gay Politicians in the Press* does something new by showing that the changing representation of gay politicians and politicians caught up in a gay "scandal" in UK newspapers can be understood using three interconnected frames within an overarching frame of representation:

1  The move towards recognition
2  Acceptability over time (in relation to "heterosexual public space")
3  Mediated personas as "constructed reality".

The use of frames in the discussion of media representation is not new in itself, but the bringing together of the above three frames in relation to gay politicians *is*. In fact, the press representation of gay politicians in the UK has never before been evaluated in such an extensive and detailed manner; while the press representation of homosexuality in general has been discussed (and within that, some gay politicians have been mentioned), it has never been examined in the way that the representation of female politicians has, with in-depth study of words, themes and stereotypes. Considering that gay politicians and politicians caught up in gay "scandal" stories have been at the very forefront of the media's attention at various times over the last fifteen years, such a study is therefore timely. The relationship between the media and politicians has also focused on discussions surrounding the (negative) impact of political spin; conversely, *Sex, Lies and Politics* explores the impact of the media on politicians/political life, through the three frames, within the overarching frame of representation.

## Full Recognition?

With the politics of recognition, groups are not just tolerated; they are recognized as equal members of society *and* for their difference (C. Taylor 1992). The research has expanded on the fact that whole recognition has not yet been reached for gay politicians, seen in the way that gay politicians are often defined as such above anything else (in a negative way, rather than as a positive affirmation), with certain criteria needing to be met before positive representation is possible. That said, gay politicians have moved closer to recognition over the years, as demonstrated by the case studies, and in recent years the personal lives of gay politicians have received similar press coverage to that of heterosexual politicians, leading to "sexual scandal equality".

It should be understood that Taylor's concept of recognition, in relation to the idea of group shared characteristics, can be problematic. Certainly, it can be debated whether or not full acceptability or recognition is even possible (and not just for gay politicians, but for any gay person or member of a minority group). Also, would such a world be a wholly positive one? In fact, one criticism of a fully recognized world, if it is taken to the extreme, could be that individuals actually end up being limited by such an approach (*i.e.* all gay people have the same opinions and ideas, as do people within other minority groups, leading to rigid groups within societies). However, gay politicians do not have to share all of the same characteristics to be recognized; recognition could mean that a gay politician is recognized as a gay *individual*, rather than as part of a homogenized group, therefore allowing for group differences.

Chari (2004) notes that recognition, as a standard-bearer, can actually contribute to the continuation of subordination, showing another problem with recognition: it can keep subjugated groups/individuals in their place. So, by relying on the recognition of others, individuals can in fact become oppressed. Consequently, it could be argued that gay people and other repressed people/groups need to act out their resistance as well as aiming for the recognition of others. If such an approach is taken, as valid and equal members of society and political life gay politicians should therefore not only look for (hope for?) the respect of "heterosexual society", they should also fight for it through their actions. The campaign of the pressure group Outrage! in the 1990s is a rather extreme example of fighting for recognition through action. In the 1990s Outrage! "outed"/attempted to "out" gay politicians and public figures because it was believed that by doing so, gay rights as a political cause would be strengthened — the "outed" gay people were collateral damage. The methods employed by Outrage! were generally thought to be unfair to the gay public figures concerned, but the organization's actions illustrate the significant impact gay public figures can have, whether or not they wish to engage with their sexuality publicly. The assertive identity politics espoused by Outrage! demonstrates that the media reacts to as well as creates gay identities. It may therefore benefit gay politicians to actively engage with their sexuality in order that outside influences (the press, pressure groups *etc.*) do not set the agenda.

Another way of contributing to recognition and liberation is by representing gay people in Parliament. Indeed, representation can be interpreted in two ways: (1) gay MPs are themselves represented by the press and the media as a whole; (2) they also represent others in Parliament — and not just *electoral* constituents. "Surrogate" representation suggests that gay MPs may find themselves representing gay people from outside their constituencies (whether or not they want to), as discussed by Mansbridge (2003). Some gay politicians may be happy to regard themselves as a surrogate representative on gay issues and engage with the advancement of gay rights in a very vocal, active manner. However, some politicians, gay or otherwise, may be reluctant to be seen as surrogate representatives, because they do not want to be seen as single-issue politicians, suggesting that it is not only the press/public that does not fully recognize gay politicians; there may also be resistance from gay politicians themselves, in response to the press/public.

## The Acceptability Threshold

Homosexuality/sexual acts can be rated in terms of acceptability within "heterosexual public space", making this frame about the acceptability of types of *behaviour* (as opposed to Frame One, recognition, which is about *public opinion* more generally). The acceptability (and press representation) of homosexuality, since its categorization as an identity, has generally moved in one direction: from negative to positive (tying in with the move towards recognition). Although the progression is on the whole linear, there have been some backwards steps, such as the 1980s and the onset of HIV/AIDS and its early classification as a "gay plague". What is acceptable has changed over the years. For example, a homosexual identity is now accepted by most of society, whereas at one time identifying as gay was illegal. Figure 2.1 demonstrated that there is an acceptability threshold in terms of acts becoming public. While a homosexual identity is acceptable in heterosexual public space (in terms of law and society as a whole), homosexual sexual acts (both private and public) have not passed the acceptability threshold, therefore becoming issues of public concern. While the placing of private homosexual sexual acts below the acceptability threshold can be debated (they are after all perfectly legal and have been for some time, hence the legality threshold also shown in figure 2.1), the amount of press attention given to issues such as the age of gay consent and Clause 28 in recent years, along with the results of public opinion polls and the contemporary press representation of various gay politicians, suggests that they are not yet accepted, at least wholly.

It could also be argued that public *heterosexual* sexual acts should be below the acceptability threshold instead of above. But, unlike public homosexual sexual acts (stereotypically categorized as immoral and dirty by the press), heterosexual public sex is often presented by the press as a fantasy to be acted out. For example, a 2000 survey in *The Sun* (YOUR SEX CONFESSIONS, 25 April 2000) found that: "*Sun* readers do it in their cars . . . not to mention lay bys, cinemas, swimming pools, department stores, hospitals and even the Ideal Home Exhibition. The strewth is out there! We asked you to tell us your sauciest secrets — and you gave us The Sex Files." Public homosexual sexual acts are not presented in such way by the "mainstream" press, hence their placing below the acceptability threshold.

The acceptability threshold and its relation to private and public spaces impacts upon the representation of gay politicians in the UK press; as homosexuality has become more acceptable, so have gay politicians. However, public space still comes into play here; gay people — including gay politicians — are expected (and may wish) to limit "displays" of their sexuality. In fact, their sexuality is marked in heterosexual public space. That does seems to be changing though, shown by the almost nonchalant approach of much of the press towards Alan Duncan's civil partnership. Of particular interest in figure 2.1 is the distinction between a homosexual *identity* and homosexual *sexual acts*. It is not necessarily the case that *being* gay in itself has always been problematic for gay people (in recent times in particular, as acceptability has improved); more accurately, it is the actual act of sodomy. It is for that reason that gay politicians or politicians caught up in a gay "scandal" whom the press have classed as "dangerous" receive such negative press coverage; their *active* sexuality (in terms of sexual acts) is at the forefront of their press coverage, unlike "safe" politicians, who are deemed less overtly sexual. Of course, it is not automatically the case that those presented as "dangerous" have engaged in penetrative sex, but this stereotype is almost representative of male homosexual sex (in the media and the minds of many heterosexual people at least).

## Mediated Reality

The final frame, mediated personas as "constructed reality", is present in a more obvious sense than the other two frames; a perceptive reader can see the framework in use on a day-to-day basis, and as such it has the most immediate impact. The binary themes defined are also constant (in that they are always present in the periods of press representation identified above — although their strength changes over time), whereas the first two frames have a (predominantly) unidirectional trajectory (*i.e.* the move towards recognition shows a move from intolerance to partial recognition, albeit allowing for backwards steps). The binary themes identified, as metanarratives/master frames (McAdam 1994), suggest that there are two main types of persona for gay politicians and politicians caught up in a gay "scandal": negative and positive. Some politicians are more strongly positive or negative than others, depending on how many of the relevant binary themes they meet, showing the graduated nature of the personas (as well as the binary themes which make up the personas). It is also not necessarily the case that the binary themes are of equal value to each other in the first place (*i.e.* being "dangerous" could contribute more strongly to a negative persona than being "bad"). Factors such as year of publication need to be taken into account; certain binary themes are more or less important at particular times, tying in with social/political/legal factors. The notion of being "in", for example, was very negative in the late 1990s with the "outings" of Mandelson and other MPs, but in more recent years the fever pitch surrounding the binary has diminished (although it is possible it could return). So, while it is not the case that the binary themes are ranked in terms of a consistent importance (*i.e.* that out/in is *always* the most important binary theme, across time), various boundaries are particularly important at different times. Table 10.1 shows how many positive binary themes Peter Tatchell, Stephen

| Name | Tatchell | Twigg | Davies |
|---|---|---|---|
| Private/public (sexual behaviour) | Private | Private | Public |
| Out/in | In | Out | In |
| Good/bad | Bad | Good | Bad |
| Safe/dangerous | N/A | N/A | Dangerous |
| Clean/dirty | N/A | N/A | Dirty |
| Positive/negative mediated persona | Negative (1/3) | Positive (3/3) | Negative (0/5) |

**Table 10.1** The mediated personas of Twigg, Tatchell and Davies.*
*The classifications apply to their original press coverage, rather than later stories.

Twigg and Ron Davies meet, demonstrating the graduated nature of mediated personas.

It was noted that anal penetration is stereotypically seen as representative of gay sex. Indeed, anal sex was represented as the homosexual sexual norm in House of Lords debates on homosexuality (Baker 2004). In relation, there is another binary theme associated with *male* politicians: passive (assumed no penetration) versus active (assumed penetration). Thus, while gay people may be accepted in a general sense (as an identity), penetrative gay sex is more contentious (something suggested in figure 2.1). The passive/active binary theme involves assumptions on behalf of the writer/reader; not only that anal sex is the default sexual act of gay men, but also that anal penetration is negative (perhaps "dirty", to utilize the clean/dirty binary theme). After some debate the binary theme was not included in Frame Three due to the fact the binary is more of an abstract one; in a sense it underlines all of the above binary themes rather than being a completely separate binary theme in itself, in the way that it underscores heterosexual conceptions of gay (male) sex. This is suggested in Chapter 2, when it was noted that it is the homosexual sexual act (deemed to be penetration) that is of most concern to people, whether or not it takes place privately or publicly. For that reason there is also no separate binary of sexual versus desexualized; even politicians who are "safe" are deemed sexual to a certain extent because of connotations about homosexuality and sex: homosexuality = anal sex. Thus, with the clean/dirty and safe/dangerous binary themes, the supposed wrongness of anal sex contributes to the negative binary; sex is dirty and/or dangerous partly because it (assumingly) involves anal penetration.

It is through negative binary themes that the press (as an informal/culture of democracy, as opposed to a formal/institution of democracy such as the parliamentary system) contributes to gay and "outed" politicians failing to reach whole recognition. In table 10.1, Twigg meets all of the positive representation criteria applicable to him, making his mediated persona extremely positive. Tatchell meets one out of the three positive representation criteria applicable to him; his reluctance to "come out" as gay and instead stay "in the closet" during his early 1980s political campaign made his mediated persona more negative. This pales in comparison, though, to Davies; as he does not meet any of the positive representation criteria, his mediated persona is extremely negative. Obviously, the *time* of press representation has to be taken into account; there is almost sexual scandal "equality" in some of the later press coverage of gay politicians and politicians caught up in a gay "scandal", as their press coverage is similar to that of politicians caught up in heterosexual sexual scandals (although the fact they are [thought to be] gay automatically makes their press coverage more "scandalous"). Thus, negative binary themes are still utilized in the 2000s, leading to negative mediated personas, but not as strongly as in earlier times. Of course, subjectivity has to be taken into account when reading newspapers (that of casual readers, but also when approaching representation academically); it is possible there could be different views about whether X politician is "good" or "bad", taking into account other contextual factors. Overall, though, most press coverage is explicit enough in tone that a similar reading is likely to be engaged with by most readers (whether or not the newspaper's view is agreed with).

Tabloid/broadsheet differences come into play when discussing mediated personas. Tabloid newspapers are more likely to pay attention to the personal lives of gay politicians and use certain (negative/stereotypical) words. In the same sense, tabloid newspapers are more likely to (or more obviously) portray gay and "outed" politicians using binary themes: they are safe *or* dangerous, clean *or* dirty. This can be seen in the press representation of Davies, who was portrayed in the tabloid newspapers as dirty and dangerous through, for example, the suggestion he had Hepatitis B, as published in the *People* (SHAMED MP HAS GAY SEX DISEASE; RON DAVIES PICKED UP HEPATITIS B SAYS EX-WIFE, 1 November 1998). One reason why tabloid newspapers use binary themes, rather than a relational approach, is because through strong characterization they can grab the attention of readers. Plus, broadsheets generally focus on opinion, comment and analysis (looking at the "bigger picture") more than scandal. The press does not act in a vacuum; stories are published according to how well they will "connect" with the public through their newsworthiness. Thus, a politician who is "out" generally receives less attention than someone who has been "outed" or who is "scandalous" because it has less novelty. In fact, the negative binaries are more "newsworthy" than the positive ones (scandals equal sales). As Chapter 1 explains, binary themes sell personas and therefore stories and newspapers (who are, after all, competing against each other in the media market).

The binary themes can be related to heterosexual press coverage as well (*i.e.* a politician whose story involves someone of the opposite sex). Private/public, safe/dangerous and clean/dirty can be applied in their original context. Out/in and good/bad only pertain to gay politicians or politicians caught up in a gay "scandal", although with a different emphasis applied they could relate to politicians involved in a hetero-sexual "scandal". Certainly, heterosexual politicians are never "in" because heterosexuality is the perceived default sexuality. But, they could be condemned for not being truthful about their sexual life. In the same manner, while a heterosexual politician is inherently "good" when compared to a gay politician (once again because heterosexuality is deemed the default sexuality and heterosexual politicians therefore do not need to hide their sexuality), they could still be perceived as being "bad" if they were not open and relaxed about their private lives. Heterosexual politicians can be represented as "dangerous" and "dirty" if they are caught, for example, having an extra-marital affair or hiring prostitutes. They can also be condemned for sexual behaviour that does not take place in private. However, heterosexual politicians benefit from the fact that they are heterosexual rather than homosexual; so, a hetero-sexual politician such as Steven Norris (Conservative MP for Oxford East 1983–7 and Epping Forest 1988–97), alleged to have had five mistresses at once, was portrayed by the press as "shagger Norris", a tongue-in-cheek reference to his so-called impressive heterosexuality (*Observer*, THE OBSERVER PROFILE: THE ULTIMATE ESSEX MAN, 15 December 1996). There is much less chance of a gay MP being portrayed in such a way, even in the 2000s.

## Implications

As Seaton (2003: 174) highlights, the press focus on the private lives of politicians has potentially democratic consequences: "A key defence of the media is that they are there precisely to expose, reveal, complain and attack. Healthy democracy depends on vigorous scrutiny, and the examination of the ways in which public power is used to further private ends is a vital aspect of this process. Yet the media — just like everything else in political systems — change. The problem is whether the role, impact and obsessions of the media have now become a democratic liability." Deacon (2004) recognizes that focusing on politics *through* the personal can inhibit the media's democratic performance. Obviously, press attention on the personal can be positive; it can expose wrongdoing, hypocrisy and illegal behaviour. It is also the case that politicians themselves have played a part in the attention paid to their private lives, through somewhat excessive media management ("spin") and promotion of political private lives for public gain. Nonetheless, excessive press attention potentially has a big impact: it could influence the amount of attention the press pays to more serious issues; it may affect the ability of politicians to do their jobs; negative/excessive press representation of homosexuality and/or gay politicians could in theory discourage gay people from becoming politicians, leading to a democratic deficit (fewer gay MPs may lead to poorer parliamentary representation of gay people and discussion of gay issues), or from being "out" or from talking about "gay issues"; gay politicians may feel they have no choice but to deny their sexuality; a focus on "scandalous" gay politicians may also encourage negative public opinion about gay politicians (either individual politicians or gay politicians as a whole) and gay people in general. The points relating specifically to gay politicians are less likely to be an issue in the 2000s than previous decades, but they are still relevant.

As suggested by Van Zoonen (2005: 150), "antidemocratic tendencies", as homophobia could be termed, exist within popular culture. Thus, the press, as an institution of popular culture, can foster homophobia or at least help to maintain the status quo in relation to attitudes towards gay men and women, as well as causing/contributing to a democratic deficit. It is through the press, as an informal/culture of democracy, that groups such as gay politicians have been excluded. So, there is a subtle cultural politics of exclusion which is operated by the media. The third frame identified (mediated personas) is therefore very important; not only is it the most obvious frame in terms of reader perceptibility, it could also, potentially, be used as a tool for maintaining negative and stereotypical representations of gay people and politicians in the press, with negative consequences for democracy. While it is not the case that framing is negative in itself — frames exist, whatever their consequences — some frames can have negative effects. Of course, Frame Three could be considered a useful one; not only is it a helpful analytical tool, but as one half of the binary themes identified are positive ones, perhaps it has been of benefit to gay politicians, as well as a disadvantage at times. While a journalist may consciously use particular words to describe a gay person/politician — "poof" in the 1980s or "exotic" in more recent years — the frameworks which arch over the process are unconscious ones.

Chapter 2 discussed how the media can be seen as reinforcing public opinion via the mirroring and shaping of boundaries, rather than directly setting public opinion. The move towards the whole recognition of gay politicians is therefore led by the public, with the media acting as a tiller. Binary themes (Frame Three) are used by newspapers as an expression of public opinion. Sometimes the press misjudges the mood of its readers and will face a backlash of public opinion, but generally the match is successful (taking into account tabloid/broadsheet differences and the political/moral opinions of newspapers/readers). As gay sexuality has become more accepted in terms of public space (Frame Two), and whole recognition has moved closer (Frame One), binary themes have become less resonant, shown by the more moderate language employed by the press in recent years. But, as their presence in the representation of gay politicians and politicians caught up in a gay "scandal" in the UK press is linked to public opinion about homosexuality, such binary themes or metanarratives will continue to be present until public attitudes shift; as many of the themes (private/public, safe/dangerous/ clean/dirty) apply to heterosexuality as well as homosexuality, it appears that these themes will be present for the foreseeable future.

# Bibliography

Abbey, R. 1999: Charles Taylor's Politics of Recognition: a Reply to Jonathan Seglow. *Political Studies* 47 (4), 710–14.

Alley, T. and Dillon, N. 2001: Sex-linked Carrying Styles and the Attribution of Homosexuality. *The Journal of Social Psychology* 141 (5), 660–6.

Arendt, H. 1958: *The Human Condition*. Chicago: University of Chicago Press.

Baker, P. 2002: *Polari: the Lost Language of Gay Men*. London: Routledge.

Baker, P. 2004: "Unnatural Acts": Discourses of Homosexuality within the House of Lords Debates on Gay Male Law Reform. *Journal of Sociolinguistics* 8 (1), 88–106.

Baston, L. 2000: *Sleaze: The State of Britain*. London: Channel 4 Books.

Baudrillard, J. 1995: *Simulacra and Simulation*. (Translated from the 1981 original by S. Faria Glaser). Michigan: University of Michigan Press.

BBC News 2011: *Residents Tackle East End "Gay Free Zone" Stickers* [online]. Available from: http://www.bbc.co.uk/news/uk-england-london-12526820 [accessed 15 April 2011].

Binnie, J. 1997: Coming out of Geography: Towards a Queer Epistemology. *Environment and Planning D: Society and Space* 15 (2), 223–37.

Boling, P. 1996: *Privacy and the Politics of Intimate Life*. London: Cornell University Press.

Brickell, C. 2000: Heroes and Invaders: Gay and Lesbian Pride Parades and the Public/Private Distinction in New Zealand Media Accounts. *Gender, Place and Culture* 7 (2), 163–78.

British Medical Association 1994: *Age of Consent for Homosexual Men: Report to the Council of the British Medical Association from the Board of Science and Education* [online]. Available from: http://www.stonewall.org.uk/documents/Scan5a.pdf [accessed 16 February 2006].

Britsocat 2011: *What about Sexual Relations between Two People of the Same Sex?* (British Social Attitudes Information System statistics) [online]. Available from: //www.britsocat.com/Body.aspx?control=Britsocat Marginals&AddSuperMap=LBHOMOSEX&JumpCrossMarginals =yes [accessed 13 April 2011].

Burridge, J. 2004: "I am not Homophobic But . . . " Disclaiming in Discourse Resisting Repeal of Section 28. *Sexualities* 7 (3), 327–44.

Cappella, J. N. and Jamieson, K. H. 1997: *The Spirit of Cynicism: The Press and the Public Good.* New York: Oxford University Press.

Chari, A. 2004: Exceeding Recognition. *Sartre Studies International* 10 (2), 110–22.

Clarke, E. 2000: *Virtuous Vice: Homoeroticism in the Public Sphere.* Durham: Duke University Press.

Cole, P. 1999: Dumbing Down: Bottoming Out? *Aslib Proceedings: New Information Perspectives* 51 (3), 72–7.

Corner, J. 2000: Mediated Persona and Political Culture: Dimensions of Structure and Process. *European Journal of Cultural Studies* 3 (3), 389–405.

Critcher, C. *et al.* 1997: The Social Production of News. In P. Elliott and P. Golding (eds), *Making the News.* London: Longman, 645–52.

D'Angelo, P. 2002: News Framing as a Multi-Paradigmatic Research Program: A Response to Entman. *Journal of Communication* 52 (4), 870–88.

Deacon, D. 2004: Politicians, Privacy and Media Intrusion in Britain. *Parliamentary Affairs* 57 (1), 9–23.

Doig, A. and Wilson, J. 1995: Untangling the Threads. In A. Doig and F.F. Ridley (eds), *Sleaze: Politicians, Private Interests and Public Perception.* Oxford: Oxford University Press, 14–30.

Downs, A. 1957: *An Economic Theory of Democracy.* New York: Harper and Row.

Driberg, T. 1977: *Ruling Passions.* UK: Jonathan Cape.

Duncan, N. 1996: Renegotiating Gender and Sexuality in Public and Private Spaces. In N. Duncan (ed.), *BodySpace: Destabilising Geographies of Gender and Sexuality.* London: Routledge, 127–89.

Dunleavy, P. and Weir, S. 1995: Media, Opinion and the Constitution. In A. Doig and F.F. Ridley (eds), *Sleaze: Politicians, Private Interests and Public Perception.* Oxford: Oxford University Press, 54–68.

Ellis, S. and Kitzinger, C. 2002: Denying Equality: An Analysis of Arguments against Lowering the Age of Consent for Sex Between Men. *Journal of Community and Applied Social Psychology* 12 (3), 167–80.

Entman, R. M. 1993: Framing: Toward Clarification of a Fractured Paradigm. *Journal of Communication* 43 (4), 51–8.

Epstein, D. *et al.* 2000: Twice Told Tales: Transformation, Recuperation and Emergence in the Age of Consent Debates 1998. *Sexualities* 3 (1), 5–30.

Evans, J. 2005: Celebrity, Media and History. In J. Evans and D. Hesmondhalgh (eds.), *Understanding Media: Inside Celebrity.* Berkshire: Open University Press, 11–55.

Foucault, M. 1998: *The Will to Knowledge — The History of Sexuality: 1*. London: Penguin Books.

Fowler, R. 1991: *Language in the News*. London: Routledge.

Franklin, B. 1997: *Newszak and News Media*. London: Arnold.

Fraser, N. 1992: Rethinking the Public Sphere: A Contribution to the Critique of Actually Existing Democracy. In C. Calhoun (ed.), *Habermas and the Public Sphere*. Cambridge, MA: MIT Press, 109–42.

Galtung, J. and Ruge, M. 1973: Structuring and Selecting News. In S. Cohen and J. Young (eds), *The Manufacture of News: Social Problems, Deviance and the Mass Media*. London: Constable, 62–72.

Gillespie, M. and Toynbee, J. 2006: Framing the Real: Beyond the Text. In M. Gillespie and J. Toynbee (eds), *Analysing Media Texts*. Berkshire: Open University Press, 187–91.

Gitlin, T. 1980: *The Whole World Is Watching: Mass Media in the Making and Unmaking of the New Left*. Berkeley: University of California Press.

Goffman, E. 1974: *Frame Analysis: An Essay on the Organization of Experience*. New York: Harper & Row.

Goffman, E. 1990: *The Presentation of Self in Everyday Life*. London: Penguin Books.

Gronfors, M. and Stalstrom, O. 1987: Power, Prestige, Profit: AIDS and the Oppression of Homosexual People. *Acta Sociologica* 30 (1), 53–66.

Grosz, E. A. 1994: *Volatile Bodies: Towards a Corporeal Feminism*. Bloomington: Indiana University Press.

Guidry, L. 1999: Clinical Intervention with Bisexuals: A Contextualized Understanding. *Professional Psychology: Research and Practice* 30 (1), 22–6.

Habermas, J. 1991: *The Structural Transformation of the Public Sphere: An Inquiry into a Category of Bourgeois Society*. (Translated by T. Burger). Cambridge, MA: MIT Press.

Hall, S. *et al.* 1978: *Policing the Crisis: Mugging, the State and Law and Order*. London: Macmillan.

Hansard 1885: *House of Commons Debates*. (Vol. 300) 6 August 1885 (column 1397).

Hansard 1896: *House of Lords Debates*. (Vol. 38) 20 March 1896 (column 1444).

Hansard 1921: *House of Lords Debates*. (Vol. 43) 15 August 1921 (column 573).

Hansard 1965: *House of Commons Debates*. (Vol. 713) 26 May 1965 (column 616).

Hansard 1966a: *House of Lords Debates*. (Vol. 275) 16 June 1966 (column 160).

Hansard 1966b: *House of Commons Debates*. (Vol. 738) 19 December 1966 (column 1078).

Hansard 1994: *House of Commons Debates*. (Vol. 238) 21 February 1994 (column 103).
Hansard 1998: *House of Commons Debates*. (Vol. 314) 22 June 1998 (column 772).
Hansard, 2000: *House of Commons Debates*. (Vol. 344) 10 February 2000 (column 440).
Hartley, J. 1995: *Understanding News*. London: Routledge.
Hattersley, M. 2004: Will Success Spoil Gay Culture? *Gay and Lesbian Review Worldwide* 11 (1), 33–4.
Hemmings, S. 1980: Horrific Practices: How Lesbians were Presented in the Newspapers of 1978. In Gay Left Collective (ed.), *Homosexuality: Power and Politics*. London: Allison and Busby Limited, 157–71.
Herek, G. M. 1990: Gay People and Government Security Clearances: a Social Science Perspective. *American Psychologist* 45 (9), 1035–42.
Hocquenghem, G. 1978: *Homosexual Desire*. London: Allison and Busby.
Inness, J. 1992: *Privacy, Intimacy and Isolation*. New York: Oxford University Press.
Jeffery-Poulter, S. 1991: *Peers, Queers and Commons: The Struggle for Gay Law Reform from 1950 to the Present*. London: Routledge.
Johnston, L. 1997: Queen(s') Street or Ponsonby poofters? Embodied HERO Parade Sites. *New Zealand Geographer* 53 (2), 29–33.
König, T. 2007: *Frame Analysis* [online]. Available from: http://www.ccsr.ac.uk/methods/publications/frameanalysis/ [accessed 3 September 2007].
Lilie, S. *et al.* 1993: On the Nature and Dynamics of Social Construction: The Case of AIDS. *Social Science Quarterly* 74 (1), 123–35.
Macintyre, D. 2000: *Mandelson and the Making of New Labour*. London: HarperCollins.
Mansbridge, J. 2003: Rethinking Representation. *American Political Science Review* 97 (4), 515–28.
McAdam, D. 1994: Culture and Social Movements. In E. Laraña *et al.* (eds), *New Social Movements: from Ideology to Identity*. Philadelphia: Temple University Press, 36–57.
McCreary, D. R. 1994: The Male Role and Avoiding Femininity. *Sex Roles* 31 (9–10), 517–31.
McIntosh, M. 1996: The Homosexual Role. In S. Seidman (ed.), *Queer Theory/Sociology*. Oxford: Blackwell Publishers, 33–40.
McQuail, D. 2005: *Mass Communication Theory*. London: Sage.
Moran, M. 2005: *Politics and Governance in the UK*. Basingstoke: Palgrave Macmillan.
Myslik, W. 1996: Renegotiating the Social/Sexual Identities of Places: Gay Communities as Safe Havens or Sites of Resistance? In N. Duncan (ed.), *BodySpace: Destabilising Geographies of Gender and Sexuality*. London: Routledge, 156–69.
Namaste, K. 1996: Genderbashing: Sexuality, Gender, and the Regulation

of Public Space. *Environment and Planning D: Society and Space* 14 (2), 221–40.

Natcen 2010: *British Social Attitudes 26th Report — Britain Becoming Increasingly Liberal* [online]. Available from: http://www.natcen.ac.uk/media-centre/press-releases/2010-press-releases/british-social-attitudes-26th-report—britain-becoming-incre asingly-liberal [accessed 12 November 2010].

Padgug, R. 1992: Sexual Matters: on Conceptualizing Sexuality in History. In E. Stein (ed.), *Forms of Desire: Sexual Orientation and the Social Constructionist Controversy*. New York: Routledge, 43–67.

Parris, M. 1995: *Great Parliamentary Scandals: Four Centuries of Calumny, Smear and Innuendo*. London: Robson Books.

Parris, M. 2002: *Chance Witness: an Outsider's Life in Politics*. London: Viking.

Pateman, C. 1988: *The Sexual Contract*. Stanford, CA: Stanford University Press.

PCC 2009: *History* [online]. Available from: http://www.pcc.org.uk/about/history.html [accessed 21 February 2011].

PCC 2011: *Code of Practice* [online]. Available from: http://www.pcc.org.uk/cop/practice.html [accessed 1 March 2011].

Philo, G. 1983: Bias in the Media. In D. Coates and G. Johnston (eds), *Socialist Arguments*. Oxford: Martin Robertson, 130–45.

Plummer, K. 2001: The Square of Intimate Citizenship: Some Preliminary Proposals. *Citizenship Studies* 5 (3), 237–53.

Plummer, K. 2003a: Re-presenting Sexualities in the Media. *Sexualities* 6 (3–4), 275–6.

Plummer, K. 2003b: *Intimate Citizenship: Private Decisions and Public Dialogues*. Seattle: University of Washington Press.

Prokhovnik, R. 1999: *Rational Woman: A Feminist Critique of Dichotomy*. Manchester: Manchester University Press.

Rayside, D. 1998: *On the Fringe: Gays and Lesbians in Politics*. London: Cornell University Press.

Reese, S. 2001: Prologue — Framing Public Life: A Bridging Model for Media Research. In S. Reese *et al.* (eds), *Framing Public Life: Perspectives on Media and our Understanding of the Social World*. Mahwah: Lawrence Erlbaum Associates, 7-31.

Richardson, D. 1996: Heterosexuality and Social Theory. In D. Richardson (ed.), *Theorising Heterosexuality*. Buckingham: Open University Press, 1–20.

Richardson, D. 2004: Locating Sexualities: From Here to Normality. *Sexualities* 7 (4), 391–411.

Ridley, F. F. 1995: Feet of Clay. In A. Doig and F. F. Ridley (eds), *Sleaze: Politicians, Private Interests and Public Reaction*. Oxford: Oxford University Press, 69–83.

Rubin, G. 1992: Thinking Sex: Notes for a Radical Theory of the Politics of Sexuality. In C. S. Vance (ed.), *Pleasure and Danger: Exploring Female Sexuality*. London: Pandora Press, 267–319.

Sanderson, T. 1995: *Mediawatch: The Treatment of Male and Female Homosexuality in the British Media*. London: Cassell.

Seaton, J. 2003: Public, Private and the Media. *Political Quarterly* 74 (2), 174–83.

Sedgwick, E. 1994: *Tendencies*. London: Routledge.

Shugart, H. 2003: Reinventing Privilege: The New (Gay) Man in Contemporary Popular Media. *Critical Studies in Media Communication* 20 (1), 67-91.

Sinfield, A. 1994: *The Wilde Century*. London: Cassell.

Snow, D. A. *et al.* 1986: Frame Alignment Processes, Micromobilization and Movement Participation. *American Sociological Review* 51 (4), 464–81.

Steinberger, P. 1999: Public and Private. *Political Studies* 47 (2), 292–313.

Stonewall 1993: *The Case for Change: Arguments for an Equal Age of Consent* [online]. Available from: http://www.stonewall.org.uk/documents/ Scan2a.pdf [accessed 11 April 2011].

Stonewall 1999: *Public Opinion on the Age of Consent* [online]. Available from: http://www.stonewall.org.uk/documents/lords_briefing_ apr00. doc [accessed 11 April 2011].

Stonewall 2006: *Age of Consent: Changing the Law* [online]. Available from: http://www.stonewall.org.uk/information_bank/criminal_law/66.asp [accessed 16 February 2006].

Storr, M. 2001: New Labour, New Britain, New Sexual Values? *Social Epistemology* 15 (2), 113–26.

Street, J. 2001: *Mass Media, Politics and Democracy*. London: Palgrave.

Swim, J. *et al.* 1999: Avoiding Stigma by Association: Subtle Prejudice against Lesbians in the Form of Social Distancing. *Basic and Applied Social Psychology* 21 (1), 61–8.

Tankard, J. W. 2001: The Empirical Approach to the Study of Media Framing. In S. Reese *et al.* (eds), *Framing Public Life: Perspectives on Media and our Understanding of the Social World*. Mahwah: Lawrence Erlbaum Associates, 7-31.

Tatchell, P. 1983: *The Battle for Bermondsey*. London: Heretic Books.

Tatchell, P. 1993: *Peter Tatchell's Evidence to the National Heritage Committee on the Press*. Available from: http://www.petertatchell.net/ media/national%20heritage.htm [accessed 3 February 2005].

Taylor, A. 1983: Conceptions of Masculinity and Femininity as a Basis for Stereotypes of Male and Female Homosexuals. *Journal of Homosexuality* 9 (1), 37-53.

Taylor, C. 1992: *Multiculturalism and "The Politics of Recognition"*. Princeton: Princeton University Press.

The Knitting Circle 2001: *Maureen Colquhoun* [online]. Available from:

http://myweb.lsbu.ac.uk/~stafflag/maureencolquhoun.html [accessed 6 January 2005].

Thompson, J. 2000: *Political Scandal: Power and Visibility in the Media Age*. Cambridge: Polity.

Valentine, G. 1993: (Hetero)sexing Space: Lesbian Perceptions and Experience of Everyday Space. *Environment and Planning D: Society and Space* 11 (4), 395–413.

Valentine, G. 1996: (Re)negotiating the "Heterosexual Street". In N. Duncan (ed.), *BodySpace: Destabilising Geographies of Gender and Sexuality*. London: Routledge, 146–55.

Van Zoonen, L. 2005: *Entertaining the Citizen: When Politics and Popular Culture Converge*. Lanham: Rowman and Littlefield Publishers, Inc.

Weeks, J. 1981a: *Sex, Politics and Society: The Regulation of Sexuality since 1800*. London: Longman.

Weeks, J. 1981b: Discourse, Desire and Sexual Deviance: Some Problems in the History of Homosexuality. In K. Plummer (ed.), *The Making of the Modern Homosexual*. London: Hutchinson and Co Ltd, 76–111.

Weeks, J. 2000: *Making Sexual History*. Oxford: Polity Press.

Wheen, F. 2001: *The Soul of Indiscretion: Tom Driberg, Poet, Philanderer, Legislator and Outlaw — His Life and Indiscretions*. UK: Fourth Estate Ltd.

Williams, K. 1998: *Get Me a Murder a Day: a History of Mass Communication in Britain*. London: Arnold.

Wolfenden, J. 1957: *The Wolfenden Report: Report of the Committee on Homosexual Offenses and Prostitution by Great Britain* (Committee on Homosexual Offences and Prostitution). London: HMSO.

Wulf, C. 2005: From the Subject of Desire to the Object of Seduction: Image — Imagination — Imaginary [online]. *International Journal of Baudrillard Studies* 2 (2). Available from: http://www.ubishops.ca/BaudrillardStudies/vol2_2/wulf.htm [accessed 30 January 2008].

Young, I. 1990: *Justice and the Politics of Difference*. Princeton: Princeton University Press.

# Index